T0326386

Markets, marketing and developing countries

Markets, marketing and developing countries

Where we stand and where we are heading

edited by: Hans van Trijp and Paul Ingenbleek

Wageningen Academic
P u b l i s h e r s

ISBN: 978-90-8686-145-3
e-ISBN: 978-90-8686-699-1
DOI: 10.3921/978-90-8686-699-1

First published, 2010

© Wageningen Academic Publishers
The Netherlands, 2010

Table of contents

Preface

The book in front of you consists of 20 essays in which the authors discuss a proposition in the domain of markets, marketing and developing countries. At a time in which high hopes exist pertaining to the role of markets in development, these essays may help to create an understanding of where we are, where we are coming from and where we are heading. The authors are established scientists in the field of marketing in developing countries, or related disciplines, and occupy senior positions within their research institutions. We have deliberately asked them to write short essays (rather than full scientific papers) to allow them to express their views and current concerns with this important field.

This book marks the celebration of Aad van Tilburg's retirement, after a career of more than three decades in the field of marketing and developing countries. All authors have in common that, in one way or another, they have a professional relationship with Aad van Tilburg. Aad has been able to develop strong networks in the field, working closely with a wide variety of colleague academics. Given Aad's experience and expertise combined with his very pleasant personality this should not come as a surprise. The present book brings together the view of Aad and several of his intimate co-workers on where this field could and should be developing after Aad's retirement.

Aad van Tilburg (June 11, 1945) joined the Marketing and Consumer behavior Group of Wageningen University in 1974, after an MSc in Economics and Econometrics at Erasmus University Rotterdam (1966-1971) and several years of business experience at Philips in the Netherlands. Although initially focusing on agricultural marketing in the Western World (in 1984 he successfully defended a PhD thesis on `Consumer choice of cut flowers and pot plants'), Aad was very early in recognizing the potential for and the challenges in the application of marketing theory for problems related to developing countries. The demand for this expertise was also recognized by professors from Development Economics and Rural Sociology and in response to their calls, a position was created in the Marketing and Consumer Behavior group that was entirely dedicated to marketing and developing countries. Aad seized the new opportunity offered to him in 1978. To familiarize himself in this field he gained field experience in Indonesia, followed by longer periods of field work in Malaysia (1982), Sierra Leone (1985), and Benin (1987). In the 1990s and 2000s, he visited research sites in among others Senegal, South Africa, Costa Rica and Bhutan.

In his work on marketing in developing countries, Aad van Tilburg has always focused on the balance between market integration and market efficiency on the one hand and to what extent this can improve the livelihood of primary producers in developing countries on the other. He has specifically focused on the role that marketing institutions can play in finding this right balance. Central to his approach was the value chain analysis, as Aad recognized early on that poverty alleviation is not purely a production problem but mainly a problem of functioning of markets. Understanding the behavioral forces that influence success and failure in these markets and chains is crucial in finding solutions for better integration and market access. As Aad's empathy was also largely with the small scale producers, he has been able to combine marketing and value chain analysis, with a livelihood approach to understand the dilemmas and restrictions that primary producers see themselves faced with.

Aad's approach was timely and full of foresight. With the increased attention for broader scope of sustainable development, the type of research questions that Aad has been focusing on have also gained considerably in social and academic relevance. This is highly visible in Aad's successes in attracting PhD students for this type of research. PhD students Clemens Lutz, Lineke van Bruggen, Xiaoyong Zhang,

Chairo Castano, Emma Kambewa, and Suresh Bhagavatula have benefited from Aad's rich experience and insight in conducting their research across the globe as a first step into their own careers. Aad was involved in the initiation of many of the current PhD projects within, or co-supervised by the Marketing and Consumer Behaviour group, i.e. those of Cathelijne van Melle, Workneh Tessema, Bukelwa Grwambi, Mênouwesso Hounhouigan, Mayra Esseboom and Suleimani Adekambi. It is fair to say that in the field of marketing for developing countries, Aad has left a footprint that will be recognizable long after his retirement.

This is a good moment to thank Aad for all his work in this important field. The essays in this book testify that Aad was right in his approach to strive for a balance between local livelihoods and global trade. The contributing authors look back with some degree of satisfaction as well as some concern. From the essays it is clear that a lot has been achieved, but with greater success in some parts of the world than in others. There is hope and we trust that future generations of academic scientists will continue the work from where Aad's contributions have brought us.

Aad, thank you very much for all of your fruitful work. Not only academically, but also as a coach to many of us. You have been a very valuable colleague to many of us, a strong leader that has stood at the start of many peoples' careers. We would like to also include in our thanks your wife Augustine, for her patience and support to the group.

Hans van Trijp and Paul Ingenbleek

Markets, marketing and developing countries: an introduction

Hans van Trijp and Paul Ingenbleek

Many of the products that consumers routinely purchase in today's supermarkets originate from long and complex supply chains, often rooted in primary production in developing countries such as for tropical fruits, coffee, tea, and cocoa. It is in this context of international chains that markets in developing countries are receiving substantial attention these days. Issues like poverty reduction at the level of smallholders and the design and coordination of international value chains that favor smallholders' livelihoods, are currently high on the agenda's of policy makers and nongovernmental organizations (NGOs). The growing attention for sustainable development has further nurtured interest at all levels. At the macro-level, reducing poverty worldwide and increasing trade with developing countries have become part of the United Nations' Millennium Development Goals to which 189 national governments have committed themselves. Also, many (international) food companies show increased focus on the developing countries and primary producers. First, they have started to recognize the collective purchasing power of consumers at 'the bottom of the pyramid', which as led to the design of products specifically for low income groups. But also, many of these companies have embraced sustainable development as the leading principle of their Corporate Social Responsibility (CSR) policies. Ensuring adequate livelihoods, through fair distribution of revenues across all parties involved in the value chain, is increasingly part of these policies. Importantly, consumers also express an increased interest for sustainability issues related to the products that they buy thereby generating a market pull for sustainable products, including Fair Trade products. Together these emerging trends bring new opportunities for development and make the role of marketing in development more salient.

This positive message of hope for the future is far from implying that the enhanced integration of smallholders into value chains against conditions that would improve their livelihood is a straightforward or simple process. As many contributors to this book argue, the track record is not particularly strong and substantial system innovations are needed to bring this desirable situation into reality. Many smallholders still lack adequate access to international value chains. Those that have access may earn incomes that fail to meet the expectations. Many primary producers are therefore still struggling to build a good livelihood from their agricultural production. This is particularly (but not exclusively) true for the situation in Sub-Saharan Africa, where despite considerable efforts, poverty among smallholders is still highly prevalent. Likewise, malfunctioning markets are a problem for food security, in particular to feed the growing urban populations, and for environmental sustainability of common pool resources like water and grazing lands.

1. Where we are and where we are heading

For this book, at the occasion of Aad van Tilburg's retirement, we have invited a number of leading academics in the field to write short essays on the state of affairs in markets, marketing and developing countries. Such short essays should allow for succinct position statements of what individual academics see as the accomplishments of the past and the challenges ahead. Each of the academics has summarized this into a short proposition at the beginning of the essay. The different contributors have not been constrained in the choice of their topics, other than that it should relate to the domain of markets, marketing and developing countries. Together these propositions and essays have sketched out a number of key themes.

Out of the many ways in which the 20 chapters of this book can be structured, we have chosen to group them in four thematic parts. The first part includes the essays that take a generic or macro approach to markets, marketing and developing countries. The second part deals with the role of agriculture in development. We include the essays on market access, value chains, and institutions in the third part. Finally, the fourth part discusses the role of marketing research also in a time perspective. Below, we elaborate further on these themes along the lines of the propositions that the authors have put central in their essays.

2. Macro perspectives on markets, marketing and developing countries

This section consists of essays that are grouped under the headings of the track record at the macro level and systems thinking in development. Three contributions look back at the success rates of previous policy approaches aimed at enhancing market access and improvement of livelihood (poverty reduction) among smallholders. Poole proposes:

Decades of agricultural marketing research has not provided solutions to the current problems of global security and poverty reduction.

Until the late 1980's and early 1990s, in many developing countries the initiative in promoting agricultural marketing was with the state rather than the individual and characterized by the establishment of marketing boards and cooperatives. The era of structural adjustment that followed led to a strong emphasis on market liberalization through generic 'free market' programs and policies and reduced involvement of national states, with the idea that trade would be a strong basis for market-led economic growth. However, these liberalization policies have only been partially successful in leading to efficiency and market-led growth. As a result, these have not provided solutions to the current problems of global security and poverty reduction. According to Poole, interventions and investments are needed in local assets, structures and institutions to truly bring benefits to communities of the poor and hungry.

Tollens picks up on this point from a slightly different angle, namely that of investment in food marketing hardware (physical infrastructure such as wholesale and retail markets telecommunications, roads, etc.) and software (the rules and regulations governing the exchange of products). Revisiting the concept of marketing margins, the difference between consumer and producer prices taking into account quality losses, he argues that a focus on reducing these marketing margins would be beneficial to the value chain:

Investing in marketing margin reduction is crucial for agricultural development and food security.

Using a simulation model he analyzes the effects of marketing margins on producer and consumer prices to show that, despite being replaced by modern concepts relating to agricultural value chain analysis, investing in marketing margin reduction is still crucial for agricultural development and food security for producers and consumers.

Heijman and Van Ophem also take a macro-level approach albeit from a different perspective. From cross-sectional data at the country level they show that there is a positive relationship between real Gross Domestic Product (GDP) per head and happiness. More specifically they also focus on how GDP per head is related to bundles of private and public goods in the field of human development, environmental health, gender related development and life expectancy and show these also to be positively related. Their overall conclusion is that for smallholders in developing countries facilitating better market access will contribute to their happiness, because this will generate a higher income for them.

Happiness is positively related to income and therefore the happiness of smallholders in low income countries will increase as a consequence of improved market access.

Two papers take a systems approach to development. Janssen and others take an innovation perspective to agricultural development. They specifically focus on the interactions between knowledge and market based development and how these can be integrated through the use of innovation system theory:

In the evolving agricultural economies of the developing world, knowledge and market development can be effectively linked through the use of innovation system theory.

They see innovation system theory as an important resource for rural-based sustainable development also from the design and implementation of new production-to-consumption systems (the so called 'new agriculture'). Based on eight case studies they identify a number of key success factors underlying successful innovation systems in developing and emerging countries.

Wierenga approaches the systems from a marketing point of view, giving a central role to the value chain (marketing channel), that connects upstream marketing and downstream marketing. He discusses how primary producers from emerging economies can connect to the channel, and which roles information systems and communication technology play in making the connection. He gives a positive message:

The ongoing of adoption of modern information and communication technology among primary producers in developing economies will significantly accelerate their connection to the third era of marketing.

3. Agriculture and agricultural markets as engines for development

The idea that development should start from the agricultural sector is well-established. It is therefore not surprising that several authors go back to these agricultural roots of development. Whereas the latter two essays within this part of the book deal with land reform and land markets, the first two stress the ineffectiveness of a one-size-fits-all approach to primary producers.

Previous policy approaches have partly been criticized for the fact that they are generic measures not specifically aligned with the specific conditions and environment with which particular groups of smallholders see themselves faced. Several contributors emphasize that policy measures can only be effective if they address the specific rather than generic conditions for livelihood improvement. As Kambewa and Nagoli state: 'much of the analysis on smallholder contribution tends to come from a managerial and policy point of view, rather than the (complementary) perspective of smallholders themselves'. They make the point that the labor of smallholders is the primary engine for development, and therefore propose that:

The worst thing that can happen is if smallholders can lay down their tools.

Lutz takes the point of the ineffectiveness of a one-size-fits-all approach further arguing that:

Strategic resources are a prerequisite for making the inclusion of smallholders in agro value chains sustainable.

According to Lutz, an individual firm perspective would require a focus on two important determinants of profitability: the attractiveness of the market and the (base line and unique) competencies of the firm. Only if these firm resources are to some extent superior and difficult to imitate, they will help to defend the long term firm's or farm's interest through enhanced negotiation power for the smallholder. Lutz pleads for more attention for rural development policy measures to develop these strategic resources at the primary producer level.

The second two papers in this part of the book deal with land reform and land markets. Land property right systems constitute an important policy measure to boost food production and to achieve more efficient distribution of food. Obi takes the unique situation of Zimbabwe as a test of different modes of implementation of land reform in the context of the Fast Track Land Reform Program in the early 21st century. He shows that the program has had a negative impact on maize yields and has weakened primary markets by creating supply bottlenecks and decreasing effective demand. He argues for proper planning in land reform when the purpose is to contribute to food security and poverty reduction.

Without proper planning, land reform can lead to supply bottlenecks as a result of declining productivity and production.

China is another example where the reform of land property is a key element of the transition from a centrally planned to a market oriented system. Heidhues and Piotrowski analyze this reform process in terms of its contribution to productivity. They identify a number of important constraints that prohibit the establishment of an efficient land and land rental market, at the social, institutional and economic level. Their analysis leads to two important policy recommendations, namely (a) that a more efficient land rental market would be facilitated by delinking land use rights and from off-farm employment and establish (another) social safety net for those working off farm, and (b) concomitantly increase agricultural productivity for small scale farming by providing higher incentives for farming household to rent-in additional land.

Land markets as instruments of efficient resource allocation require appropriate economic and institutional framework conditions. Reform policies need to address these constraints if they are to establish more efficient land markets.

4. Market access, value chains and institutions

In a book on markets, marketing, and developing countries, substantial attention for international value chains, smallholder access to these chains and institutions influencing chains, is of course inevitable. The eight essays in this part of the book are clustered in four topics that respectively deal with institutions and institutional arrangements, certification and standards, technological impact on chains and markets, and financial institutions.

Two papers focus on institutions and institutional arrangements designed for facilitating market access of smallholders. Van Huylenbroeck and colleagues formulated the proposition that:

Institutions are needed to create incentives for people to invest, increase their knowledge and organize the markets they are involved in.

They emphasize the importance of institutions in linking primary producers to markets by creating incentives for people to invest, increase their knowledge and organize the markets they are involved in. However, illustrated by two case studies, they also point at some important limitations specifically if such institutions only focus on economic rationality of output markets ignoring the specific other rationalities of producers and market players. These may be particularly due to dependency of small producers on credit facilities given by local shops and traders and by unequal distribution of transaction costs to the disadvantage of primary producers. To be successful new institutional arrangements should address the particular challenges of the people concerned and the vicious poverty cycles that many of them are caught in.

Staatz and Ricks focus on one specific institution, namely that of value chain participant councils (VCPCs), which are voluntary organizations, typically organized along value chain lines, that engage in joint analyses and problem-solving by a broad spectrum of key participants in a specific value chain. These VCPCs typically include representatives from farmers and trader organizations, processors, shippers, exporters, retailers, government agencies, and research and outreach organizations, with the goal to improve economic coordination and promote effective and inclusive economic growth. The authors provide evidence that these VCPCs, when carefully designed and implemented, provide a valuable institutional arrangement for vertical coordination and effective and inclusive economic growth. A number of design issues for such organizations are identified. Staatz and Ricks state the following:

Purely individualistic competition among the various participants in agricultural value chains often leads to poor vertical coordination and ineffective market performance. Value chain participant councils can play a critical role in improving effective vertical coordination, thereby improving the capacity of agricultural markets to contribute to sustainable, broad-based economic development.

Certification schemes and standards form a specific set of institutions that may serve in (international) chains as an important mechanism to manage and align quality levels of the primary product, while at the same time potentially leading to a fairer distribution of revenues. Fair Trade has taken a leading role in this development. Currently, as Ruben argues there is also an increased interest for business-to-business labeling schemes such as Utz and Rainforest Alliance and private sector certification schemes. These certification schemes have in common that they aim at delivery under market-conform conditions. In these schemes, higher prices emerge from improved efficiency and from better quality performance. Ruben compares different certification schemes, both on production standards (Fair Trade, Utz and Rainforest Alliance), company standards (CAFÉ and AAA) and verification standards (4C). His conclusion is that Fair Trade may be useful for initial market access, but that the private (brand) certification schemes may be a necessary follow up to guarantee sustained market participation in light of increasingly stringent market demands. He proposes:

For maintaining long-term competitiveness private labels offer better prospects to enhance quality upgrading.

Certification requires substantive changes in the structure, organization, and governance of value chains. In other words, it necessarily adds to the complexity of the value chain. Beuchelt and others analyze coffee value chains in Nicaragua to assess the price effects at the level of primary production in certified chains versus conventional chains. Interestingly they show that using certification to add value is not benefitting producers as expected. This is attributed to information asymmetry, governance issues in cooperatives and long chain structures in consuming countries causing high transaction costs:

In certified coffee value chains, the added value evaporates at the cost of primary producers; due to long chain structures in consuming countries causing high transaction costs, information asymmetry and bad governance in intermediating cooperatives.

Technology can be an important facilitator for enhanced market access of smallholders in many different ways. Jansen and colleagues focus on the role of telecommunication technology in improving information services. They propose:

In rural areas investments in telecommunications have the highest impact on welfare .... Governments have an important role to play in generating public content and optimizing the complementarities of infrastructure investments.

From a number of case studies they illustrate the effect of telecommunications on rural welfare through increased market access and reducing market inefficiencies. However, their important point is that this potential can only be optimally exploited if it is accompanied by other complementary infrastructural measures. There is an important role here for public policies, complementary and aligned to the private initiatives to enhance the market services and high penetration of telecommunications access.

As a food technologist, Van Boekel looks with a bit of surprise to the situation where the debate on food security and poverty reduction has focused heavily on quantity of crop production and nutritional quality of the crops, but much less on the food quality issues involved in post harvest processing. As most of these products are highly perishable, he argues that food technology expertise in storage, packaging and processing can help tremendously to reduce the large post-harvest losses (up to 30-40% in some developing countries). This would not only help in reducing the issues of food safety and food security, but with prolonged shelf life it would also improve the smallholders' negotiation power within the value chain. Food technology can also play a crucial role in product (quality) differentiation to better align primary production with the different types of value chains (local, regional and global) that primary producers are potentially part of. Van Boekel argues:

Food technology and marketing are complementary in improving the quality of food and the position of smallholders in developing countries.

Two papers specifically focus on the financing and financial risk management of procedures in developing countries. Huijsman and colleagues take microfinance as a central topic of their research. Microfinance is seen by many as one of the most effective tools to fight poverty as it promotes the economic development of the poor presumably leading to a higher standard of living. They are also considered a very stable source of financing as microfinance institutions (MFIs) are generally believed to be rather immune against the 'turmoil' on financial markets. The authors use the economic crisis as a research context to explore this 'immunity'. They report on an empirical study using both survey data and time series analysis to identify structural breaks in the MFIs profitability, growth and portfolio quality. Their main conclusion is that the microfinance sector is not as disconnected from formal markets as commonly assumed and they discuss many explanations why that is the case in the current structure of MFIs:

The current financial crisis adversely affects microfinance institutions and the extent of the adverse impact depends on the funding structure of MFIs.

Pennings looks at value chains from the perspective of risk management. He makes the point that due to low equity position of primary producers in the value chain, their capacity to absorb price risk is limited. Because agricultural value chains have the potential to benefit welfare levels at all stages of the chain, developing risk benefit tools that fit the needs of producers in developing countries seem particularly important. The paper addresses the issue of developing successful commodity future contracts for developing countries. In addition to hedging effectiveness, the market microstructure of the commodity futures exchange, the financial- and transportation infrastructure, and the market advisory structure, amongst others, are key to the success of futures exchanges in these countries. Market Advisory Services are crucial in this process in advising producers regarding selling their crops. Pennings therefore proposes that a road map is necessary:

A road map is needed that provides the necessary and sufficient conditions for successful commodity futures exchanges in Least Developed Countries (LDCs).

5. The marketing research agenda in past, present and future

The final two papers look back and ahead on the role of the academic marketing discipline (marketing research) in research on developing countries. In line with the developments sketched by Wierenga in his essay, Ingenbleek distinguishes three phases of marketing thought. He relates the negative attributions of marketing to development to the phase of marketing management, but recognizes that more recent work in marketing relates stronger to the original marketing concept. The marketing concept, he claims, has an inherent promise to development:

Marketing can provide a unique contribution to development thinking. Recent developments in marketing theory help to remember that marketing is inherently part of the solution rather than part of the problem.

According to Ingenbleek, marketing research can make a contribution to development by increasing the understanding of responsiveness to customer wants and needs on consumer and business markets. Responsiveness can be studied at the level of individual entrepreneurs, the level of value chains that connect producers to final consumers, and on the level of marketing systems that also include institutions, NGOs, governments, and other third parties.

In the final essay, somewhat different from the others, Van Tilburg looks back on his career from both a theoretical and a practical point of view. It includes a brief overview of the literature sources that guided Van Tilburg during his career and the theories and key concepts that helped him find new ways to approach marketing and market problems in developing countries. He shares the highlights of his rich field experience to illustrate the development of thinking in this field. He concludes that a single approach is unlikely to deal with all problems. Rather researchers should choose a perspective dependent on the context, because the functioning of a market or chain is as strong as its major weakness:

The supply or value chain for primary producers in developing countries is as strong as the weakest link whether this is entrepreneurship including marketing, market performance, horizontal or vertical coordination in the supply chain, or combinations of these factors.

As a final advise to his colleagues, Van Tilburg recommends more attention to be given to the roles and functions of entrepreneurs and institutions as the key forces that shape markets. To avoid overlooking potential weaknesses, he also pleads for broadening the scope of performance measurement from financial performance only to measures that cover a broader part of the sustainability concept.

6. In summary

Thanks to all individual contributions, we believe that the book contains a rich collection of ideas on markets, marketing and developing countries with regard to their past present and future. In general, the essays reflect the current hope in the development community, that markets are part of the solutions to poverty, distribution of agricultural lands, food security, and sustainable development at large. The essays also critically reflect that markets, shaped by opportunistic human self interests, are in many cases too vulnerable to be let free entirely. Proper institutions are required to guide the development of markets and value chains in the right direction. Marketing, as an activity by which entrepreneurs and companies develop markets, may help to make the high hopes for the future come true.

Part 1.

Macro perspectives on markets, marketing and developing countries

Track record on the macro level

From 'marketing systems' to 'value chains': what have we learnt since the post-colonial era and where do we go?

Nigel Poole

The recent world food crisis of 2007-08 has changed perceptions of the global importance of agriculture, but also suggests that decades of food and agricultural marketing research have not provided solutions to current problems of global security and poverty reduction. Small-scale interventions and investments in local economies are necessary to address the specific problems of the poorest.

Abstract

Analyses of agrifood marketing systems in poor countries since the post-colonial era have been characterized by waves of enthusiasm, circumspection, disillusion, new insights and renewed enthusiasm. In the same period, an extra 3 billion or so people have been fed; on the other hand, at least 1 billion people, the same total as at the beginning of the 1960s, are still hungry, of whom maybe 200 million are children. It is timely to consider what have we learnt during the last four decades of agricultural marketing research, and also what has been achieved in improving agricultural commerce in developing countries. This chapter reviews experience and comments how ideology has driven policy approaches which have often left agricultural marketing problems unresolved. It suggests that small-scale institutional innovations and investments in local economies are superior to the current imperative of 'upscaling' and 'generalizability', and need to be founded on specific studies through agricultural marketing research undertaken at a disaggregated level.

Keywords: agricultural marketing, policy shifts, public intervention, private initiatives, value chains, targeting, local investment, disaggregated agricultural marketing research

1. Introduction

Reflecting on the first two decades after the Second World War, Jones (1974: 4) commented on the concerns about the role of marketing systems in stimulating and facilitating agricultural development and assuring the availability of foodstuffs to rural and urban populations. Studies of Africa by outsiders discovered that marketing was not a new phenomenon, but was 'much more common in the pre-colonial period than was previously thought'. Much more has been learnt since then by outsiders about how markets actually function. The context of agricultural marketing has also changed dramatically. The recognition then of the opportunity to create marketable surpluses and to exchange goods and services over larger distances in order to make these foodstuffs available anticipated the explosion of international trade together with social, economic and political processes of globalization which are now familiar. This was facilitated by liberal market economics, technological change and expanding commercial strategies, and was affected by institutional intervention for and against international agricultural development and trade. On the one hand, poverty has been overcome through local and international economic growth in many contexts; on the other the complexity of production systems, disadvantageous economic geography, bad governance and now climate change continue to assail and define the poorest populations. Inequality has probably increased, and many marketing problems remain unresolved in many countries.

2. Changing policy approaches

For many developing countries, the balance of initiative in promoting agricultural marketing lay with the state rather than with the individual until the late 1980s or early 1990s. The expansion of public sector marketing could not have been undertaken without the provision of aid from bilateral and multilateral donors, whose policies constituted an endorsement of a state-led strategy. Marketing boards and cooperatives were a convenient counterpart agency for donors whose programs of food aid, infrastructural investment and rural development projects were increasing in importance. But intervention in agricultural markets did not generally work in Africa.

The era of structural adjustment followed, with diverse patterns of market reform, from the redefinition of parastatal roles through a range of radical changes to abolition of state intervention. The nature of the policies being adopted depended partly on ideology, and on assumptions about the capacity of the private sector to respond, the estimate of risk of failure in unprofitable markets, the importance accorded to social or 'public' objectives such as stockholding, the existence of scale economies, and the danger of emerging privatized monopolies.

The potential for a response from the private sector to economic incentives and opportunities should have created a sense of optimism in creating efficient and competitive markets, and overcoming the livelihood constraints of poor producers and traders. The propensity of many African peoples to engage in trade should have been a sound foundation for market-led economic growth.

The resurgence of faith in liberal market mechanisms towards the end of the twentieth century was paralleled by international policy neglect in respect of the rural economy, an uninterested attitude to, even a disengagement from, agriculture. But liberalization policies did not generally lead to efficiency and market-led growth. As traders were not willing or able to fill the void, farmers were left without market outlets. The radical reduction in scope of state intervention and not infrequent collapse of organized marketing systems did not stimulate a strong private sector response, nor generate higher levels of competition, but precipitated a decline in agricultural trading. Most farmers without commercial knowledge or experience have been unable to engage successfully in marketing their produce on their own account, and the possibility of engaging in high value export markets for many smallholders is remote.

3. Newer analyses and intervention approaches

Making markets work

The policy climate has continued to evolve substantially since the reforms of the 1980s and 1990s. Newer policies have encouraged the provision of business development services to stimulate the private sector. Recently, considerable attention has been attached to improving the performance of the wider business environment. 'Making markets work for the poor' (MMW4P) stresses the process of creating opportunities through increasing access to markets, achieving equitable and remunerative prices for goods and services, and reducing risk. While MMW4P envisages commercial interventions and is 'pro-competitive structures', it is weak in the policy dimension and draws back from advocating innovative public policy interventions and radical resource reallocation (Poole, 2009). Linkages of enterprise concepts to movements advocating collective organization are also weak.

Value chain approaches

Latterly NGOs have become a significant channel for linking poor people to markets, and together with international donor-practitioners have drawn on the value chain approaches more commonly used in advanced economies and international commodity exports. The emergence from industrial organization of value chain analysis as an analytical framework can be traced, *inter alia*, to Porter's exposition of competitive strategies (1985) which provided a tool to enable firms to look beyond their own boundaries, to examine linkages with other organizations and to identify ways of creating and sustaining better business performance. Gereffi (1994) developed the concept in relation to global commodity chains, focusing on the locus of power in chain management, being either buyer-led or supplier-led.

The early analytical precision in value chain analysis derived from the focus on the resources and activities of the individual firm within its own value chain, and the competitive strategies whereby the firm could add value and increase profitability. Adoption and diffusion of the value chain concept has led to an emphasis on a wide range of stakeholders and a loss of analytical distinctiveness: commonly, 'The value chain describes the full range of activities which are required to bring a product or service from conception, through the different phases of production (involving a combination of physical transformation and the input of various producer services), delivery to final consumers, and final disposal after use' (Kaplinsky and Morris, 2002). Porter still focuses on the firm as the unit of analysis in the chain but himself has expanded the scope of the concept to embrace business performance in a broad sense, including corporate social responsibility (Porter and Kramer, 2006).

Value chains and the poor

Through the advocacy of international and non-governmental organizations value chain approaches have become a policy mechanism, even moving towards an all-inclusive 'task-force' approach, such as that used in the development of the cassava sector in Zambia (Chitundu *et al.*, 2009). The extent to which economic development and wellbeing can be generated by supporting the agricultural activities of the poorest is still a moot point. Reduction of poverty among the poorest may be more likely to come through interventions targeted at the not-so-poor, and the resulting multiplier effects through the labor market, for example. Commercial enterprise may well select against the extreme poor in such a way that agriculture, producer organization and market integration are not a viable pathway out of poverty. These limits are not well understood, but they circumscribe the scope of effective agricultural marketing policy.

4. Ideology and empiricism

It is evident that donor ideology has also influenced the choice of organizational forms and marketing interventions. Donor policies are in turn influenced by pragmatic considerations such as how aid can be most easily dispensed. This probably applies just as much at the beginning of the 21st century as during the 20th century, and the danger of interventions representing prevailing conventional wisdom remains.

Re-evaluation of the positive role of the state in facilitating the Green Revolution, and a resurgence of interest in collective organizations, the stakeholder concept, comparative approaches to political economy and network approaches to business are beginning to vindicate a hybrid policy approach, drawing on models of both 'liberal' and 'coordinated' market economies (Hall and Soskice, 2001). That is to say, while private sector activity accounts for most successful economic activity, at the same time market failures are still pervasive in developing countries and require initiatives from the private sector and interventions from the state and the 'third sector'.

Scale and type of intervention and initiative

From the history of state and market failure in the last couple of decades, we can say with some confidence that often it is small-scale institutional innovations and investments in local market structure and conduct and a range of other non-price factors, that are likely to stimulate the participation of poorer smallholders in markets, particularly those for staple foods (Poole and De Frece, 2010). Efficient market organization not only involves more but also better linkages between different economic players, which in turn require investment in many and various forms of human skills and social capital in addition to physical infrastructure and communications:

- For collective organization, innovative business models can be made to work: new and alternative cooperative management structures exist with access to innovative financial resourcing; either philanthropic support, or external equity investment, or bondholders with a financial stake but without governance rights. These strategies offer the possibility of external capitalization without diluting membership control.
- The approach of external supporting organizations must be patient and realistic in achieving threshold levels of asset requirements and of external support. Enterprises are 'organic': they learn and grow, sometimes fail, and sometimes need to rise from the ashes of incompetence and corruption. But there is no 'one size-fits all', and no guarantee that individual successes can be upscaled and replicated.
- The purpose of the formal legal and regulatory framework, such as competition and business laws and cooperative laws is, in part, to shape the environment and enable business to operate effectively. In this context, the needs of smallholders may be unrecognized and underprovided. Policies and priorities are critical to economic empowerment of the rural poor. Direct intervention should have a 'light', 'enabling' touch: correcting specific market failures, without otherwise intervening in commercial chain activities.
- Most successful cases of collective enterprise creation have depended on a substantial degree of intervention from NGOs and international donors. International donors can best employ their financial and human resources to address sectoral failures that cannot be addressed by the state or the private sector.
- Commercial partnership programs can provide the essential capacity building to create viable business relationships in competitive markets. But agribusiness partnership programs cannot necessarily be mainstreamed. Where commercial linkages work, donors and the state should not crowd out the private sector. Nevertheless, it is not philanthropy but profitability that drives the private sector.

5. Lessons learned: local solutions to local problems

While there have been notable achievements in agricultural development and marketing over recent decades, food and agricultural marketing research have not provided widespread solutions to the current problems of global security and poverty reduction. Among the inferences to be drawn from past experience, the most important that can be deduced is that ideological shifts have not resulted in viable policies to boost the contribution of agricultural marketing to poverty and hunger reduction in many situations.

Because poverty problems are specific to a given development context, the demand for 'generalizability' and 'upscaling' of interventions is often ineffective and misplaced. Consequently, it is necessary to emphasize empirical approaches to policy formulation based on precise and disaggregated studies. Effective interventions are likely to be local and particular, and therefore more costly than the ranges of RORs and NPRs to which economists are accustomed. Targeting the local economy through interventions and investments in local assets, structures and institutions is more likely to bring significant benefits to communities of the poor and hungry.

References

Chitundu, M., Droppelmann, K. and Haggblade, S. (2009). Intervening in value chains: lessons from Zambia's Task Force on Acceleration of Cassava Utilisation. Journal of Development Studies 45: 593-620.

Gereffi, G. and Korzeniewicz, M. (eds.) (1994). Commodity Chains and Global Capitalism. Greenwood Press, Westport, CT, USA.

Hall, P.A. and Soskice, D. (2001). Varieties of Capitalism: the Institutional Foundations of Comparative Advantage. OUP, Oxford, UK.

Jones, W.O. (1974). Regional Analysis and Agricultural Marketing Research in Tropical Africa: Concepts and Experiences. Food Research Institute Studies 13: 3-28.

Kaplinsky, R. and Morris, M. (2002). A Handbook for Value Chain Research. Prepared for IDRC.

Poole, N.D. (2009). Making markets - and institutions - work for the poor. Eurochoices 8: 40-45.

Poole, N.D. and De Frece, A. (2010). A Review of Existing Organisational Forms of Smallholder Farmers' Associations and their Contractual Relationships with other Market Participants in the East and Southern African ACP Region. AAACP Paper Series – No. 11. Rome, Food and Agriculture Organization of the United Nations.

Porter, M.E. (1985). Competitive Advantage: Creating and Sustaining Superior Performance. Macmillan, New York, NY, USA.

Porter, M.E. and Kramer, M.R. (2006). Strategy and society: the link between competitive advantage and corporate social responsibility. Harvard Business Review 84: 78-92.

The neglect of food marketing in developing countries revisited

Eric Tollens

Investing in marketing margin reductions is crucial for agricultural development and food security.

Abstract

This essay is based on the seminal article by Frank Meissner 'Effective food marketing - A tool for socioeconomic development in the Third World', published in Food Policy, May 1989. The article focuses on the benign neglect of agricultural and food marketing as a tool of agricultural and rural development, explores the causes of this neglect and the roads ahead. This lag between production and marketing of food is often referred to as the second generation of Green Revolution problems. Although emphasis is still squarely on increasing food production, more attention is now paid to market access, marketing information and reducing marketing margins. We explain the pivotal role of reducing marketing margins and improving the marketing performance to increase prices paid to producers and to reduce prices paid by consumers. We use a simulation model to illustrate the effects of a reduction in the marketing margin, ceteris paribus, for various price elasticities of supply and demand for agricultural products. The causes of the relative neglect of agricultural marketing in poor countries are revisited, for marketing hardware as well as for software. Reducing marketing margins, which are typically excessive in developing countries, is still imperative for a green revolution to succeed. This is often overlooked as ineffective marketing systems, although completely liberalized, are so common in poor countries. Investing in markets and market development still takes the back seat in agricultural investment programs. The chapter concludes by examining what can be done to give agricultural marketing its proper place in the fight against hunger and destitution.

Keywords: marketing margins, reduction of marketing costs, effects on producers and consumers, effective food marketing, neglect of food marketing, simulation of effects

1. Introduction

Frank Meissner's article in Food Policy on 'Effective food marketing - A tool for socioeconomic development in the Third World', (1989) is best known by food marketing economists as the article that put the benign neglect of food marketing in developing countries on the spot, explored the causes of benign neglect and the roads ahead. It became mandatory reading of my students. Indeed, agricultural development economists almost naturally focus on increasing food production, somehow hoping that the food produced will reach the consumer at affordable cost. But the high marketing margins – simply defined as the difference between consumer and producer prices, taking into account quantity losses because of processing, storage, transport and distribution – found in most developing countries show that this is illusory. Frank Meissner reviewed data on food marketing margins and derived some clues about tentative goals for what should be 'reasonable' investments in food marketing hardware (physical infrastructure such as wholesale and retail markets, telecommunications, roads, etc.) and software (the rules and regulations governing the exchange of products, including weights and measures, quality standards, dispute settlement, opening and closing hours, etc.). He also tried to explain why investment in food marketing has lagged behind food production. Meissner (1989: 94) argued that the causes for the benign neglect of food marketing are:

- Marketing is seen by many political leaders in poor countries as a wasteful, parasitic and socially irrelevant activity.
- The merchant class in many poor countries often belongs to a foreign minority, accused of 'exploiting' the indigenous population. Political leaders therefore tend to assign marketing improvement activities a very low priority, actively putting up barriers to their effective performance.
- Most professionals in agricultural development are traditionally agronomists, with prime concern for increasing on-farm production.
- Incremental on-farm production is easier to measure than benefits generated by improvements in marketing functions.
- Policy makers tend to believe that marketing institutions spring up spontaneously to bring agricultural commodities to markets and inputs to farms.
- Hunger in the midst of plenty is primarily caused by inequitable income distribution, a matter outside the scope of marketing.
- The marketing profession has been incredibly inept at marketing to policy decision makers and implementers in poor countries.

Meissner's focused very much on what the CGIAR (Consultative Group on International Agricultural Research) could and should do, saying: '... what the CGIAR accomplished in food production can also be done in marketing, the function that gets commodities from farmers to consumers, in the process doubling or tripling value added to the raw products that leave the farm gate.' He recommended to set up a TACAM: Technical Advisory Committee on Agricultural Marketing.

This essay revisits these issues: the neglect of food marketing in developing countries, the importance of marketing margins and their effects on producer and consumer prices, using a simulation model, and the importance of investments in food marketing hardware and software in poor countries.

2. The neglect of food marketing in developing countries revisited

The World Bank named its 2008 World Development Report 'Agriculture for Development'. For the fist time in 25 years, agriculture is at the centre of attention again. Partly, this is due to the realization that without development in agriculture, reaching Millennium Development Goals on poverty and hunger will remain elusive. Partly, it is a reflection of the fact that growth in demand for food is outpacing supply. Partly, it is recognition of the fact that if agriculture has to provide not only food, feed and fibre, but also fuel, then renewed investment in agriculture is required (World Bank, 2007). Although the WDR is a very timely and excellent report, again food marketing in poor countries is neglected in it. Food marketing or agricultural marketing do not appear in the index and neither does the term marketing margins. New terms and concepts such as agribusiness, value chains, modern supply chains, commodity trading, etc. are in the report and receive a lot of attention. But the costs of getting food from producers to consumers only receive scant attention. It seems that food marketing economists are now more preoccupied by new institutional economics concepts such as information asymmetry, moral hazard, adverse selection, transaction costs (which are part of marketing margins), principal agents, etc.

Most food markets, if not all, in developing countries are now liberalized, but not necessarily effective nor efficient. Many papers are published showing that these markets are high cost, with lack of physical infrastructure, high losses and wastage, poor regulation, manipulation by cartels or informal power brokers, lack of adequate marketing information, lack of economies of scale, lack of market integration. But such food markets, including wholesale markets, are usually under the responsibility of cities, or the Ministry of Commerce, not the Ministry of Agriculture. Hence, the Ministry of Agriculture has not and will not invest in them.

Over the last decade, characterized by rapid urbanisation and low investments in agriculture and related downstream sectors such as food marketing, the absolute and relative cost of getting food from producers to consumers in cities has probably been growing in poor countries, although we have no hard data to back this assertion up. In developing countries, food marketing is traditionally very labour intensive, including food transport, processing and distribution. Meissner reported that in developing countries, at least 25% of the total funds invested in the food system (including production) should have been into marketing functions, including all software and hardware related to assembly, processing, transport, distribution, finance and information activities involved in getting staple foods from producers to consumers. I personally do not believe that this has happened or is happening. The primacy and overriding consideration of investing in agriculture means that probably much less that 25% has been invested. But even for Meissner, the 25% minimum is just for the sake of argument with no hard calculation to back it up.

Some of the major studies on food marketing margins in the 1980s were 'Marketing costs and Margins for Major Food Items in Developing Countries' by Mittendorf and Hertäg (1982). A major methodological study on how to measure marketing costs and margins is 'A Methodology for Measuring Marketing Costs and Margins for Foodstuffs in Developing Countries' by L.D. Smith (1981) of the University of Glasgow. A major comparison of marketing margins is 'Marketing and Price Incentives in African and Asian Countries: A Comparison' by Ahmed and Rustagi (1987).

FAO conducted for the first time in 1979-80 a survey on the magnitude and composition of marketing costs and margins in a number of developing countries. The Mittendorf and Hertäg (1982) article is the outcome of that survey. Since then I am not aware of any worldwide comparisons of marketing costs and margins, except for IFPRI's work by Ahmed and Rustagi (1987). In the meantime, FAO has scaled down its Marketing and Credit Service in the Agricultural Services Division and also IFPRI (International Food Policy Research Institute) has changed its strategy and is focusing less on 'traditional food marketing' research.

The issue of marketing margins is important in judging the efficiency of marketing chains. Recently, there has been a lot of discussion on marketing cost ratios retail/farmer for various commodities on the internet as part of CTA's (Technical Centre for Agriculture and Rural Cooperation) discussion forum on Promoting Second Generation Market Information Services (MIS) in Developing Economies (mis@dgroups.org). Vinay Chand, a MIS expert, states that a ratio of 3:1 is normal for the United Kingdom (i.e. the marketing margin is 75% of the retail price). For imported products, 5:1 or more is normal. The ratio does not tell you what the farmer got, but tells us what proportion of retail he/she received. It is however dangerous to draw conclusions from ratios. If for a particular developing country a ratio is found of e.g. 1:8 for horticulture, it is not evidence of rampant exploitation of farmers. That is too simplistic a conclusion. It most often means that the chain is inefficient, due to a number of possible factors. It may be that it is a low value business with little investment and thus high wastage. It may be a fragmented chain with too many links none making good money. It may be geography with difficult and long access to markets. It may be low productivity, poor infrastructure or differing degrees of concentration in the sub sectors. Several factors may conspire in an inefficient chain to yield poor returns to farmers and usually everyone else in the chain also.

In our studies on cassava marketing for the Kinshasa market in the Democratic Republic of Congo, we found ratios of 4:1 for cassava chips (*cossettes*) from Bandundu province and about 3:1 from Bas Congo province, which is closer to Kinshasa, now a city of 8 million inhabitants (Goossens *et al.*, 1994).

One of the main problems encountered in marketing margin analysis is that there are no real benchmarks for comparison. There is no way to judge objectively whether marketing costs are too high or not. Each marketing chain is different and one can only use experience and judgement to evaluate whether efficiency can be gained somewhere in the chain, thus reducing pragmatically marketing costs. And there are many different ways of reducing marketing costs. Non specialists usually tend to equate marketing costs with transport costs only, but that is a big simplification. In many poor countries, the absence of organized wholesale markets, or the non separation of the wholesaling function from the retail function, contributes to marketing inefficiency and high marketing margins. The main benefit of a well functioning wholesale market is the price discovery mechanism, resulting from the confrontation of all of supply with all of demand. Such an equilibrium price automatically clears the market and in fact sets the price for all market participants (Tollens, 1997).

3. How does reducing the marketing margin benefit producers, consumers and traders?

Hereafter, we present an analytical framework or model that helps to understand why it is so important to invest in food marketing by reducing marketing margins. In this analysis, it does not matter by what means the food marketing margins are reduced: either a new road which reduces transport costs, a new marketing technology, enhanced competition in the marketing chain, etc. The model is based on Shepherd (1963) and Shepherd and Futrell (1968) but follows standard agricultural price analysis theory. Two basic assumptions underlay the model:
1. Perfect competition, as otherwise the gains from a reduction in marketing margins are possibly 'pocketed' by a powerful trader.
2. Homogeneous food products and no quantity losses from farm to consumer. This is just to facilitate the analysis, otherwise it becomes messy.

The *ceteris paribus* conditions also have to be considered: i.e. the marketing margin decreases, but nothing else changes. In Figure 1, two demand functions and two supply functions are drawn. The consumer demand function Dc is the primary demand function, with Dp the derived demand function at the level of the producer. The vertical difference between the two is the marketing margin.

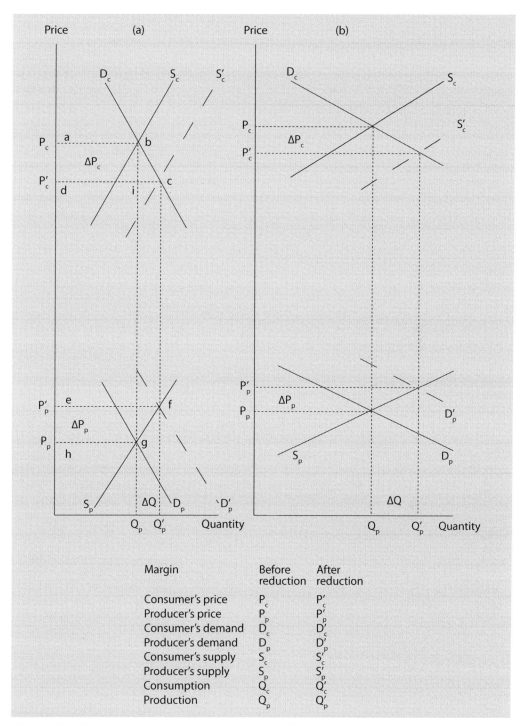

Figure 1. *The effect of a decrease in the marketing margin: (a) inelastic supply and demand, (b) elastic supply and demand.*

The producer supply function Op is the primary supply function while Oc is the derived supply function at the level of the consumer. Again, the vertical difference between the two is the marketing margin.

A reduction of the marketing margin has the following effects (Figure 1):
- a decrease in the consumer price from P_c to P'_c
- an increase in the producer price from P_p to P'_p
- an increase in production from Q_p to Q'_p
- an increase in consumption from $Q_c=Q_p$ to $Q'_c= Q'_p$, i.e., the consumed quantity and the produced quantity increase both in the same way
- both the derived supply and the derive demand functions shift in the same way. The primary demand and supply functions do not move.

It becomes clear that under perfect competition, a reduction in the marketing margin benefits both producers and consumers and this shows the importance of increasing the efficiency of marketing systems. The decrease of the consumer price ΔPc ($P_c-P'_c$) and the increase in the quantity consumed ΔQ ($Q_c-Q'_c$) benefits the consumer with the area a, b, c, d, the consumer surplus. The producer also benefits from a reduction in the marketing margin by the area e, f, g, h, the producer surplus. When demand and supply functions are inelastic, the price effect is larger than the quantity effect (Figure 1a). When they are elastic, the quantity effect ΔQ is relatively more important than the price effect (Figure 1b). Thus, the relative importance of the quantity and price effects depend on the relative importance of the price elasticities of supply and demand. If both elasticities of supply and demand are the same, the effect on consumer prices equals that on producer prices ($\Delta P_p=\Delta P_c$). With different price elasticities, the price effects are different: an inelastic supply results in a relatively larger increase in the producer price, while an inelastic demand results in a relatively larger decrease in the consumer price compared to the increase in the producer price.

In Table 1, we have simulated these different effects of a 10% reduction in the marketing margin, *ceteris paribus*, for different elasticities of supply and demand (linear functions). We assume here that the producer price is one-fourth of the consumer price, i.e. a ratio of 4:1. We use for simulation a mathematical model (which can be obtained from eric.tollens@biw.kuleuven.be) of Figure 1. It is this mathematical model that allowed us to calculate Table 1. The following example makes it clear. For a price elasticity of demand of -0,3 and a price elasticity of supply of 0,6, a reduction in the marketing margin by 10% will have the following effects:
- an increase in the producer price of +10%;
- a decrease in the consumer price of -5%;
- an increase in the quantity sold of +6%.

These benefits will occur year after year, *ceteris paribus*, and it is possible to calculate the net present value of the effect of a reduction in the marketing margin over several years. But it will not be realistic to assume that the effect is immediate. Markets adjust only slowly, even under competitive conditions. Moreover, the reduction in the marketing margin will probably also be a gradual slow process, except for e.g. opening up a new road, or opening a new wholesale facility. How fast the benefits will be realized depends very much on the competitive character of the market. It is to be noted that the benefits realized are Pareto better; everyone gains and nobody loses.

As food markets in poor countries are characterized by relatively inelastic demand for food staples and relatively elastic supply, it is clear that consumers gain most in this case. In the example of demand elasticity

Table 1. *The effects of a reduction in the marketing margin by 10% on the producer price and consumer price and on the marketed quantities (in %) when one assumes that the producer price is one-fourth of the consumer price (based on simulations using a mathematical model of Figure 1).*

Demand elasticity		Supply elasticity				
		0.2	0.6	1.0	1.4	1.8
-0.1	Producer	+10.0	+4.3	+2.7	+2.0	+1.6
	Consumer	-5.0	-6.4	-6.8	-7.0	-7.1
	Volume effect	+2.0	+2.6	+2.7	+2.8	+2.9
-0.3	Producer	+18.0	+10.0	+6.9	+5.3	+4.3
	Consumer	-3.0	-5.0	-5.8	-6.2	-6.4
	Volume effect	+3.6	+6.0	+6.9	+7.4	+7.7
-0.5	Producer	+21.4	+13.6	+10.0	+7.9	+6.5
	Consumer	-2.1	-4.1	-5.0	-5.5	-5.9
	Volume effect	+4.3	+8.2	+10.0	+11.1	+11.7
-0.7	Producer	+23.3	+16.1	+12.3	+10.0	+8.4
	Consumer	-1.7	-3.4	-4.4	-5.0	-5.4
	Volume effect	+4.7	+9.7	+12.3	+14.0	+15.1
-0.9	Producer	+24.5	+18.0	+14.2	+11.7	+10.0
	Consumer	-1.4	-3.0	-3.9	-4.6	-5.0
	Volume effect	+4.9	+10.8	+14.2	+16.4	+18.0
-1.1	Producer	+25.4	+19.4	+15.7	+13.2	+11.4
	Consumer	-1.2	-2.6	-3.6	-4.2	-4.6
	Volume effect	+5.1	+11.6	+15.7	+18.5	+20.5
-1.3	Producer	+26.0	+20.5	+17.0	+14.4	+12.6
	Consumer	-1.0	-2.4	-3.3	-3.9	-4.4
	Volume effect	+5.2	+12.3	+17.0	+20.2	+22.7

-0.1 and supply elasticity of 1 in Table 1, the effects are: +2,7% producer price; -6,8% consumer price; +2,7% volume. Usually a lot of non price constraints limit supply response in developing countries, and it is more realistic to also assume inelastic supply. But we should not forget that for a ratio of 4:1, the consumer price is four times the producer price and a 1% change in the consumer price equals in absolute terms 4% at the producer level. This is what many farmers worldwide have difficulty with understanding and accepting.

For producers, the volume or quantity effect may be more important than the price effect. Also, the more supply and demand are elastic, the higher the volume effect and it becomes quickly larger than the price effects. Surprisingly, traders also always gain through the volume effect. But at low elasticities of supply and demand, the volume effect is low, in the order of 2-3%.

It is the competition in the system that ensures that the gains from the reduction in the marketing margin cannot be captured by traders and go entirely to producers and consumers. Traders will make extra profit only through the volume effect in the case of perfect competition. The competitiveness of the system ensures that all their costs are covered with a reasonable profit margin, but nothing more. This holds an important lesson for governments: they need to ensure competition in the marketing system as otherwise public investments to reduce marketing costs (marketing margins) are likely to be captured by traders, and will not go to (poor) producers and consumers.

4. What can be done? - roads ahead

The TACAM that Meissner recommended never materialised and TAC in the CGIAR itself was changed to the Science Council which will now become the Science and Partnership Council in the new CGIAR. What Meissner wanted is also to establish an international network of marketing research centres designed to (a) pull together existing knowledge, (b) define missing links, (c) assign priorities, (d) develop a research agenda, (e) help prepare projects, (f) assign responsibility for research, (g) guide implementation, and (h) mobilize the required funds. He saw IFPRI as the best location and initial home.

In the proposed draft Strategy and Results Framework for the CGIAR (Von Braun *et al.*, 2009), new Mega Programs (MP) are defined and one of them is 'Institutional Innovations and Markets': knowledge to inform institutional changes needed for a well-functioning local, national, and global food system that connects small farmers to agricultural value chains through information and communications technologies and facilitates policy and institutional reforms.

Will this do? Certainly not in Meissner's view. But recently, more interest has been shown in linking farmers to markets and market access issues, particularly by AGRA (Alliance for a Green Revolution in Africa), financed by the Rockefeller and Bill and Melinda Gates Foundations. Market development has become much more prominent, but it is usually packaged in new terms, such as value chain development, from farm to fork. The critical role of improved markets for inclusion of the poor is recognized. Low market access in fact means high marketing margins and institutional innovations are probably the mechanism by which marketing margins are to be reduced. Also, reducing risk in marketing is now high on the agenda. One aim of this MP is to reduce transaction costs of small farmers by 30% by 2025, while mitigating risks. Transactions costs need probably to be understood in a broad sense and stand for marketing margins.

5. Conclusions

In conclusion, food marketing is now certainly recognized as an important driver of economic development in poor countries, but the traditional emphasis on food marketing and marketing margins has been replaced by more modern concepts relating to the agricultural value chain, transaction costs, institutional innovations, market access, etc. To some extent, Meissner is still right that there is benign neglect of food marketing as compared to food production. But as demonstrated, investing in marketing margin reductions is crucial for agricultural development and food security for producers and consumers. Thus, food marketing has retained what Meissner called its Cinderella status – a sleeping beauty still largely ignored in economic development – and this is exactly why this essay has been written in honor of colleague and friend Aad van Tilburg, a more traditional agricultural and food marketing economist like myself.

References

Ahmed, R. and Rustagi, N. (1987). Marketing and Price Incentives in African and Asian Countries: A Comparison. In: D. Eltz (ed.), Agricultural Marketing Strategy and Pricing Policy. World Bank, Washington DC, USA.

Meissner, F. (1989). Effective Food Marketing - A Tool for Socioeconomic Development in the Third World. Food Policy 14: 90-96.

Mittendorf, H.S. and Hertäg, O. (1982). Marketing Costs and Margins for Major Food Items in Developing Countries. Food and Nutrition 8: 27-31.

Goossens, F., Minten, B., and Tollens, E. (1994). Nourrir Kinshasa - L'approvisionnement local d'une métropole africaine, Paris. L'Harmattan & K.U.Leuven, Paris, France.

Shepherd, G., (1963). Agricultural Price Analysis. 6th Edition. Iowa State University Press, Ames, IA, USA.

Shepherd, G. and Futrell, G. (1968). Marketing Farm Products. Iowa State University Press, Ames, IA, USA.

Smith, L.D. (1981). A Methodology for Measuring Marketing Costs and Margins for Foodstuffs in Developing Countries. In: Post Harvest Operations: Workshop Proceedings. FAO Network and Centre For Agricultural Marketing Training In Eastern and Southern Africa, Harare, Zimbabwe, pp. 37-83.

Tollens, E., (1997). Wholesale Markets in African Cities - Diagnosis, Role, Advantages and Elements for Further Study and Development. FAO and University of Leuven, AC/05-97, Rome, Italy.

Von Braun, J., Byerlee, D., Chartres, C., Lumpkin, T., Olembo, N., and Waage, J. (2009). Towards a Strategy and Results Framework for the CGIAR. Draft report by the Strategy Team.

World Bank (2007). Agriculture for Development. World Development Report 2008, 20433, Washington D.C., USA.

Income, happiness and socio-economic bench marking across countries

Wim Heijman and Johan van Ophem

Happiness is positively related to income and therefore the happiness of people in low income countries will increase as a consequence of improved market access.

Abstract

In this paper the relationship between real income and happiness will be analysed, based on literature and the authors' own original empirical research. The topic is addressed at the level of a particular society or nation state. From cross sectional data on the country level, it is found that the real GDP per head and happiness are positively related. People in the richer part of the world are happier than in the poorer part of the world. Furthermore, it appears that, on the one hand, GDP per head and, on the other hand, bundles of private and public goods in the field of human development, environmental health, gender related development and life expectancy are positively related. Finally the relationship between these bundles and income provides the basis for socio-economic bench marking and the setting of priorities for socio-economic bench marking across countries.

Keywords: happiness, income, socio-economic bench marking, smallholder

1. Introduction

In general, happiness is considered to be the ultimate goal of life, or at least desirable (Frey and Stutzer, 2002b, 2005; Layard, 2005; Veenhoven, 2004, 1997). Happiness can be defined as the degree to which people positively evaluate their overall life situation (Veenhoven, 1997). Happiness may be considered as the affective aspect of the general concept of subjective well-being, whereas life satisfaction captures the cognitive aspect (Diener, 1984; Veenhoven, 1984). The most commonly used concept of subjective well-being in economic surveys is happiness (Easterlin, 2001b; Frey and Stutzer, 2002a). In economic surveys happiness is studied in various ways.[1]

When we turn to a diachronic perspective, we observe the Easterlin paradox (Easterlin, 2001b). Easterlin found that there are differences in happiness across income groups in cross-sectional surveys, but that

[1] Including one's income, housing, leisure, friends, marriage (Cohen, 2002; Easterlin, 2001a; Van Praag and Ferrer-i-Carbonell, 2004), children, gender, age (Argyle, 1999; Frey and Stutzer, 2004; Oswald, 1997; Plug, 1997), level of education and work (Argyle, 1999; Bowling and Windsor, 2001; Easterlin, 2001; Frey and Stutzer, 2002; Gerdtham and Johannesson, 2001; Oswald, 1997), smoking (Delfino *et al.*, 2001; Koivumaa-Honkanen *et al.*, 2003; Rabois and Haaga, 2003;) and religion (Cohen, 2002; Koenig *et al.*, 2001; Levin and Chatters, 1998; Myers and Diener, 1995).

no happiness differences over the individual life cycle and across different generations can be established despite substantial income growth. Furthermore, subjective reports of happiness in the past (future) are lower (higher) than in the present. However, present happiness is constant over the life cycle. Easterlin (2001a) gives the following explanation for these results: aspirations (for material goods) rise with increasing income. Since high aspirations make people unhappy, so the income effect on happiness 'leaks away'.

Furthermore Easterlin (2001b) shows that in the same cohort (assuming that aspirations are similar at an early age), higher education leads to more happiness than lower education (because education enables one to achieve one's aspirations at a higher income). There is evidence that more goods are desired and more goods are owned for groups with higher education, so income seems to drive aspirations. There is a strong positive correlation between income and material aspirations over the course of the life cycle. The assumption is that at early ages, social classes are mixed, thus breeding similar aspirations. At later ages, social classes tend to segregate, thus breeding diverging aspirations. Also, at later ages, aspirations may increase in proportion to income. This causes the 'leaking away' of happiness with increasing income.

A similar conclusion is drawn by Schor (1998). She points at the fact that when a considerable portion of American consumers are keeping up with the Jones's they no longer refer to their neighbours but to the, often conspicuous, consumption of celebrities in the mass media, especially television. So, the demonstration effect has shifted from the relatively attainable consumption level of the middle classes to one of the very rich.

The upward preference and reference shift was already analysed by Kapteyn and Van Praag in the 1970s, see e.g. Van Praag and Kapteyn (1973) and Kapteyn (1977). They use the concepts preference and reference drift to analyse this change in their individual welfare functions of income (WFI) approach, also labelled the Leyden welfare approach. For an overview of the individual welfare approach, we refer to Plug (1997) and Van Praag and Ferrer-i- Carbinell (2004).

In their study on income and happiness across Europe, Caporale *et al.* (2007) using data from the European Social Survey (ESS), come to the conclusion that relative income is indeed an important determinant of subjective well-being or happiness. Their results support the relative utility hypothesis; the income of a reference group exerts a negative effect on well-being even after controlling for absolute income and demographic characteristics.

So, relative income is of importance in affecting happiness. Given the high penetration and effect of mass media, it is reasonable to assume that relative income is no longer the income of the Jones's, but the income of the richest part of the population. This means that the growth in income disparities in the past 25 years in the Western world, especially at the top where real incomes and greed have risen considerably, must have a negative effect on happiness. Happiness in the Western world has not increased over recent decades.

However, in this contribution we will demonstrate by using various sources that at the societal level happiness as well as other amenities or facilities that make live more comfortable are positively related to the level of income of a society, the GDP per head. We will test three hypotheses. We will see in Section 2, happiness and real income is positively related although not necessarily linear. From cross section data for European countries, it is found that the real GDP per head and happiness are positively related. People in the richer part of the world are happier than in the poorer part of the world.

Furthermore, it appears in Section 3, using global data, that, on the one hand, GDP per head and, on the other hand, bundles of private and public goods in the field of human development, environmental health, gender related development and life expectancy are positively related. This gives opportunities for socio-economic bench marking, which can be found in Section 4. Section 5 contains a number of conclusions.

2. Happiness and income at the national level

In this section Hypothesis 1 is tested: happiness is positively related to income. Furthermore, the levelling off effect with respect to this relationship is tested (Hypothesis 2). If this holds true it means that an increase of happiness at a certain increase of income is smaller at higher levels of income than at lower levels.

Figure 1 illustrates the relation between Happiness H and income Y for European countries. The data stem from the Special Eurobarometer 'Mental Well-being' (European Commission, 2006). In the framework of this research in 29 European countries the question was asked: Have you felt happy during the past four weeks? In the Netherlands 86% of the respondents answered this question with 'all the time' or 'most of the time'. In Bulgaria this percentage was only 42%. Taking this as a measure for happiness H it is now possible to test the hypothesis that there is a positive relationship between happiness and income (GDP) per head (Hypothesis 1). Figure 1 shows the scatter diagram of this relationship.

The results of the regression procedure are given in Table 1. The estimated regression equation 1 is:

$$H = \gamma Y + \delta \tag{1}$$

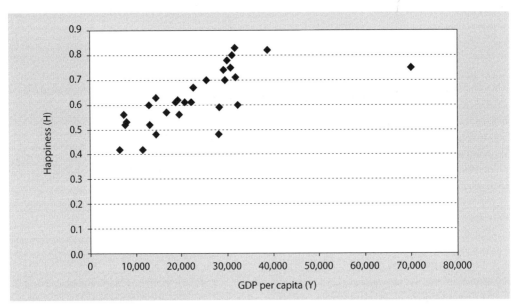

Figure 1. *Scatter diagram of the relation between happiness (H) and GDP per capita (Y) for 29 European countries (European Commission, 2006).*

Table 1. *Happiness as a function of income, linear estimation.*

γ	t-value γ	δ	t-value δ	R²
0.00000619	4.877	0.483	14.389	0.468

The result is quite satisfactory. However, because the score for happiness H cannot exceed 100, one might expect a levelling-off-effect (Hypothesis 2). In order to test whether happiness levels off when income grows the following regression equation 2 was also tested:

$$H = \varepsilon + \frac{\sigma}{Y+1}$$
(2)

which may be called the levelling-off-function. Table 2 provides the results.

Table 2. *Happiness as a function of income, levelling off-function.*

σ	t-value σ	ε	t-value ε	R²
-2,216.37	-4.956	0.755	24.93	0.476

From Table 2 it can be concluded that there is a positive relationship between happiness and income per capita and that there is some levelling-off-effect when income grows, but this is not spectacular.[2]

3. The decomposition of happiness

In this section we test Hypothesis 3 that utility or happiness H can be decomposed in partly overlapping bundles of private and public goods and that there is a positive relationship between each of the bundles and income. The bundles of private and public goods are part of the utility function (Equation 3). The variables used in the utility function are: Human Development Index (X_1), Environmental Health score (X_2), Gender related development index (X_3), Health (X_4), Life expectancy (X_5), and Research and Development (X_6).[3] This is shown in Equation 3:

$$H = H(X_1(Y), X_2(Y), X_3(Y) \, X_4(Y) \, X_5(Y) \, X_6(Y))$$
(3)

---

[2] The levelling off might be more visible if low income countries were involved.

[3] Of course the choice for these variables is more or less arbitrary. Other variables like 'democracy' (assumed positive relation with income) or 'corruption' (proved negative relation with average GDP) are also possible (The Economist, 2007).

The variables represent more or less 'composite goods' consisting of public and private elements (Casamiglia, 1978).[4] For each of these variables it is assumed that they contribute in a positive way to human well-being or happiness H. The relation to average global income, Engel's functions, is examined in a cross country setting. The central hypothesis to be tested is that there is a positive relationship between these variables and average income. If confirmed, the utility function of these variables might as well be reduced to Equation 4:

$$H = H(Y) \tag{4}$$

From Section 2 we already know that the assumed positive relationship between happiness and income is supported by the data (Hypothesis 1). Assumptions in the approach of the paper of Camiglia are that there is not only a relationship between the consumption of private goods and average income, but also between the consumption of public goods and average income, and further that the Engel's functions found for the Average Global Consumer (AGC) reflect the optimum consumption level of each national average consumer at each level of average income. In other words, the hypothesis (3) is tested that the consumption level of the six composite goods mentioned in equation (3) is determined by income (GDP). To test Hypothesis 3 we have used the data from the Pocket World in Figures (The Economist, 2006).

Figure 2 shows the relationship between the Human Development Index X_1 and GDP per head Y (in $ PPP), Figure 3 shows the relationship between Environmental Health X_2 and Y, Figure 4 the relationship between the Gender Related Development Index (GRDI) X_3 and Y, Figure 5 the relationship between Health spending per head X_4 and Y, Figure 6 Life Expectancy X_5 against GDP, and Figure 7 R&D expenditures X_6 per head against Y.[5] Except for Life expectancy (Figure 6), the scatter diagrams do not show a 'levelling off' of the consumption as income grows.

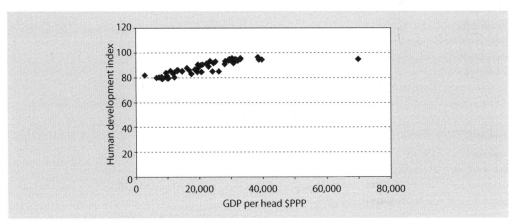

Figure 2. *Scatter diagram of Human Development Index (HDI) X_1 against GDP per head $PPP in 2004, 60 countries, Norway ranking 1, Romania ranking 60 (The Economist, 2006).*

---

[4] According to Hicks' aggregation theorem the use of composites is justified under a number of conditions (Hicks, 1939).

[5] Human Development Index: a knowledge variable consisting of average years of schooling and adult literacy. Environmental Health score: index based on child mortality, indoor air pollution, safety of drinking water, quality of sanitation, and quantity of urban air particulates. Gender Related Development Index (GRDI): indicator of the disparities between men and women in individual countries. The lower the index, the greater the disparity. Health spending per head: percentage of GDP times GDP per head ($PPP), Life expectancy: the number of years a baby born today can expect to live; Research and Development (R&D) expenditures per head: percentage of GDP spent on R&D times GDP per head $PPP.

Markets, marketing and developing countries

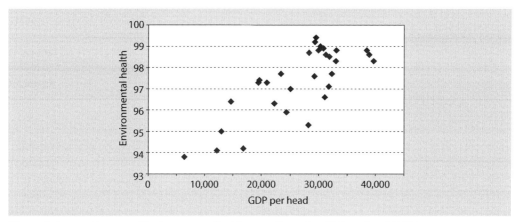

Figure 3. *Scatter diagram of Environmental Health scores X_2 against GDP per head $PPP in 2004, 39 countries, Norway ranking 1, Kuwait ranking 39 (The Economist, 2006).*

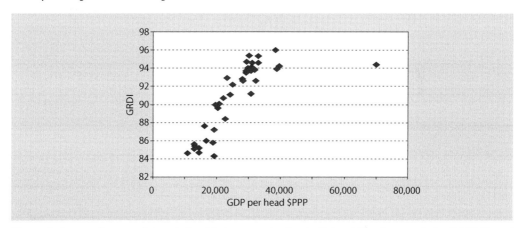

Figure 4. *Scatter diagram of the relationship between the Gender Related Development Index (GRDI) X_3 and GDP per head $PPP: 39 countries, Norway ranking 1, Kuwait ranking 39 (The Economist, 2006).*

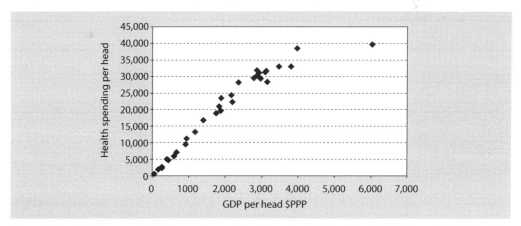

Figure 5. *Scatter diagram of Health spending per head X_4 against GDP per head $PPP: 31 countries, US ranking 1, Malawi ranking 31 (The Economist, 2006).*

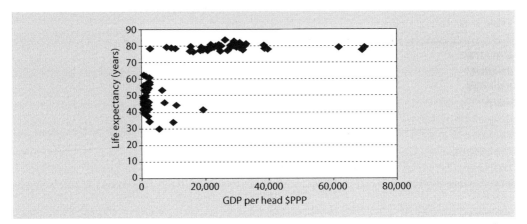

Figure 6. *Scatter diagram of Life expectancy X_5 (years) against GDP per head $PPP: 100 countries, Andorra ranking 1, Swaziland ranking 100 (The Economist, 2006).*

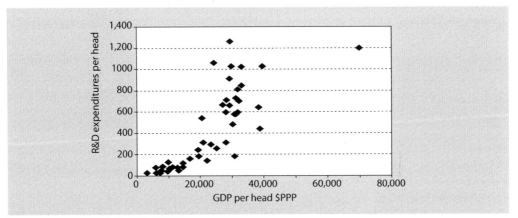

Figure 7. *Scatter diagram of the relationship between the R&D expenditures per head X_6 and GDP per head $PPP: 46 countries, Sweden ranking 1, India ranking 46 (The Economist, 2006).*

Table 3 shows the results of the regression analysis of Equation 5:

$$X_i = \gamma_i Y + \delta_i \qquad (5)$$

The results are quite convincing. Apart from δ_4 and δ_6 all coefficients are significant at the 1% level (one-tailed test). So, Hypothesis 3 is supported by the results. To a large part, all variables concerned depend on the value of income per head. Also, because $\delta_1, \delta_2, \delta_3$ and δ_5 are positive, income elasticity's of Bundles $X_1, X_2, X_3,$ and X_5 are between 0 and 1, which means that these 'goods' are considered by the Average Global Consumer(AGC) to be basic goods and not luxury goods. This means that, where there is under-performance in the supply of these goods there is a high urgency to increase the supply (see Section 5). As far as Goods 4 and 6 are concerned, δ_4 and δ_6 are negative. However the value of these coefficients is non-significant. It means that Goods 4 and 6 are considered by the AGC to be 'origin goods', which

Table 3. *Relationship between X$_i$ and GDP per head Y.*

Variable	γ	t-value γ	δ$_i$	t-value δ$_i$	R^2
X$_1$ (HDI)	0.000406	11.914	79.439	95.607	0.710
X$_2$ (Environmental health)	0.000153	6.563	144.858	144.858	0.606
X$_3$ (GRDI)	0.000275	7.306	83.672	78.491	0.591
X$_4$ (Health exp. per head)	0.109894	17.446	-206.049	-1.393	0.913
X$_5$ (Life expectation)	0.000786	11.221	52.248	34.583	0.562
X$_6$ (R&D)	0.023788	8.674	-114.542	-1.588	0.631

GRDI: Gender Related Development Index, HDI: Human Development Index.

means that their income elasticity's equals 1. Therefore, they can be classified in between basic goods and luxury goods.

To finish this section, Table 4 shows the AGC's estimated income elasticity's for the six composite goods[6].

Table 4. *Average Global Consumer's income elasticities for the six composite goods.*

X$_1$ (HDI)	X$_2$ (Env. health)	X$_3$ (GRDI)	X$_4$ (Health exp.)	X$_5$ (Life exp.)	X$_6$ (R&D)
0.044	0.014	0.029	1	0.118	1

GRDI: Gender Related Development Index, HDI: Human Development Index.

4. A benchmarking procedure and its consequences for socio-economic policy

Section 4 indicates a possible application of the above results. Section 3 concluded that there is an AGC's optimum consumption of the indicated bundles for each income level. Further, the plausible assumption is that each of the bundles contributes to AGC's happiness. This implies that policies that would bring the consumption of the bundles in line with the optimum consumption would contribute to a nation's welfare. The socio-economic happiness benchmarking procedure is based on the Engel's functions for the six composite goods. The actual score of a country for a bundle was evaluated against the normative score computed with the bundle's specific Engel's function. Where the actual value was too low the country was given a minus for under performing on this good; it was given a plus in the case of over performing. A

---

[6] Though the specific value of the income elasticity may change with the GDP per head, because the derived Engel's functions are linear, the character of the good (basic, luxury, origin) does not depend on the GDP per head. This follows directly from Marshall's rule in the case of linear Engel's functions.

minus indicates that a country should improve on the issue, whereas a plus implies that a country could do less on a specific indicator. For a number of selected countries, the results of the benchmarking procedure are listed in Table 5.

These results indicate, for example, for the Netherlands that, taking into account the Dutch average GDP, the country could do better on Environmental Health, on Health expenditures and on R&D. Further, it is striking that Hungary has only negative scores, whereas Germany has only positive ones. Clearly, these scores could play a role in the evaluation of a country's socio-economic policy.

Table 5. *Results of socio-economic happiness benchmarking for selected countries for the six composite goods.*

Country	X_1 (HDI)	X_2 (Env. health)	X_3 (GRDI)	X_4 (Health exp.)	X_5 (Life exp.)	X_6 (R&D)
Australia	+	+	+	?	+	-
Canada	+	+	+	-	+	-
France	+	?	+	-	+	+
Germany	+	+	+	+	+	+
Hungary	-	-	-	-	-	-
Italy	+	-	+	-	+	-
Japan	+	-	+	?	+	+
Netherlands	+	-	+	-	+	-
Slovenia	+	+	+	?	+	?
Spain	+	-	+	?	+	-
Switzerland	+	-	+	+	+	+
United Kingdom	+	+	+	?	+	-
United States	-	-	-	+	-	+

GRDI: Gender Related Development Index, HDI: Human Development Index.
+ : over performance; - : under performance; ? : missing data.

5. Conclusion and discussion

In the previous sections we have seen that at a societal level the following hypotheses are corroborated: There is a positive relation between happiness and income per capita (Hypothesis 1) and that there is some levelling-off-effect when income grows (Hypothesis 2) and the consumption level of the six composite goods or bundles mentioned in the happiness equation is determined by income (Hypothesis 3). So, happiness and income are positively related.

If we take a specific look at developing countries, then under the present circumstances the levelling-off-effect will be weaker and subsequently the relationship between income and happiness stronger there than in higher income countries. With respect to happiness especially countries with a low income will benefit from an improved market access, because this will generate a higher income for them.

The overall conclusion must be that one way or the other happiness is positively related to income. We may safely conclude that if average world income increases in a situation where income distribution hardly changes (as is the case in the past few years) people's well being is positively influenced. Possibly, a growing income is a necessary, and not a sufficient, condition for increasing happiness. If this is the case then at present, with a more or less constant global income distribution between countries and a growing average income per capita, this necessary condition for increasing happiness is being fulfilled for more people than in the past.

References

Argyle, M., (1999). Causes and correlates of happiness. In: D. Kahneman, E. Diener and N. Schwarz (eds.), Well-being: the foundations of hedonic psychology. Russell Sage Foundation, New York, NY, USA, pp. 353-373.

Bowling, A. and Windsor, J. (2001). Towards the good life: a population survey of dimensions of quality of life. Journal of Happiness Studies 2: 55-81.

Caporale, G.M., Georgellis, Y., Tsitsianis N. and Ping Yin, Y.A. (2007). Income and happiness across Europe: do reference values matter? Working paper Brunel University and University of Hertfordshire.

Casamiglia, X. (1978). Composite goods and revealed preference. International Economic Review 19: 395-404.

Cohen, A.B. (2002). The importance of spirituality in well-being for Jews and Christians. Journal of Happiness Studies 3: 287-310.

Delfino, R.J., Jamner L.D., and Whalen, C.K. (2001). Temporal analysis of the relationship of smoking behavior and urges to mood states in men versus women. Nicotine and Tobacco Research 3: 235-248.

Diener, E. (1984). Subjective well-being. Psychological Bulletin 95: 542-575.

Diener, E., Diener M., and Diener, C. (1995). Factors predicting the subjective well-being of nations. Journal of Personality and Social Psychology 69: 851-864.

Easterlin, R.A. (2001a). Life cycle welfare: trends and differences. Journal of Happiness Studies 2: 1-12.

Easterlin, R.A. (2001b). Income and happiness: towards a unified theory. The Economic Journal 111: 465-484.

European Commission (2006). Mental Well-being. Special Eurobarometer 248/Wave 64.4-TNS Opinion and Social Research.

Frey, B.S. and Stutzer, A. (2002a). Happiness and economics. Princeton University Press, Princeton, NJ, USA.

Frey, B.S. and Stutzer, A. (2002b). What can economists learn from happiness research? Journal of Economic Literature 40: 402-435.

Frey, B.S. and Stutzer, A. (2004). Happiness Research: State and Prospects. Working Paper No. 190, Institute for Empirical Research in Economics, University of Zürich, Zürich, Switzerland.

Frey, B.S. and Stutzer, A. (2005). Happiness research: state and prospects. Review of Social Economy LXIII: 177-207.

Gerdtham, U. and M. Johannesson (2001). The relationship between happiness, health, and socio-economic factors: results based on Swedish microdata. Journal of Socio-Economics 30: 553-557.

Heijman ,W.J.M. (1998). The Economic Metabolism. Kluwer, Dordrecht, the Netherlands.

Hicks, J.R. (1939). Value and Capital. Oxford University Press, Oxford, UK.

Kapteyn, A. (1977). A theory of preference formation. Ph.D Leiden University, Leiden, the Netherlands.

Koenig, H.G., McCullough, M.E. and Larsson, D.B. (2001). Handbook of Religion and Health. Oxford University Press, Oxford, UK.

Koivumaa-Honkanen, H., Honkanen, R., Koskenvuo, M. and Kario, J. (2003). Self-reported happiness in life and suicide in ensuing 20 years. Social Psychiatry and Psychiatric Epidemiology 38: 244-248.

Layard, R. (2005). Happiness. Lessons from a new science. Penguin: Allen Lane, London, UK.

Levin, J.S. and Chatters, L.M. (1998). Research on religion and mental health: an overview of empirical findings and theoretical issues. In: H.G. Koenig (ed.), Handbook of Religion and Mental Health. Academic Press, San Diego, CA, USA, pp. 33-50.

Myers, D.G. and Diener, E. (1995). Who is happy? Psychological Science 6: 10-19.

Oswald, A.J. (1997). Happiness and economic performance. The Economic Journal 107: 1815-1831.

Plug. E. (1997). Leyden welfare and beyond. Tinbergen Institute Research Series, Amsterdam, the Netherlands.

Rabois, D. and Haaga, D.A.F. (2003). The influence of cognitive coping and mood on smokers' self-efficacy and temptation. Addictive behaviours 28: 561-573.

Schor, J.B. (1998). The overspent American. Upscaling, downshifting and the new consumer. Basic Books, New York, NY, USA.

The Economist (2006). Pocket World in Figures 2007 edition. Profile Books and The Economist, London, UK.

Van Praag, B. and Ferrer-i-Carbonell, A. (2004). Happiness quantified. A satisfaction calculus. Oxford University Press, New York, NY, USA.

Van Praag, B.M.S. and Kapteyn, A. (1973). Further evidence on the individual welfare function of income: an empirical investigation in the Netherlands. European Economic Review 4: 33-62.

Veenhoven, R. (1984). Conditions of happiness. Reidel, Dordrecht, the Netherlands.

Veenhoven, R. (1997). Advances in understanding happiness. Revue Québécoise de Psychologie 18: 29-74.

Veenhoven, R. (2004). The greatest happiness principle. Happiness as an aim in public policy. In: A. Linely and S. Joseph (eds.), Positive psychology in practice. Wiley & Sons, Hoboken, NJ, USA.

Veenhoven R. (2005). Apparent quality of life in nations: how long and happy people live. Social Indicators Research 71: 61-86.

Systems thinking in development

Linking market and knowledge based development: the why and how of agricultural innovation systems[7]

Willem Janssen, Andy Hall, Eija Pehu and Riikka Rajalathi

While knowledge based development is key for sustainable productivity increases, market based development is essential for creating and accessing income opportunities. Together they achieve a lot more than each one on their own. This paper argues that in the evolving agricultural economies of the developing world, knowledge and market development can be effectively linked through the use of innovation system theory.

Abstract

This paper explores how knowledge and market based development interact and can be integrated through the use of innovation systems theory. It will first identify some major – market based – changes in the context of agricultural development. Next it will explain how this has modified the ideas about supporting innovation processes, defined here as the generation or application of new knowledge; it will then introduce the concept of 'new agriculture' and eight case studies in four countries that were undertaken to explore and better understand the potential of innovation systems theory to support sustainable development. The paper finishes with some selected conclusions that further highlight the interaction between knowledge generation and market development and that suggest the need to keep on investing in farmer organization.

Keywords: agricultural innovation, value chain coordination, knowledge based development, market based development, innovation systems, sustainable development, farmer organization

1. Introduction

Agricultural development depends to a large extent on how successfully knowledge is generated and applied. Investments in knowledge – especially in the form of science and technology – have featured prominently and consistently in most strategies to promote sustainable and equitable agricultural development at the national level. Although many of these investments have been quite successful the context for agriculture is changing rapidly – sometimes radically – and the process of knowledge generation and use has to change as well (Janssen and Braunschweig, 2003).

---

[7] This paper is based on the following publication prepared by the same authors: World Bank, 2006: Enhancing Agricultural Innovation: How to go beyond the Strengthening of Research systems.

This paper will briefly explore how in this new context knowledge and market based development interact and can be integrated through the use of innovation systems theory. It will first identify some major – market based – changes in the context of agricultural development. Next it will explain how this has modified the ideas about supporting innovation processes, defined here as the generation or application of new knowledge; it will then introduce the concept of 'new agriculture' and eight case studies in four countries that were undertaken to explore and better understand the potential of innovation systems theory to support sustainable development. The paper finishes with some selected conclusion from these case studies that further highlight the interaction between knowledge generation and market development.

2. The changing context of agricultural development

Several changes in the context for agricultural development stress the need to specifically examine how the generation and use of new knowledge can be made more market oriented. Four of those are of particular relevance to this essay.

First, markets – not production – increasingly drive agricultural development. For most of the 20th century, major progress in agricultural development was inextricably linked to major improvements in the productivity of staple food crops, but this situation is changing. The falling staple food prices and rising urban incomes that many developing countries experienced during the first decade of the 21st century shifted the attention to strategies that enhance agricultural diversification and increase the value added of agricultural production (Bhargouti *et al.*, 2004). And while the 2007-2009 Food and Economic Crises increased the attention to staple foods, market as much as production potential are guiding the investments to overcome those crises.

Second, the production, trade, and consumption environment for agriculture and agricultural products is increasingly dynamic and evolving in unpredictable ways. If farmers and companies are to cope, compete, and survive in contemporary agriculture, they need to innovate continuously. Drivers for innovation include, for example, emerging health and disease problems such as avian flu and HIV/AIDS; changing patterns of competition in local but particularly in global markets; changing trade rules and the need for continuous upgrading to comply with them; and changing technological paradigms, such as biotechnology and information technology and the opportunities and challenges that they present (World Bank, 2005).

Third, knowledge, information, and technology are increasingly generated, diffused, and applied through the private sector. Private businesses develop and supply a substantial number of the technologies that farmers use or introduce (examples include seed, fertilizer, pesticides, and machinery). The role of the private sector is expected to grow with the increasing intensification of agriculture (Hall, 2006).

Fourth, agricultural development increasingly takes place in a globalized setting. The domestic market is not the only market that defines demand; environmental and health issues cross the borders of any country; knowledge from abroad may be more important than domestically generated knowledge and ICT allows information to spread through international networks. Globalization causes quality standards to be defined increasingly by international markets and leads small sectors suddenly to confront huge potential demand. It raises the stakes in agricultural development: success, for example in the export of nontraditional products, may assume larger dimensions than in a more insular world, but failure to adapt to new conditions will also have larger consequences and may cause traditional trade patterns to erode rapidly (World Bank, 2007).

3. Changing approaches for supporting agricultural innovation

As the context of agricultural development has changed, ideas of what constitutes innovation have changed, and so have approaches for investing in it. In the 1980s, the concept of the 'national agricultural research system' or NARS[8] was developed to guide knowledge investments in agricultural development. Development activities based on the NARS concept generally focused on strengthening research supply by providing infrastructure, capacity, management, and policy support at the national level.

Strengthened research systems may increase the supply of new knowledge and new technologies, but they may not necessarily improve the capacity for innovation throughout the agricultural sector (Rajalahti *et al.*, 2005). Recently more attention has been given to the demand for research and technology and to the development of wider competencies, linkages, enabling attitudes, practices, governance structures, and policies that allow this knowledge to be put into productive use. The concept of an innovation system[9] has guided this more holistic approach to planning knowledge production and use. While the concept found its origin in industrial theory (Lundvall, 1992; Nelson, 1993) it has, with proper modifications, also proven useful for agriculture in developing countries (Hall *et al.*, 2004; Spielman, 2005).

An innovation system may be defined as comprising the organizations, enterprises, and individuals that together demand and supply knowledge and technology, and the rules and mechanisms by which these different agents interact. The innovation systems concept focuses not merely on the science suppliers but on the totality and interaction of actors involved in innovation. It extends beyond the creation of knowledge to encompass the factors affecting demand for and use of new and existing knowledge in novel and useful ways. Thus innovation is viewed in a social and economic sense and not purely as discovery and invention. Figure 1 is a stylized presentation of an innovation system and of the context in which it might operate. While the innovation systems concept does not ignore the importance of research investments, it recognizes more explicitly that change can be brought about in other ways and is not only based on what scientists come up with.

4. Grounding the innovation systems concept in the 'new agriculture'

Although staple food production will remain very important, an exciting agricultural trend in many countries is the rapid emergence of many new production-to-consumption systems. Agricultural sectors around the world are increasingly diversifying into vegetables and fruits, spices, aquaculture products, and nonfood products (such as medicinal plants and cut flowers); the production of animal protein is increasing; and the importance of postharvest handling and processing is growing to meet (mostly urban) consumers' demand for storability and convenience (CGIAR/Science Council, 2005). These new

---

[8] The NARS comprises all of the entities in a given country that are responsible for organizing, coordinating, or executing research that contributes explicitly to the development of its agriculture and the maintenance of its natural resource base (ISNAR, 1992).

[9] Within innovation systems not so much the notion of *novelty* is fundamental, but the notion of the *process of creating local change, new to the user*. A change that may have been adopted in one part of the world years before, may still be an innovation in another part.

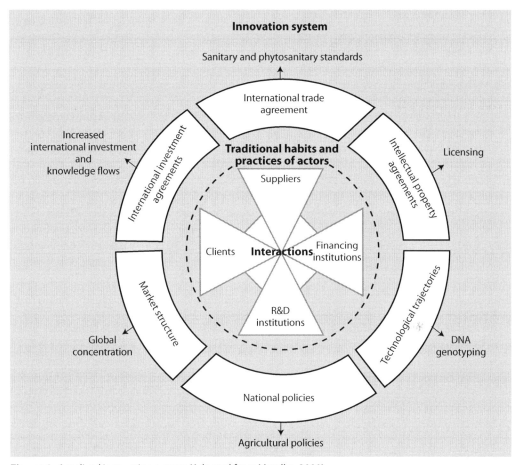

Figure 1. *A stylized innovation system (Adapted from Mytelka, 2000).*

agricultural activities are highly volatile, but frequently they provide considerable income and employment opportunities. Their development can make a large contribution to rural-based sustainable development.

Many of these new agricultural activities and products emerge when private entrepreneurs respond to new market opportunities. Often the production and marketing efforts for these new products are quite sophisticated. Although the overall value of new agricultural activities can be considerable, the large number of products makes it impossible to develop national research programs for each one, except perhaps in very large countries such as China and India. Consequently, countries must develop new approaches to support innovation in these knowledge-intensive activities.

This 'new agriculture' provides many opportunities for developing an operational framework based on the agricultural innovation systems concept, because it typifies several important new patterns in the agricultural sectors of many developing countries:
- The delineation of new, dynamic, and very knowledge-intensive niche sectors, such as export horticulture and agroprocessing.

- Rapid evolution in production, consumption, and marketing conditions, driven by new technologies, globalization, and urbanization.
- Industrialization of the food chain.
- The importance of these new sectors as income sources for the poor: farmer-owners as well as laborers.
- An important role for organizations other than state organizations; particularly private organizations, but also cooperatives and civil society organizations.
- The need to compete in rapidly evolving international markets and the consequent importance of innovation as a source of competitive advantage.
- The importance of upgrading and innovating, not only in hi-tech sectors but also in sectors such as agriculture, which are considered more traditional and low-tech.
- The need to tailor innovation capacities to extremely heterogeneous and volatile conditions.

New agriculture is also an area where developing countries are competing successfully with developed countries. Table 1 shows that between 1992 and 2001 the export growth from developing countries was more than double the growth from the developed countries. For later years there are no good data available, but the experience of World Bank projects in India, Colombia, Peru, Bolivia, Indonesia and several African countries would suggest that new agriculture has remained a strong source of demand growth.

Table 1. *World value[1] of nontraditional agricultural exports (million US$), 1992 and 2001 (FAO, 2004).*

Exports	1992	2002	Growth (%)	Average annual growth rate (%)
From developing countries	4,412	8,606	95	6.91
From developed countries	4,783	6,902	44	3.74

[1]Excludes citrus and bananas.

5. Case studies on the potential of innovation systems theory

Eight case studies from four countries – Bangladesh, India, Ghana and Colombia – spanning the three main regions of the developing world – Asia, Africa and Latin America (Table 2) – were used to explore the potential of the innovation systems concept for supporting sustainable agricultural development. Four case studies (one per country) focused on truly new or nontraditional activities. The other four concentrated on more traditional sectors that are experiencing rapid mainly market driven transformation. The combination of traditional and nontraditional subsectors allowed us to evaluate the suitability of the innovation systems concept across a wide range of conditions. The list of case studies is presented in Annex 1.

A checklist for conducting diagnostic assessments in the eight settings based on an innovation systems framework was used in the comparative analysis. The checklist focused on a central insight of the innovation systems framework: any innovation system must be analyzed in its historical and contemporary context to define the opportunities and necessities for innovation, especially where rapid change is occurring. This

Table 2. *Case studies by country and subsector.*

Case study country	Traditional subsector in rapid transformation	Nontraditional subsector
Bangladesh	Food processing	Shrimp
India	Medicinal plants	Vanilla
Ghana	Cassava processing	Pineapple
Colombia	Cassava processing	Cut flowers

context includes policy, market, and trade conditions and the challenges they present, as well as other contextual factors, such as the sociopolitical environment and the natural resource base. The checklist includes the following major issues:

- *Actors, the roles they play, and the activities in which they are involved,* with an emphasis on diversity of public and private sector actors and on the appropriateness of their roles.
- *Attitudes and practices of the main actors,* with an emphasis on collaboration, potential inefficiencies, patterns of trust, and the existence of a culture of innovation.
- *Patterns of interaction,* with an emphasis on networks and partnerships, inclusion of the poor, and the existence and functions of potential coordination and stakeholder bodies.
- *Enabling environment (policies and infrastructure),* with an emphasis on the role of policies related to science, technology, and fiscal concerns; the role of farmer and other organizations in defining research and innovation challenges; and the significance of legal frameworks.

Three salient findings of the case studies will be discussed here. First, the importance of value chain coordination stood out. It leads to stronger interactions, greater agreement on challenges to a sector, and greater willingness to pursue innovation, as shown for flowers and cassava in Colombia. The value chain approach provides a useful organizational principle for identifying the key actors in the production-to-consumption chain. However, the actors, their roles, and the types of interaction need to be analyzed from an innovation systems perspective. The potential synergy of combining the effective market-based and knowledge-based interactions needed for innovation in the value chain could form the basis for a powerful new form of intervention. The Colombian cases, and the cassava case in Ghana, provided evidence for the potential of this approach.

Secondly, in many of the cases studies the innovation system could not take advantage of the existing enabling environment. The capacity to enforce standards effectively or implement a certification system was absent, or the ability to submit competitive proposals to a grant fund was deficient. Owing to this lack of capacity, the actors in the sector did not benefit from the support that the enabling environment could offer. As shown in Bangladesh, it was not the enabling environment but weak patterns of interaction – and the attitudes and practices that fostered those patterns – which created the major bottleneck in the innovation process. In many cases, improvements in the enabling environment will be effective only if they are combined with activities to strengthen other aspects of innovation capacity, particularly the patterns of interaction of the main actors in the innovation system.

Thirdly, the patterns of interaction necessary to create dynamic systems of innovation are frequently absent. The case studies in India showed that too often farmers, micro entrepreneurs, and companies have not been part of the network of research, training, and development organizations required to bring about a continuous process of innovation. The problem is not that candidate organizations for this network are absent. Usually many of these organizations are present, but they are not playing the required roles, or they have not formed the relationships required to support the dialogue that leads to fruitful interaction, learning, and innovation. Reluctance to form such relationships is reinforced by deep-seated behavioral patterns and mistrust (for example on public and private sector roles).

6. Conclusions

The case studies provided many conclusions on what drives innovation and on the generic interventions that promote the capacity to innovate. Most of these have been summarized in World Bank (2006). And while many of these conclusions go beyond the link between market and knowledge based development, the interdependency of the two types of development was a major highlight. This paper will focus on those highlights.

Conclusion 1: innovation systems and value chains may have the same partners but different goals. Innovation systems and value chains[10] often have many shared partners, and although they respond to different organizational principles, they are highly complementary and overlapping. From a value chain perspective, the key challenge is to link supply and demand in the most effective way, and information sharing is very important for enabling these producer-consumer linkages. Organizations that help to link producers, transporters, and distributors to consumer markets are vital if value chains are to function effectively. When participants in a value chain pass along information on demand characteristics, for example, or on standards and regulations affecting the market (such as sanitary and phytosanitary standards), at the same time they are providing important information to shape the direction of the innovation process. If, in addition to well functioning value chain, an effective innovation capacity exists, this market information will be combined with new and existing knowledge on technological opportunities and information, such as farming techniques, postharvest processes and marketing to innovate in response to these market signals. One of the innovation challenges with respect to sustainable agriculture is to expand opportunities and means for resource-poor farmers to become actors and stakeholders in these innovation systems.

While a value chain brings partners together in their desire to integrate production, marketing, and consumption issues in the most profitable way, both in the long and in the short run, the innovation system brings actors together in their desire to bring about change in the value chain, in response to market, policy, and other signals. The innovation system perspective allows creating and applying the new knowledge required for the development, adaptation, and future profitability of the value chain.

Conclusion 2: in the contemporary agricultural sector, competitiveness depends on collaboration. The context of agriculture is continuously evolving. New regulations, consumer preferences, competitors, pests and diseases, climate change, and human health problems such HIV/AIDS are just some of the

---

[10] A value chain may be defined as the set of interconnected, value-creating activities undertaken by an enterprise or group of enterprises to develop, produce, deliver, and service a product or service. See also: Webber and Labaste, 2009.

changes that agricultural systems may face. Different sources of knowledge are needed to deal with these challenges, which require dense networks of connections. Information may come from public research organizations, technical services in the public and private sectors, development agencies, as well as other entrepreneurs or producers. Many problems cannot be solved by the producer alone; they often require changes in different segments of the value chain. Quality improvement, for example, is as much about production as about postharvest innovation, and it may require collaboration between growers, assembly agents, warehousers, exporters, and shipping agents. Such collaboration is even more important when a sector wants to build a national brand image, which may even require collaboration among competing exporters. Companies need to collaborate to compete, and governments need to be a nurturing partner in this process.

Conclusion 3: social and environmental sustainability are integral to economic success. Social and environmental concerns increasingly are embedded in consumer preferences in global markets. Ethical and green trade is an increasing consumer concern in many markets, though the economic crisis of 2008/2009 has apparently reduced the momentum. Companies and governments need to interact with actors engaged with these agendas (mainly civil society organizations). Dealing with social and environmental issues may require new types of expertise and insights into the social structure, asset base, and functions of farming communities, which can guide interventions to bring these communities into innovation systems as partners.

Conclusion 4: the market is not sufficient to promote interaction; the public sector has a central role to play. Even when competitive incentives to innovate are very strong, they are not always sufficient to bring together all of the actors needed for innovation to function or to reach sufficient scale. The public sector's role is important in four ways:
- To improve interaction between all relevant players and to use its convening power.
- To provide and enforce an enabling regulatory framework for the differentiated product markets.
- To support small-scale farmers in becoming partners in innovation systems and adding value to their assets and skills (for example, through public-private partnerships).
- To provide financing and infrastructure to bring inventions to market (science parks) or to reach a sufficient share of the global market.

Conclusion 5: the organization of rural stakeholders is a central development concept: it is a common theme in innovation systems and in market development. Successful innovation systems are often based on organizing rural stakeholders. It mobilized innovation in Colombia's cassava and cut flower industries and in India's medicinal plant and vanilla industries. The organization of rural stakeholders is also a common element of value chain approaches and community-driven development. Given that investments in organization extend across most development efforts in agriculture they offer important possibilities for synergy of market and knowledge based development efforts. Organization can foster two capacities that rural stakeholders tend to lack: the ability to articulate and gain a hearing for their demands, and the ability to negotiate. Investing in rural organizations thus tends to make agricultural innovation systems more effective at the same time that they improve value chains. Agricultural organization improves the ability to articulate and communicate needs for particular kinds of technology, it increases the likelihood that technology is used, and at the same time strengthens the negotiation and coordination ability in the market.

References

Barghouti, S. Kane, S., Sorby, K., and Ali, M. (2004). Agricultural Diversification for the Poor: Guidelines for Practitioners. Agriculture and Rural Development Discussion Paper 1. World Bank, Washington DC, USA.

CGIAR (Consultative Group on International Agricultural Research), Science Council (2005). System Priorities for CGIAR Research, 2005-2015. Science Council Secretariat, Rome, Italy.

FAO (Food and Agriculture Organization) (2004). The Market for Non-traditional Agricultural Exports. FAO, Rome, Italy.

Hall, A.J. (2006). Public-Private Sector Partnerships in a System of Agricultural Innovation: Concepts and Challenges. International Journal of Technology Management and Sustainable Development 5: 3-20.

Hall, A.J., Mytelka L. and Oyeyinka, B. (2004). Innovation Systems: Concepts and Implications for Agricultural Research Policy and Practice. United Nations University, Maastricht, the Netherlands.

ISNAR (International Service for National Agricultural Research). 1992. Service through Partnership: ISNAR's Strategy for the 1990s. ISNAR, The Hague, the Netherlands.

Janssen, W. and Braunschweig T. (2003). Trends in the Organization and Financing of Agricultural Research in Developed Countries: Implications for Developing Countries. ISNAR Research Report no. 22. The Hague: International Service for National Agricultural Research (ISNAR).

Lundvall, B.-Å. (ed.) (1992). National Systems of Innovation: Towards a Theory of Innovation and Interactive Learning. Pinter, London, UK.

Mytelka, L.K. (2000). Local Systems of Innovation in a Globalised World Economy. Industry and Innovation 7: 15-32.

Nelson, R. (1993). National Innovation Systems: A Comparative Analysis. Oxford University Press, Oxford, UK.

Rajalahti, R., Woelcke, J. and Pehu, E. (2005). Development of Research Systems to Support the Changing Agricultural Sector. Proceedings. Agriculture and Rural Development Discussion Paper 14. World Bank, Washington DC, USA.

Spielman, D.J. (2005). Innovation Systems Perspectives on Developing-country Agriculture: A Critical Review. ISNAR Discussion Paper 2. International Food Policy Research Institute (IFPRI), Washington DC, USA.

Webber C.M. and Labaste, P. (2009). Building competitiveness in Africa's agriculture: a guide to value chain concepts and applications. World Bank, Washington DC, USA.

World Bank (2005). Agricultural Growth for the Poor: An Agenda for Development. World Bank, Washington DC, USA.

World Bank (2006). Enhancing Agricultural Innovation: How to Go Beyond the Strengthening of Research Systems. World Bank, Washington DC, USA.

World Bank (2007). Agriculture for Development. World Development Report 2008. World Bank, Washington DC, USA.

Annex 1. Case studies and authors

A diagnostic innovation system study of the shrimp sector in Bangladesh
Zahir Ahmed, Professor of Anthropology, Jahangirnagar University, Dhaka, Bangladesh

The innovation of the cassava sector: the Ghana experience
George Essegbey, Science Technology Policy Research Institute, Council for Scientific and Industrial Research, Accra, Ghana

Innovation of the pineapple sector: the Ghanaian experience
George Essegbey, Science Technology Policy Research Institute, Council for Scientific and Industrial Research, Accra, Ghana

Medicinal plants in India: challenges and opportunities to develop innovation capacity
Rasheed Sulaiman V., Director, Centre for Research on Innovation and Science Policy, Hyderabad, India

Small-scale food processing in Bangladesh: a diagnostic innovation system study
Muhammad Taher, Technology Policy and Development Consultant, Dhaka, Bangladesh

The story of vanilla in Kerela - shifting from sector forgetting to sector learning
Rasheed Sulaiman V., Director, Centre for Research on Innovation and Science Policy, Hyderabad, India

Strengthening the agricultural innovation system in Colombia: an analysis of the cassava and flower sectors
Lynn K. Mytelka, Professorial Research Fellow, United Nations University – Maastricht Economic and social Research and training centre on Innovation and Technology (UNU-MERIT), Maastricht, the Netherlands
Isabel Bortagaray, PhD candidate, Georgia Institute of Technology, Atlanta, Georgia, USA

Connecting developing economies to the third era of marketing

Berend Wierenga

The ongoing of adoption of modern information and communication technology among primary producers in developing economies will significantly accelerate their connection to the third era of marketing.

Abstract

The development of marketing can be divided into three eras: marketing as distribution (1900-1960); marketing as (brand) management (1960-2000); and customer-centric marketing (2000-present). Marketing of developing countries is still mainly in the first era, but it can leapfrog to the third era. Most significant condition is its connection to the overall marketing channel, which makes it possible to attune the upstream supply (agricultural and food products) to the downstream demand (manufacturers and supermarkets). What customer relationship management (CRM) is for the downstream part of the marketing channel, is supplier relationship management (SRM) for the upstream part. For their connection to the markets it is important that primary producers (e.g. farmers) have access to modern information and communication technology (ICT). Especially mobile communication technology offers great perspectives, because it is cheap and very suitable for low-density remote areas. An acceleration in the adoption of mobile ICT by producers in developing countries can already be observed, and there is also empirical evidence that this helps to make markets function better. Mobile technology is a driving factor for propelling marketing of developing countries into the third era of marketing.

Keywords: eras of marketing, marketing channel coordination, CRM, SRM, mobile communication technology, third era marketing

1. Introduction

The field of marketing started out by studying the flow of goods from their initial agricultural production to the ultimate consumers (Kohls and Downey, 1972). So, marketing took its point of departure at the farm. The cradle of marketing stood on the cornfield, so to speak. And it is not by coincidence that the great icons of marketing, companies such as Unilever and Nestlé, are basically food companies. These companies belong to the fast-moving consumer goods industry (FMCG), and it was in this industry that marketing came to glory. Since then marketing has gone through an impressive development, conquering virtual all industries, but its beginnings in the agriculture and food industry are still visible. Also it was not by coincidence that the first university chair in marketing in the Netherlands was established at the then Agricultural University, now the Wageningen University. The first holder of that chair, Mathieu Meulenberg, was appointed in 1965.

Markets, marketing and developing countries

2. Three eras of marketing

Broadly speaking, we can distinguish the following eras in marketing:

- Marketing as distribution (1900-1960)

  Marketing began with an emphasis on distribution. As just mentioned, researchers were interested in how products go through the distribution channel from the original producer (farmer) to the end consumer. Products were seen as commodities, anonymous products, going to anonymous consumers. Marketing was studied at the macro/industry level rather than as a managerial activity of individual companies. During this period, agricultural marketing and 'general' marketing were basically similar (Meulenberg, 1986).

- Marketing as management (1960-2000)

  In the fifties of the last century, after the 'invention' of the marketing mix, marketing changed completely. From a field that studied interesting phenomena in distribution channels, it became a managerial field with the main purpose of finding the values for the elements of the marketing mix that maximize total profit (or some other organizational goal) of a company. Not the flow of the goods through the distribution channel was the most interesting subject anymore, but how an individual company can influence these flows in a way that is favorable for its products. Marketing became *marketing management*. And marketing management was not about anonymous products in the form of commodities anymore, but brands became all important. Therefore, marketing management in the second era of marketing became practically identical to brand management. The most important marketing metric of this era is the market share of a brand. Agricultural products served, in commodity form, as inputs for the manufacturing of branded products, but were in no way retractable to their production origins. In this period a gap developed between agricultural marketing and (general) marketing management (Meulenberg, 1986).

- Marketing as customer orientation (customer-centric marketing) (2000-present)

  Towards the end of the twentieth century, another major change took place. Information technology had made it increasingly easy to collect and retain information about individual customers, not only demographic information (e.g. family status, age and education), but also information about their purchase histories, and their responses to marketing campaigns. This means that individual customers were not anonymous anymore but obtained their own identity in the marketing process. With information about individual customers, a company knows precisely with whom it is dealing, and can figure out the best way of interacting with a particular customer. This is a rigorous departure from the previous era. The individual customer has now come center-stage. Whereas the product had lost its anonymity (and became recognizable as a brand) in the second era of marketing, the third marketing era gave an individual identity to the customer. The customer is increasingly replacing the brand as the unit of analysis, and variables such as customer share, customer satisfaction, and customer lifetime value (CLV) have become important marketing metrics. As a consequence, customer relationship management (CRM) has become the new mantra of marketing (Winer, 2001). In the third marketing era a lot of effort is being put in the development of customer data bases, which is the starting point for any interaction with individual customers.

How does the marketing of products from developing economies, the research area of Aad van Tilburg to whom this volume is dedicated, fit in this picture? In these economies the agricultural sector is mostly dominant and in that sense, these countries are in the first era of marketing as described before. What are the possibilities of (re)connecting marketing of agricultural and food products of the developing countries to mainstream marketing, that is to third era marketing? This is the subject of the remainder of this essay.

3. Coordinating the marketing channel

Figure 1 is a sketch of the classical marketing channel, covering the complete trajectory from the initial (agricultural) producers until the ultimate consumers. The developments discussed before have moved marketing's centre of gravity in the downstream direction of the vertical marketing channel. It moved from agricultural producers, via the collecting trade, on to processing and manufacturing companies, and then to supermarkets, food service companies, and online retailers. Especially these latter parties strongly focus on the (individual) end consumer. In the lower part of the marketing channel, through CRM the different parties can mutually coordinate their actions. Customers can give signals to suppliers and these suppliers can respond with matching offers.

Marketing channels have to be coordinated and channel coordination is a basic condition for a marketing channel to deliver its full potential (Jeuland and Shugan, 1983). Channel coordination is achieved if all channel partners have the incentive to act in a way that maximizes the overall performance of the channel. It may occur that a complete marketing channel is owned by one party, which makes it relatively easy to coordinate such a channel. However, most often a marketing channel consists of a (vertical) chain of

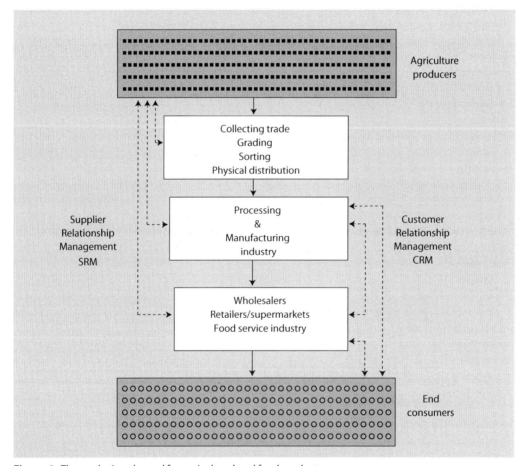

Figure 1. *The marketing channel for agricultural and food products.*

different parties, all making their own decisions, which are not necessarily in the interest of the channel as a whole. This leads to a suboptimal result, which in the end can be harmful for all channel members. Situations of sub-optimality caused by a lack of channel coordination can easily be found, for example in the area of sales promotions (Wierenga and Soethoudt, 2010).

Information exchange between channel partners is a fundamental condition for a marketing channel to function properly. As we have seen, in the downstream part of the marketing channel the possibilities for information collection and information exchange have tremendously improved over the last 20 years, especially in FMCG. First came the 'scanner revolution' which by means of optical reading of barcodes on products made it possible to monitor the entire flow of products from manufacturers, through the different distribution stages, until the end consumer. More recently, electronic commerce data has been added to that. When resellers and end consumers make their purchases through the Internet, there is detailed information about these purchases, not only about when, how much, and from whom purchases were made, but it is also possible to follow consumer search behavior preceding these purchases. This information is used by suppliers to fine-tune their offerings to individual customers, dependent on their observed preferences, which can greatly improve the match between demand and supply. As we have seen before, the activities on the part of the suppliers to fine-tune their offerings to the demands of individual customers are called customer relationship management (CRM).

So CRM helps for the coordination of the downstream part of the marketing channel, but what about the upstream part? The developed economies have come a long way of being able to completely monitor the flow of products from the original upstream producers to their ultimate downstream destinations. For example, in the Netherlands, a dairy company like Friesland-Campina is able to identify the raw materials at the entry of its processing and manufacturing operation (in this case milk) from individual suppliers, that is dairy farms. In the same way, a supermarket chain such as Albert Heijn is able to trace back the fruits and vegetables in its stores to the individual growers. And when it sells these products to its customers through its on-line delivery service Albert.nl, it also has the data about the individual end users. So here, in principle the whole marketing channel is electronically connected, from the individual growers at the basis to the individual customers at the end. Such a situation makes it possible to not only to practice customer relationship management to optimally attune with the downstream customers, but also to directly exchange information about qualities and quantities with the upstream suppliers. By giving them the right information and incentives, these suppliers will deliver the varieties and quantities that match with the demand downstream. Just like this is the case for the consumers at the end of the marketing channel, also for the producers at the beginning it is important to go to the level of the *individual* farm. In this time with an emphasis on sustainability and health, it should be possible to trace back products to the individual producer. In analogy with customer relationship management (CRM) for the downstream part, we can call relationship management with the upstream part of the marketing channel *supplier relationship management* (SRM), see Figure 1. CRM and SRM together make it possible to coordinate the whole marketing channel for agricultural and food products. This can truly be called third era marketing. With the right communication systems in place, we can connect the upstream part of the marketing channel to the downstream part, creating the conditions for optimal coordination of the channel as a whole.

4. Marketing channels in developing economies and the role of ICT

Full coordination of the marketing channel may be possible in developed economies, but how about marketing in developing economies? In the literature the need for functioning vertical) marketing channels in developing economies is well recognized. (Van Tilburg *et al.*, 2007). Such channels should exchange quality and quantity information back and forth between the growers on the one hand and downstream parties on the other hand. Consequently, there is a clear need for linking the producers in developing countries to marketing channels (Van Tilburg *et al.*, 2007). Smallholders have to participate in exchange networks in order to reach the final consumer with the required quantities and qualities in an optimal way. Preferred supplier relationships can already be seen emerging in developing countries. This may result in 'tropical food chains' which can play an important role in coordinating the marketing channels for these products. At the same time it is not always easy in practice to connect fundamentally different marketing systems, for example the pastoral livelihood system in Ethiopia with the culture of multinational corporations of modern management practices (Ingenbleek and Van Tilburg, 2009). Relationship marketing may help there, in this case a specific form of supplier relationship management (SRM).

However, just like for CRM, also for successful SRM the most critical element is adequate information and communication technology (ICT). With the right ICT, primary producers in developing countries can be connected to marketing channels. If these farmers have the possibility of electronically connecting to traders, purchasing companies, cooperatives and to sources of market information, this will not only benefit the performance of the marketing channel as a whole, but also the economic position of the individual producers. Therefore, the availability of ICT for the actors at the origins of the marketing channel is a key success factor for effective supplier relationship management in developing economies. Here the news seems to be good. Especially the perspectives for mobile communication technology are very promising. In a recent paper comparing the development of mobile communication technology in the BRIC countries (Brazil, Russia, India, and China), with a set of developed countries such as France, Germany, United States, Canada, and Japan, Chircu and Mahajan (2009) reported that in terms of penetration (the authors call this 'depth') the BRIC countries may still be behind developed countries (47 versus 95%), but they have a higher growth rate. Some individual BRIC countries are even ahead of developed countries, for example Brazil has overtaken Canada on mobile technology. Interestingly, in developing countries mobile phones are used for a greater variety of functions (the authors call this 'breadth' of use), not only as communication devices, but also as information, entertainment, and Internet access channels. This is especially the case in countries such as India and China. Chircu and Mahajan (2009) suggest that developing countries can leapfrog the developed countries with mobile communication technology. Furthermore, it has been found that mobile technology is stimulating GDP growth in developing countries at twice the rate as in developed countries (Waverman *et al.*, 2005). This will fuel further adoption. Mobile technology is relatively cheap, because of low cost infrastructure, which is particularly relevant for low-density, rural, and remote areas. Mobile communication technology costs are much lower than the costs of PCs. Low-cost mobile devices are available at 30-60$ per handset. The availability of mobile communication technology makes it easy for producers of primary products in developing countries to connect to the marketing channel, both for receiving information about markets and for keeping in contact and coordinating with (potential) downstream buyers. Mobile communication technology is also used now in emerging economies for the dissemination of weather information to farmers and for offering farming advices, for example about disease control in tomato plants or how to plant bananas. Google Trader is a text based system that matches buyers and sellers of agricultural product and commodities (The Economist, 2009).

There is also empirical evidence that the availability of ICT in developing countries makes markets function better. Goyal (2010) describes a market intervention in the market for soy beans in the central Indian State of Madhya Pradesh. In the old situation farmers sold their products in regional open auctions. At each auction there were only a few buyers, with better market information than the farmers and who also were easily able to collude. The marketing intervention implied the introduction of Internet kiosks in the villages, displaying minimum and maximum prices paid for soy beans in 60 wholesale regions, updated once a day, along with agricultural information and weather forecasts. This market information increased the competition among the traders, thereby raising prices. Farmers' profits increased with 33% and in districts with kiosks the better market information made the cultivation of soy beans increase with 19%. Own Internet connections were too expensive for individual farmers, but through the kiosks the market information became accessible. This is an example where electronic links to information made it possible for farmers to connect to the market with better functioning of the marketing channel as the result.

In another study, Jensen (2007) found that the access to mobile phones made the fish markets in southern India more efficient, bringing down consumer prices by 4% and increasing fishermen's profits by 8%. Aker (2008) found that the adoption of mobile phones reduced price variations between markets (especially remote and hard to reach markets) by 6.4%. The lower transaction costs lowered the prices for consumers, and increased the profits of the traders, in this way increasing consumer and trader welfare.

Interestingly, since many years, there are high expectations about mobile marketing at the downstream end of the marketing channel, that is end consumers employing their mobiles for all kind purchasing activities. However, so far the use of mobile phones beyond interactive conversations is comparatively low (Shankar and Balasubramanian, 2009). It is interesting to observe that mobile technology does have an important influence on marketing, however at the very other side of the marketing channel where primary producers use them to connect to the market, and for their production, cultivation and selling decisions.

5. Conclusions

These examples demonstrate that the availability of (cheap) information and communication technology helps to link producers in developing economies to the market and in this way to become part of the overall marketing channel. The adoption of modern information and communication technology greatly improves marketing channel coordination in developing economies, and accelerates their connection to the third era of marketing.

References

Aker, J. (2008). Does Digital Divide or Provide? The Impact of Cell Phones on Grain Markets in Niger. BREAD Working paper, UC Berkeley, CA, USA.

Chircu, A.M. and Mahajan, V. (2009). PERSPECTIVE: Revisiting the Digital Divide: An Analysis of Mobile Technology Depth and Service Breadth in the BRIC countries. Journal of Product Innovation Management 26: 455-466.

Goyal, A. (2010). Information, direct access to farmers, and rural market performance in central India. American Economic Journal: Applied Economics (in press).

Ingenbleek, P.T.M. and Van Tilburg, A. (2009). Marketing for pro-poor development: deriving opportunities for development from the marketing literature. Review of Business and Economics, LIV: 327-361.

Jensen, R. (2007). The Digital Provide: Information (Technology), Market Performance and Welfare in the South Indian Fisheries Sector. Quarterly Journal of Economics 122: 879-924.

Jeuland, A.P. and Shugan, S.M. (1983). Managing Channel Profits. Marketing Science 2: 239-272.

Kohls, R.L. and Downey, W.D. (1972). Marketing of agricultural products, 4th ed. MacMillan, New York, NY, USA.

Meulenberg, M.T.G. (1986). The evolution of agricultural marketing theory: towards better coordination with general marketing theory. Netherlands Journal of Agricultural Science 34: 301-315.

Shankar, V. and S. Balasubramanian (2009). Mobile Marketing; A Synthesis and Prognosis. Journal of Interactive Marketing 23: 118-117.

The Economist (2009). Mobile marvels. A special report on telecoms in emerging markets. September 26th, The Economist Newspaper Limited.

Van Tilburg, A., Trienekens, J., Ruben R. and Van Boekel M. (2007). Governance for quality management in tropical food chains. Journal on Chain and Network Science 7: 1-9.

Waverman, l., Meschi M. and Fuss, M. (2005). The Impact of Telecoms on Economic Growth in Developing Countries. 33rd Annual Telecommunications Policy Research Conference.

Wierenga, B. and Soethoudt, H. (2010). Sales promotions and channel coordination. Journal of the Academy of Marketing Science 38: 383-397.

Winer, R.S. (2001) A Framework for Customer Relationship Management. California Management Review 43: 89-105.

Part 2.

Agriculture and agricultural markets as engines for development

The ineffectiveness of a one-size-fits-all approach

Barriers to economic growth in Malawi: reflections on smallholders

Emma Kambewa and Joseph Nagoli

The worst thing that can happen to Malawi's economy is if smallholders can lay down their tools.

Abstract

The contribution of smallholders to the economic growth in developing countries and Malawi in particular may be a well know fact. Malawi's economy is agro-based where the agriculture sector contributes 42% of national GDP. Despite the smallholder agriculture's contribution to the economy (30% of GDP), their everyday challenges have tended to be obscured by problems at the macro level and, thus they are often not well understood and documented. This chapter reflects on the everyday production, marketing and socioeconomic challenges facing smallholders. The paper concludes that whereas Malawi's prospects for economic growth will continue to be driven by the agriculture sector, sustained growth will depend on whether smallholders can overcome their barriers.

Keywords: Malawi, smallholders, agricultural production, marketing, production constraints, socio-economic challenges

1. Introduction

Malawi is one of the world's least developed countries located in Southern Africa (World Bank, 2009). Malawi has an estimated population of 13 million. Since independence in 1964, poverty remained prevalent until the past decade when notable economic growth and a reduction in poverty levels have been registered. People living under the poverty line decreased from 54% in 1990 to 40% in 2006, and the proportion of the 'ultra-poor' decreased from 24% in 1990 to 15% in 2007. Poverty is more prevalent in the rural areas, where 85% of the population lives. Food insecurity and poor access to basic social amenities are the continuing major threats to better living standards for the poor. Income inequality persists in Malawi where the richest 10% of the population have an annual per capita median income that is eight times higher than that of the poorest 10% (Malawi Government, 2006).

The role of smallholders in developing countries and Malawi in particular may be a well known fact. The economy of Malawi is critically dependent on the inputs and efforts of smallholders; recent history has convincingly shown that well developed smallholder production does not only improve the rural economy but also the macro-economy of the country, yet the institutions including markets and physical infrastructure does not support this to the full extent. The barriers that smallholders face such as: poor access to markets and information, inadequate institutional and credit support, high transaction costs, poor access to modern technologies, are not new either (Carr, 1997). In Malawi, like in other developing countries, government intervention in the production and marketing sectors (e.g. through input subsidies and price controls) was believed to create dependency and retard innovation and economic growth. The market liberalization efforts under the Structural Adjustment Programs (SAPs) imposed by World Bank and International Monetary Fund removed major distortions but did not ensure that small-scale farmers, particularly those without easy access to roads and markets, could benefit. The inefficiencies that ought to have been removed by the SAPs increased instead and resuming public support to smallholders was increasingly felt necessary. The re-introduction of agricultural input subsidies in Malawi over the past decade and the economic growth and food security achievement since 2005 has thus been seen as a model for green revolution in Africa (Block 2009). Yet smallholders – the force behind the success story – continue to face major challenges that can only be felt if one walks through their everyday production and marketing agenda. This paper describes the plight of smallholders and their everyday realities and gives some of the lessons that can be learnt from the challenges facing smallholders.

2. The smallholders

Who smallholders are

The English dictionary (Thesaurus) does not define 'smallholder' probably suggesting that there is no common definition. Hence, the definition of 'smallholders' and the cutting point from large scale producers may vary across countries, agro-ecological zones, enterprises and sectors. 'Smallholder' is a common term in agriculture where it is defined by the land they either own or cultivate. In aquaculture, smallholders are defined by the size and number of fish ponds they have. In capture fisheries, small scale fishers – commonly referred to as artisanal fishers – are defined by the type and size of fishing gear and craft they own or use.

In Malawi, there are nearly 3 million farm families cultivating over 70% of the country's arable land held under customary tenure. Of these 70% cultivate equal or less than 1hectare. Orr (2000) classified Malawi as moving towards an agrarian structure where more than half of rural households can be considered as 'functionally landless' as their average land holding size is below the minimum required for sustainable livelihoods from agriculture.

The role of smallholders and how they carry on with their everyday activities in developing countries is perhaps felt nowhere stronger than in Malawi. Smallholders have penetrated the production of all major cash crops although the estates have not actively engaged in food production. The contribution of smallholders to Malawi's economy facilitated by government's provision of essential agro-services, credit, extension and training, and input supply and marketing services has a long history (Sofranko and Fliegel, 1989). The recent achievement in food security facilitated by agricultural input subsidies to smallholders (Box 1) is thus a repeat of history and a testimony that smallholders continue to drive Malawi's economy.

However, much of the analysis on smallholder contribution to the economy tends to come from a managerial and policy point of view (Peters, 2006). What is missing is the (complementary) view that truly reflects the smallholder perspective to better understand what are their realities and constraints. It is certainly not a lack of motivation (as the economic perspective and personal livelihood go hand in hand), but rather a matter of constraint for the smallholders to become really integrated into value chains.

> **Box 1. The Malawi maize miracle.**
> Malawi emerged from the worst harvest in a decade in 2004 which prompted the Government to implement an ambitious assault on hunger in the history of the African continent. Targeting the smallholders with a national input (fertilizer and seed) subsidy program, maize production doubled in 2006 and almost tripled in 2007. Malawi registered a 53% surplus food (i.e. maize) production in 2007 from a 43% national food deficit in 2005. Some of the maize was exported and donated in relief to some neighboring countries. The surplus production also brought about a decline in the price of maize thereby relieving budgetary constraints for low-income urban and peri-urban households that are net food buyers. Maize traders also flourished as they increased their trade volumes. Maize, takes up about 80% of cultivated land in the smallholder agriculture sector and is grown by 97% of smallholder farming households. It accounts for 60% of total calorie intake.

Like large scale producers, smallholders too tend to be vulnerable to economic and environmental shocks but their everyday realities in production, marketing and socio-economic activities may be unique.

Production challenges

Walking along the corridors of the country and seeing smallholder gardens on steep mountain and hill slopes, and in the valleys of rivers and dambos (wetlands) reveal the extent of land constraints. One wonders how smallholders tirelessly go up and down the slopes either carrying inputs to the garden or produce down to their homes on their heads or shoulders. Neither bicycles nor oxcarts can be pushed up the hills or mountains.

Opening of marginal land to cultivation is increasing and environmental problems emerging from the practice are alarming. Sedimentation of rivers and streams is increasing and lake levels and water flow for power generation are reducing drastically. Ironically, cultivation of marginal land contributes to the success story that Malawi has witnessed in food security. Portions of arable land are still available in Malawi but some of it is either protected public forest reserves or leased land belonging to some rich people.

When the need for land overcomes smallholders understanding of the importance of game reserves or property rights, illegal encroachment of supposedly 'idle' land becomes a solution. Incidences of land conflicts between smallholders and estates or game reserves are increasing. While illegal encroachment cannot be condoned, it is land that smallholders need. Moreover they may not always have any legal means to acquire land apart from the customary land tenure. Traditional leaders too – the custodians of customary land – need land for themselves and have sometimes been part of the encroachment.

Over-dependence on rain-fed agriculture even when Malawi has abundant water resources (20% of the total land area), brings a different perspective to smallholders production nightmares. Walking along the corridors of Malawi when there is a dry spell one would see (sometimes irreversibly) withered crops that are just few meters from flowing rivers and lakes. While it may be concluded that lack of government policies – especially failure to promote sustainable irrigation – impoverishes the poor smallholders, they too may share the blame for complacency and lack of innovativeness. But the question may be whether they have the ability, knowledge, skills and facilities to divert or harvest water for use in the event of rain failure. Paradoxically, national prayers have been organized seeking divine intervention to bring rain even when water flows through rivers and streams out of the communities and the country as a whole.

Not all is lost though. The past decade has witnessed increased government and non-governmental organizations' support to small-scale irrigation through provision of treadle pumps for instance. However, the promotion of small-scale irrigation in some areas is being done without following proper guidelines. More river banks are being opened up and/or being continually used for irrigation. As a result river-bank slides and flooding are becoming common even with minimal rainfall.

Marketing challenges

Whether smallholders produce adequate commodities or not, they often sell a portion in order to buy what they cannot produce e.g. salt, clothes or pay for education or medical services. Taking the produce to the markets is another hurdle. Designated market places and infrastructure are inadequate and not always easily accessible. Market places including homesteads and road sides are common (Figure 1). When trading takes place, main roads tend to be blocked and risks and/or accidents of being run–over by vehicles are high. The phenomenon of mobile markets is increasing where trading is organized at various places in different days and times. Mobile markets keep smallholders almost always on the move to sell their commodities or buy inputs. Distance to where such markets are organized may be long and transport costs (by foot, public transport, bicycle or oxcarts) can be high in terms of time, money and volume of commodities that can be carried at a time. Rural areas are usually impassable during the rainy season; the critical time for farmers to acquire inputs. Vehicles reaching the remotest places are usually barely road worthy (commonly referred to as 'better than walking'), yet they pack people like goods. The people themselves desperate to reach markets or homes, no longer observe the roadworthiness of the vehicles or load limits, if they knew them in the first place.

Wastage of the smallholder commodities is characteristic of their trading practices. Post harvest losses and wastage become more evident in places where smallholders are trading. Lack of post harvest storage facilities coupled with poor physical handling of the commodities increase the levels of wastage of perishable commodities such as tomatoes, bananas and mangoes. Marketing places tend to be littered with commodities that are either damaged through poor handling; rotten due to failure to sell on time coupled

Figure 1. *Mango farmers along the main road of Malawi.*

with lack of storage facilities or abandoned because producers can no longer afford to transport them back home. Such losses are not often accounted for and do not appear in the national statistics. Commonality of the produce means that trading amongst smallholders is very limited. The only hope of obtaining better sales is when urban and peri-urban buyers patronize the smallholder markets. Not surprising: road side markets become increasingly important because rich people driving past the roads are more likely to stop and buy some commodities at a higher price than smallholders would otherwise get.

Some smallholders know of customer royalty. Women especially those selling along the main roads tell buyers their names or children's names so that on the buyers repeat visits to such markets, they should particularly look for them. Farmers or traders give the buyers a reasonable amount of commodities for free in addition to what they may have bought. The questions though are whether or not farmers or traders would have sold all the produce in the first instance, how many customers do they give free produce to, how much or whether the price of the commodities offsets the cost of the free commodities, and whether such buyers indeed come back to buy from the farmers.

Seasonality of supply complicates the marketing challenges for smallholders even more. Malawi has one rainy season (usually November to April) during which all agricultural production must take place and after which excess produce must be disposed off. Due to seasonality of production, lack of processing and storage facilities, and high supply that often outstrips demand, a considerable amount of these commodities especially citrus fruits, pineapples, guavas, bananas, apples, mangoes, tomatoes, onions, cabbages and Irish potatoes is wasted. Often times, some excess produce especially fruits (e.g. mangoes) are left to rot in the fields. Value adding processing and storage of these commodities is an obvious solution. But the agro-processing sector that should absorb and add value to excess produce has been relentlessly declining.

Smallholders too can add value to their produce. But this raises many questions than solutions. Do they have the right technologies and facilities? Would they be able to process all the excess produce? Smallholders too have been persuaded to believe that modern technologies for food processing are the best. Hence they have gradually abandoned their traditional ways of processing and preserving food products and who can blame them.

One would just need to visit a few rural markets or drive through the main roads to appreciate how seasonality of supply leaves the desperate smallholders and traders scrambling to sell their commodities when potential buyers stop by. Impatient buyers would never stop at rural markets for fear of what may seem as too much and possibly 'disheartening' persuasion by smallholders to buy their commodities. Downward bidding by sellers to attract buyers is a common practice where smallholders trade. Organizing these producers and linking them to agro-processing units could not only relieve smallholders of their relentless chase of would-be buyers but more importantly add value to the home grown produce that is often wasted.

Socioeconomic challenges

Smallholders may sometimes face the worst risks of their lives. In times of food scarcity, households in Malawi are usually faced with two life-threatening risks: HIV/AIDS and famine. Depending on the level of stress, they concentrate on the more immediate concerns of meeting their daily food needs. They sometimes engage in high-risk transactional affairs, as a means of alleviating hunger (Bryceson and Fonseca, 2006). For instance, research evidence shows that women traders succumb to engaging in 'sex for fish' to secure fish supply which is increasingly scarce. In the process, their vulnerability to HIV and AIDs increases.

Everyday realities for smallholders are many. In short smallholders endure a number of challenges. Although their production often adds up to national production statistics, their challenges and losses are not always accounted for at the higher level of analysis. Smallholders nonetheless continue their production and marketing activities with renewed zeal to secure their livelihoods. What matters is what lessons can be drawn from the everyday realities of smallholders.

3. Lessons and conclusions

First and foremost Malawi's prospects for economic growth will continue to be driven by agriculture and the smallholder subsector in particular. Smallholder agriculture, the predominant source of livelihoods and national economic growth may prove to be at least as efficient as larger farms when small farmers receive similar support services and inputs (e.g. seed and fertilizer) as attested by the 'Malawi Maize Miracle'. In view of the long history of smallholders' driving force for the economy, one can with reasonable confidence conclude that economic growth will never be sustained without unblocking the barriers that smallholders face. While there may never be a 'one solution fits all' smallholders, generic solutions need to be highlighted.

The production bottlenecks that smallholder farmers face may be lessened by a more secure tenure over production resources (land and water); enhanced availability of and access to improved seed, fertilizers and advanced irrigation methods and technology packages. Whereas the current national agricultural input subsidy program seems to improve access to seed and fertilizer, continued cultivation of marginal land (steep slopes and river banks) only increase the environmental problems. Environmental and smallholder friendly irrigation methods and technologies are urgently needed especially with the inevitably increasing droughts and floods. Both public and private policy need to develop and disseminate more productive agricultural and environmental friendly technology packages.

Public policy reforms that provide more access to markets and marketing infrastructure and services (e.g. roads, shelters, storage facilities, information) are needed to ensure a more structured means towards 'guaranteed' market access. The private sector needs to strengthen its linkages with and support to smallholders through for example, support in farmer organization, capacity building, and quality control and market information. The public policy should develop the public infrastructure and service sectors; and provide appropriate incentives for the private sector to engage with smallholders considering that such transactions and engagement may likely be costly.

A vibrant agro-processing sector is needed to absorb excess smallholder produce. Public policy needs to strengthen the role of research in development to enable the country to diversify and move beyond the production of 'unrecognizable' commodities and value adding technologies to reduce postharvest losses. This is important if the government's ambition to move the country from a predominantly producing and consuming into a producing and exporting nation is to come true. Smallholders as well as traders need to be more proactive, aggressive and innovative in engaging with the agro-processing sector including the wholesale and retail markets. They should engage in collective action to bulk up their produce as well as their voice to bargain with other value chain actors. The agro-processing sector including the retails markets should explore niche markets for the indigenous products.

In short, smallholders have to date persevered sometimes extreme conditions. Instability of incomes and inability to hedge against livelihood uncertainties lead them into taking desperate decisions that sometimes endanger their lives. Nevertheless, smallholders remain steadfast in their pursuit of better livelihoods and like a local Malawian saying that goes: *kuche kuche osauka satopa* (day and night poor people work without tiring); they timelessly and tirelessly drive the country's economy.

As smallholders account for over 80% of the country agricultural production, with renewed focus and support, they have the potential to take the economy to greater growth through unlocking their entrepreneurial capacity to diversify and increase production. Conversely, smallholders also have the potential to halt the economy if they can lay down their tools and that will be the worst thing that can happen to the economy of Malawi. If it happens, the plight of smallholders will be written in the history of Malawi.

References

Block, B. (2009). African Leaders Pursue 'Malawi Miracle'. Available at: www.worldchanging.com. Accessed on 26th January, 2010.

Bryceson, D.F. and Fonseca, J. (2006). Risking Death for Survival: Peasant responses to Hunger and HIV/AIDS in Malawi. World Development 34: 1654-1666.

Carr, S.J. (1997). A Green Revolution Frustrated: Lessons from the Malawi Experience. African Crop Science Journal 5: 93-98.

Malawi Government (2006). Malawi Growth and Development Strategy: From Poverty to Prosperity 2006-2007: Ministry of Economic Planning and Development.

Orr, A. (2000). 'Green Gold'?: Burley Tobacco, Smallholder Agriculture, and Poverty Alleviation in Malawi. World Development 28: 347-363.

Peters, P.E. (2006). Rural Income and Poverty in a Time of Radical Change in Malawi. Journal of Development Studies 42: 322-345.

Sofranko, A.J. and Fliegel, F.C. (1989). Malawi's Agricultural Development: A Success Story? Agricultural Economics 3: 99-113.

World Bank (2009). World Development Indicators (WDI) database. Washington DC, USA.

Agro-markets and pro-poor development in Sub-Saharan Africa: the quest for 'golden fishes'[11]

Clemens Lutz

Strategic resources are a prerequisite for making the inclusion of smallholders in agro value chains sustainable.

Abstract

Attacking poverty through the 'inclusion' of smallholders in agro-markets is a laudable pursuit that deserves support. The debate on this issue among policy makers and researchers knows a long history. However, the track record of policy making regarding agriculture and pro-poor development in Sub-Saharan Africa is rather bleak. This paper argues that successful inclusion of smallholders requires the deployment of strategic resources and capabilities in the smallholder farming systems. Farmers' organizations (shared resources) or vertical linkages can be helpful to develop these resources. However, not all smallholders are able to create these resources and, therefore, successful inclusion in agro-value chains remains an illusive dream for many of them. At present policy makers are too optimistic about opportunities for pro-poor development in the agricultural sector. The role of strategic resources in farm performance is neglected and, therefore, we have to be prepared for new disappointments.

Keywords: agro value-chains, inclusion, smallholders, strategic resources, Sub-Saharan Africa

1. Introduction

For decades the functioning of agro-markets is one of the key topics in the debate on rural development (World Bank, 2007). It started with a discussion on prices, structural adjustment and the retreat of government intervention. A decade of privatization and liberalization resulted in a shift in the debate towards the importance of coordination in supply chains and the need for proper institutions. The results of agro-policy making for pro-poor development in Sub-Saharan Africa are quite disappointing. Rural poverty rates hardly changed during the last three decades. In this paper we argue that a crucial element has been missing in the policy debate. The participants were right in stressing the importance of proper prices, institutions and coordinating mechanisms. All these issues facilitate the functioning of market mechanisms but do not provide a sufficient condition for the improvement of smallholder income. Mechanisms of value appropriation show that competitive pressures transfer profits to the strongest link in the supply chain. We argue that the inclusion of smallholders in agro-markets can be a successful

---

[11] The title refers to the name 'Poisson d'Or' Aad van Tilburg gave to a very successful relatively young food trader in Benin in 1987. Amidst poverty she was able to develop a flourishing wholesale business.

instrument in the struggle against poverty, but only if these smallholders deploy strategic resources, as these resources are needed to defend income improvements.

2. Policy making in the past

In the 60s and 70s the policy debate started with a discussion on government failure versus market failure. In particular the mandate of marketing boards and parastatals in Sub-Saharan Africa was discussed. After independence a strong foothold for governments in domestic food markets and export markets was widely adopted as an instrument to avoid market failures. Interestingly, the control mechanisms (marketing boards) were copied from governance structures that had been deployed by the colonial powers for export crops. During the seventies many of these policies resulted in major supply deficits and havoc. Mismanagement, inherent difficulties in organizing agricultural markets and political pressure by the urban poor resulted in disincentives for farmers.

This situation was the background of a discussion on 'getting the prices right'. Food deficits, major public budget deficits and macro economic instability forced most governments in Sub-Saharan Africa to accept structural adjustment programmes. The policy instruments proposed in these programmes reflected the debate on getting the prices right. Privatization (many marketing boards were dissolved) and liberalization (many formal rules of the game were abolished) reduced the role of governments and reinstalled market mechanisms to coordinate exchange. One of the positive outcomes of this policy change was that the net agricultural taxation between 1980-84 and 2000-04 declined on average from 28% to 10% in agriculture based developing countries (World Bank, 2007).

This was more or less the time that I started to do some research on market integration in Benin with Aad van Tilburg. Marketing Boards did not play a very important role on the rural food markets in this country, but formally government control was extensive. In the popular debate traders were suspects exploiting poor farmers. Being appointed at the Faculty of Agricultural Sciences of the University of Abomey-Calavi (Benin) I took the initiative to collect data on transaction costs and market prices. Nowadays these data are easily available at websites of MIS offices (Promoting Second Generation Market Information Services). At that time, 1986-1990, time series on prices were not existing. Data collection required a major effort of researchers and policy makers. Information was a major strategic resource for traders. At that time our research question was straightforward and in line with the debate on getting the prices right: are markets integrated? Time series analysis allowed us to confirm our expectation that the large number of petty traders and wholesalers active on the food markets were able to guarantee the functioning of market forces and that markets were indeed integrated in the long run. However, the results also made clear that improvements were needed with regard to integration in the short run (Kuiper *et al.*, 2003; Lutz *et al.*, 1995).

Although the structural adjustment policies contributed to more stable macroeconomic environments, it did not result in major improvements for smallholder incomes in Sub-Saharan countries (World Bank, 2007: 45). The debate evolved in a general consensus that getting the prices right (or: getting markets integrated) was not a sufficient condition for poverty reduction. Consequently, the World Bank changed their attention to the development of market institutions for attacking poverty (World Bank, 2001). These discussions broadened the scope of the debate and improved our insights in the functioning of markets in Africa. An important observation was that coordination mechanisms in supply chains are deficient and explain why smallholders still get unattractive prices in rural markets.

In Benin we came to the conclusion that the road is not yet half travelled (Adegbidi *et al.*, 2003). Despite the debate and the numerous project investments no structural changes have been observed in the organization of the food market. The role of farmers organizations is still weak. The selling of surpluses is mainly coordinated through regional food markets (spot-markets). The role of formal contracts is still at its infancy stage. The major change we observed is the widespread use of mobile phones. The transfer of market information improved significantly, although not as a result of a change in market organization, but as a result of technological development. Of course, it is an important contribution to the functioning of the market, leading to reduced transaction costs and, hopefully, to more effective market policies. However, in 2000 we were not able to identify a major improvement of market integration in the short run (Lutz *et al.*, 2007).

3. Policy making at present

In the last World Development Report on the role of agriculture for development (World Bank, 2007), several pathways out of poverty are discussed: 'smallholder farming and animal husbandry, employment in the 'new' agriculture of high value products, and entrepreneurship and jobs in the emerging rural, nonfarm economy.' The report proposes 6 instruments to make smallholder farming more productive and sustainable (World Bank 2007: 10):
- improve price incentives and increase the quality and quantity of public investment;
- make product markets work better;
- improve access to financial services and reduce exposure to uninsured risks;
- enhance the performance of producer organizations;
- promote innovation through science and technology;
- make agriculture more sustainable and a provider of environmental services.

These are relevant, but general guidelines. The problem is that the report is not clear on how these development processes work and how the rural poor can create positions that allow them to attain and sustain higher incomes. In particular this will be a problem if the target group concerns the large majority of the rural population. We recall that the literature on entrepreneurship shows that failure rates of new business ventures are high: 'Many are called but few are chosen' (Aldrich and Martinez, 2001). This means that fine-tuning between resources and market opportunities at smallholder level is key for success.

Scarcity of fertile land and slow progress in production techniques constrain the number of feasible solutions. Moreover, the pathways neglect another problem: value creation does not guarantee value appropriation. With increasing yields it is well possible that farm-gate prices simply decrease. Price elasticity explains part of this process, however there is another important element: value distribution between actors in the chain. Smallholders can create a lot of value in agricultural supply chains, but fierce competition does not guarantee the appropriation of this value by farmers.

4. A more strategic approach is needed

With regard to the debate on rural development this implies that the functioning of markets and competition is important, but not sufficient to improve the position of smallholders. A perfect market is interesting from an economic, social welfare, point of view. However, in such a market the individual firm will face only mediocre benefits. A more strategic approach (firm level) may add useful insights to the existing debate and may indicate pathways for smallholders to create strategic resources that allow them to appropriate at least a reasonable part of the value created (Teece *et al.*, 1997). Firms have to position themselves properly in order to be able to defend their position in the market.

Basically the profitability of a firm is determined by two factors: the attractiveness of the market and the competencies of the firm. In markets where competition is strong, like most agricultural output markets in Sub-Saharan Africa, a critical aspect of competitiveness concerns the development of competencies, i.e. resources and capabilities at firm level. The fit between critical success factors in the market and the competencies of the firm is key for success. This requires fine tuning as the difference between success and failure is a thin line. Also in the Sub-Saharan agro-markets resource heterogeneity is important. Major differences can be observed with regard to seasonality in production, differences in climate and soil, proximity of markets and infrastructure, knowledge about production and processing, access to capital and labour.

Even if a fit between market opportunities and capabilities exists, fulfilment of an additional condition is needed in order to be able to sustain this position: the deployed resources and capabilities have to be superior and difficult to imitate by competitors (Barney 2001). Resources fulfilling those latter conditions have strategic value as they provide the possibility to defend the firm's or farm's interests in the market: they create negotiation power for the smallholder.

These strategic aspects are not getting much attention in rural development policies. This is one of the reasons why changing prices and institutions do not necessarily change the rural poverty problem. If smallholders do not create strategic resources or capabilities it will be impossible to defend higher rates of return and to create a higher income. Without these resources profits higher than normal rates of return will be absorbed by other actors in the chain, having superior negotiation power, or will be transferred to final consumers. This transfer of value in the chain may result in a condition of 'immiserising growth' (Kaplinsky, 2001): smallholders produce more value, are included in the chain, but fail to reap the benefits.

This implies that we need the right prices and institutions, but also farming systems that are able to exploit strategic resources. Without sufficient attention for strategic positioning it will be difficult to escape the poverty trap and, consequently, the rural poor will continue to raise the question why the markets pay such unattractive prices. This problem cannot be solved by raising the wrong question. It would be more promising to phrase the question as follows: what can I do to create strategic resources and capabilities to position myself better in the markets.

5. Lessons for policy-makers

Many farmers in Sub-Sahara Africa supply a bulky product to regional spot-markets. Traditional policy making focuses on market functioning and argues that, if market mechanisms work, income improvements depend on price elasticity, higher yields per hectare and/or an increase in the number of hectares. This perspective neglects the need for organizational change. Farmers can differentiate their products, assume marketing functions, create horizontal or vertical alliances. Here a more strategic question comes in. For which product markets do individual farmers or farmers organizations have strategic resources. How to exploit these opportunities in the future and how to strengthen these strategic resources? These questions are getting insufficient attention in the present debate, which focuses on market mechanisms and, therefore, opportunities for individual farmers are missed. More attention should be paid to entrepreneurial and innovative farmers. They are expected not only to create, but also to appropriate, more value and therefore generate more income in rural areas.

The consequence of this argument is that the 'inclusion' of smallholders unable to create strategic resources will not be a sustainable strategy to escape from the poverty trap. For these groups alternative pathways out of poverty should be developed: wage employment in agriculture, wage or self-employment in the rural nonfarm economy, and migration out of rural areas; or some combination thereof (World Bank, 2007: 18).

This does not mean that the perspectives for smallholders are bleak. We admit that smallholders have difficulty to benefit from the economies of scale in production, marketing and research. However, the organization of smallholders in clusters and industrial districts makes it possible to attenuate the disadvantages of smallness through shared resources. Moreover, large firms face higher agency costs that can be avoided in small farms. We conclude that fine-tuning is key: inclusion should be based on the possibilities to create resources and capabilities at farm level. Policy making should not only address market functioning but also organizational change to create strategic resources and market opportunities for smallholders and/or their organizations.

References

Adegbidi, A., Dédéhouanou, H., Kpénavoun, S. and Lutz, C. (2003). Dix Ans de Libéralisation du Marché de Maïs au Bénin, Research Report No. 20, Centre for Development Studies, University of Groningen, Groningen, the Netherlands.

Aldrich, H.E. and Martinez, M.A. (2001). Many are called but few are chosen: an evolutionary perspective for the study of entreprenurship. Entrepreneurship: Theory and Practice 25: 41-57.

Barney, J. (1991). Firm Resources and Sustained Competitive Advantage. Journal of Management 17: 99-120.

Kaplinsky, R. (2000). Globalisation and Unequalisation: What Can Be Learned from Value Chain Analysis? Journal of Development Studies 37: 117-146.

Kuiper, E., Lutz, C. and Van Tilburg, A. (2003). Testing for vertical price leadership within marketing channels of local maize markets in Benin: Coïntegration, long-run causality and the common factor. Journal of Development Economics 71: 417-433.

Lutz, C., Van der Kamp, B. and Van Tilburg, A. (1995). The process of short and long term price integration in the maize market of Benin. European Review of Agricultural Economics 22: 191-212.

Lutz, C., Kuiper, E. and Van Tilburg, A. (2007). Maize market liberalization in Bénin: A case of hysteresis. Journal of African Economies 16: 102-133.

Teece, D.J., Pisano, G. and Shuen, A. (1997). Dynamic Capabilities and Strategic Management. Strategic Management Journal 18: 509-533.

World Bank (2001). World Development Report 2002. Building Institutions for Markets, Washington DC, USA.

World Bank (2007). World Development Report 2008. Agriculture for Development, Washington DC, USA.

Land reform and land markets

Impact of Zimbabwe's fast track land reform programme on the production and marketing of maize in the smallholder sector

Ajuruchukwu Obi

Without proper planning, land reform can lead to supply bottlenecks as a result of declining productivity and production and eventually lead to weakening of the primary markets that serve smallholders, with negative consequences for smallholder livelihoods and welfare.

Abstract

Many parts of the developing world face situations whereby the meagre farm produce of resource-poor farmers are either not sold at all or are only sold on terms that penalize the producers and severely hurt their livelihoods. Government and market failures arising from, and worsened by, weakened primary markets, are often blamed for this situation and cause serious concern as impediments to economic development. Such failures commonly arise from improper attention to the critical conditions for the success of programmes whose traditional developmental goals are indisputable. This chapter examines the impact of the most recent Zimbabwean land redistribution programme. The chapter explores the issues around the implementation of the fast track land reform programme and suggests that the programme has negatively impacted on maize yields and weakened primary markets by simultaneously creating supply bottlenecks and lowering effective demand as a consequence of depressed earnings and restrictions on cross-border trading in maize. Elements for the restoration of productive capacities and enhanced livelihoods are discernible.

Keywords: land reform, fast track land reform, land invasions, war veterans, maize, supply bottlenecks, primary markets, market failures, hyper-inflation, smallholder

1. Introduction

Low production levels, poor product quality and thin markets characterise the smallholder sector in much of Southern Africa. With the exception of South Africa, Botswana and Namibia, these countries experience food shortages, with domestic food requirements often being met through substantial commercial imports and food aid. In June, 2001, a joint UN Mission to Lesotho reported a decline in the cereal production in the order of 55% below previous year results and 60% below average results for the 5 years preceding the mission (Joint UN Mission, 2001). By 2002, this situation had placed about 444,800 persons in at least 3 districts on the verge of starvation (The Economist, 2002). In August 2003, similar situations were reported in Tanzania, Malawi, Swaziland, Mozambique, Zimbabwe, etc (WFP, 2003). Maize production in Swaziland improved marginally in 2009 but not enough to reduce the need for substantial commercial imports of maize to address the domestic cereal gap (FAO, 2010). Estimates for

2009 put the proportion of food insecure Swazis at about a fifth of the total population, a situation that complicates the crises already caused by the HIV/AIDS pandemic (FAO, 2010). This is a truly Southern African story.

Expectedly, governments in the region are adopting a wide range of strategies that seek to boost food production and achieve more efficient distribution of food. For Zimbabwe, land reform was identified at Independence in 1980 as a central strategy for ensuring food security by promoting greater equity in land distribution and enhanced agricultural productivity (Groenewald, 2003). Studies in the region (for example, Chirwa, 2004, Jayne *et al.*, 2006, 2007) suggest that the extent of market-orientation of maize production is positively associated with the household's land holding, and that those households whose maize crop failed had the least landholding. But, as Groenewald (2003) has observed, successful land reform is not possible in the absence of a set of proper planning in respect to the goals, fiscal arrangements, beneficiary selection, timing of key aspects and phases, among others.

The Zimbabwean land reform experiment is unique in the way it provides opportunities to examine different land reform options in terms of their goals and implementation arrangements within a matter of one generation and under the same political system. It is now well-known that the fast track land reform programme has been characterized by poor planning, with little or no attention being paid to the crucial need to match resources with capabilities. In some instances, agricultural extension and rural development personnel were sternly instructed to simply ensure that small farmers were allocated land for crop production, disregarding questions of land suitability and similar considerations (Muchara, 2009; Ndou, 2010: personal communication). The chapter therefore makes the challenging proposition that without proper planning, land reform can lead to supply bottlenecks due to declining productivity and production and culminate in weakening of the primary markets that serve smallholders.

To test the challenging proposition in a real-life context, a rapid appraisal of the production and marketing of maize was undertaken in the Mwenezi District of the Masvingo Province of Zimbabwe where all alternative landholding patterns are evident. The aim was to determine the impact of the Fast Track Land Reform Programme (FTLRP) on the production and marketing of maize which is an important dietary staple and famine reserve crop in Zimbabwe. The rest of this chapter will provide some more detail on the antecedents and nature and implementation of the Fast Track Land Reform Programme, the changes in maize production and marketing since the FTLRP with particular reference to physical production changes and associated supply bottlenecks, as well as the adjustments made by producers and consumers, culminating in emergence of new production areas and modes of exchange for maize. The chapter will draw conclusions from these insights to accept or refute the challenging proposition and then proffer a set of recommendations.

2. The Fast Track Land Reform Programme in Zimbabwe

Following years of bitter armed struggle triggered by intolerable levels of oppression and deprivation that revolved around access to land, peace finally came to Zimbabwe as the 1970s drew to a close. Driven by commitments made at the Lancaster House Agreement that reinforced faith in the crucial steering role of Britain, Zimbabwe launched its ambitious land resettlement programme in September 1980, a mere 5 months after political independence was granted to this former British colony. The programme was intended to redress the huge imbalance in land distribution and enhance access to land for victims of the liberation struggle and the landless, while consolidating commercial agricultural production. However, by the end of the 1990s, there was widespread disenchantment with the slow progress in resettling the indigenous population. At that time, in spite of nearly two decades of implementation of land reform, a mere 4,500 white farmers still controlled 28% of the land while more than a million black farmers struggled to eke out a desperate existence in largely unproductive and dry 'communal areas' (Mushunje, 2005). In between these two extremes, the political élites received preferential treatment in allocation of land expropriated from white owners even though much of that was promptly abandoned or mismanaged, with disastrous consequences for farm production and food prices. At the same time, Zimbabwe's macro economy began to experience serious balance of payment problems for which a structural adjustment programme was launched. As the hardships deepened, political interests capitalized upon the situation to manipulate an electoral process to seemingly obtain a popular mandate to accelerate the land transfers.

The ensuing FTLRP that began in July 2000 was marked by violent invasions of white-owned farms in which war veterans and their sympathizers unleashed a wave of terror on the large-scale farm sector. Subsequently, legislation was passed to institutionalize the 'fast track' process, adopting two key implementation models, namely Model A1 (to decongest communal areas by targeting the tribal areas suffering severe land constraints), and Model A2 (to promote agricultural commercialization at various scales) (Muchara, 2009; Zikhali, 2008). But in the view of the donor community in Zimbabwe who had privileged access to the ideas as the land invasions were just beginning, this process 'had no goal, no plan, no timetable, no budget, no capacity and no transparency' (Kinsey, 1999).While the FTLRP clearly led to substantial repossessions and transfers of land, it seemed to have created a number of other problems.

At one level, the FTLRP is blamed for directly leading to a 30% drop in agricultural production, a hyper-inflationary situation, and a 15% contraction of the economy that culminated in 2008 to an unemployment rate estimated to exceed 80% (Zikhali, 2008). At the other level, the human rights abuses came to a head with members of opposition parties being victims of extreme persecution, beatings and murders. Not even the landmark ruling by the Southern African Development Community (SADC) Tribunal on the court challenge mounted by the Commercial Farmers Union of Zimbabwe could stop the farm seizures which continued unabated (SADC, 2008). The installation of a transitional government of national unity in which the opposition party is playing a limited role has also not moderated the level of political intolerance. Targeted sanctions on the regime in Zimbabwe are still in place to force the regime's hands. Whether or not these sanctions are worsening the political and economic crises in Zimbabwe is now being debated but a recent effort by the South African government to secure some easing-off of the sanctions has failed as Britain insists on seeing real changes first (BBC-News, 2010).

3. Maize production and marketing since FTLRP

On the basis of data collected as outlined above, it can be concluded that four categories of changes have taken place in agricultural production and marketing in Zimbabwe following the FTLRP. The first is a noticeable decline in maize yields, the second is the emergence of new maize production areas, while a third major change was in relation to the sources of domestic/household maize supplies. The fourth major development relates to the nature of the transactions in the maize market.

Declining maize production

To more accurately isolate the impact of the FTLRP on maize production, it is necessary to delineate it from the previous phases of the land reform programme in Zimbabwe. Production levels in the different phases can then be compared to determine the extent to which the programme has exerted an impact on maize yields and production. Table 1 is an attempt to delineate the land reform phases according to their more specific focus or outcome. The first phase of the land reform programme launched in 1980 and lasting up to 1989 targeted farms in the high potential agro-ecological regions which were largely dominated by the large scale commercial farmers (LSCF) who were all white and numbered about 6,000. Also targeted was a small number of black farmers engaged in small-scale commercial farming and who numbered about 8,500. Land was to be withdrawn from the LSCF for redistribution. In order to decongest the communal areas, the programme implemented a parallel process of moving smallholders to Resettlement Areas (mostly state land) in which subsistence farming predominated. These processes were largely over by 1996, following which land redistribution came to a virtual halt while land hunger grew. Efforts to mobilize international funding to sustain the programme failed. The British Government that financed the first phase was uncertain about its special responsibility to meet the costs of land transfers and could therefore not confirm its continued involvement (Short, 1997). Agitations subsequently grew and culminated in the invasions of the late 1990s and gave rise to the 'fast track' under which Models A1 and A2 were introduced in an attempt to bring some order to the ensuing chaos. Even in the absence of

Table 1. Maize production in the districts of Masvingo province of Zimbabwe (tonnes/ha) (Ministry of Agriculture, Mechanisation and Irrigation Development, 2009).

District	LSCF Yield-t/ha	SSCA Yield-t/ha	A2 Yield-t/ha	A1 Yield-t/ha	OR Yield-t/ha	CA Yield-t/ha	District average
Bikita	0	0.95	0	0	0.71	0.57	0.60
Chiredzi	1.0	0.73	1.46	0.74	0.50	0.45	0.64
Chivi	0	0.76	0	0	0.93	0.61	0.60
Gutu	3.78	1.32	2.62	1.06	1.32	0.70	0.70
Masvingo	2.01	0.82	1.30	0.94	0.74	0.61	0.82
Mwenezi	0	0	0	0.51	0.71	0.60	0.55
Zaka	0	0	0	2.13	2.00	0.60	0.65
Average	1.94	1.01	1.47	0.79	0.87	0.50	0.68

LSCF: refers to large scale commercial farms which are not part of the Fast Track Land Reform Programme.

SSCA: refers to Small Scale Commercial Areas which are not part of the Fast Track Land Reform Programme.

A2: A2 Farmers are medium-large scale commercial farmers who benefited in Zimbabwe's Fast Track Land Reform Programme between 2000 and 2009.

A1: A1 Farmers are small scale farmers who benefited in Zimbabwe's Fast Track Land Reform Programme between 2000 and 2009.

OR: refers to Old Resettlement areas that were formed from 1980-1998 under the government's Land Reform and Redistribution Programme.

CA: refers to Communal Areas that have never been reformed by any of Zimbabwean government's land reform programmes.

longitudinal data, it is possible to gain a snap-shot insight into the way different phases of the land reform programme have impacted on maize production and therefore be in a position to comment on the specific impact of the fast track process.

With the foregoing in mind, data on the differential productivities of maize for 2008 are presented in Table 1. The national average maize productivity in 1999 (the year preceding the inception of the FTLRP) was estimated at 1.516 tonnes/ha. According to the estimates (Table 1), average maize productivities at the district levels were uniformly lower than the national estimate for 1999. This was also true for the provincial average which was estimated at 0.68 tonnes/ha in 2008. Thus, except in two isolated cases, namely the A2 farms in Gutu District and A1 farms in Zaka district where productivities exceeded the 1999 national average, it was clear that performance of maize has been poorer since FTLRP. Focusing exclusively on commercial agriculture, while the A2 model generated a provincial average of 1.47 tonnes/ha, the performance was as much as 30% less than what was obtained under Large Scale Commercial farming which also represented pre-FTLRP performance. These results confirm other suggestions that the FTLRP may have resulted in a 30% decline in agricultural production in Zimbabwe (Richardson, 2004; USDA, 2009; Zikhali, 2008).

Among the several reasons for the decline in maize yield, it is suggested that shortages of seeds, fuel, fertilizers, and tractors are the most important (Muchara, 2009; USDA, 2009; Zikhali, 2008). As the area planted to maize also fell, by between 16-37% over the nine year period (Table 2), it is indisputable that the fast track programme has resulted in an overall decline in maize production, among other commodities (USDA, 2009). As Table 2 indicates, the cultivated areas have fallen quite significantly since 2000 for the obvious reasons of the economy-wide hardships that impaired the ability to raise production capital. As noted above, widespread shortages in vital inputs such as seeds, fuel, fertilizers and mechanical equipment meant that farmers could not bring sizeable hectarages under cultivation, regardless of whether or not the land was available. The indication is that large scale farms recorded the highest area reduction while the old resettlement areas experienced the least area reduction. It is estimated that the combined effect of the productivity shortfall and area reduction has been 'economic collapse and 45% malnutrition' (Muchara, 2009).

Table 2. Changes in area cultivated in Zimbabwe, 2000-2009 (USDA satellite-based estimates of area changes 2000-2009).

Farm class	Percentage (%) change in cultivated area (2000-2009)	Comments
A1 Farms	-26	Areas covered by FTLRP
A2 Farms	-19	Areas covered by FTLRP
Communal lands	-34	Covered under first phase
Large scale commercial	-37	Covered under first phase
Old resettlement areas	-16	Covered under first phase
Small scale commercial areas	-36	Covered under first phase
Total	-30	

FTLRP: Fast Track Land Reform Programme.

Maize supply bottlenecks

The effect of the depressed yield on overall supply of maize was assessed by reviewing the data maintained by the Grain Marketing Board (Table 3) since 2001 as well as satellite estimates of area change provided by the USDA (Table 2). The Grain Marketing Board (GMB) is the strategic grain reserve for the country. Its main responsibility is to buy all cereal produce from farmers and sell the cereals to millers, institutions and individual consumers at affordable prices. GMB is the sole importer and exporter of government cereal products. Table 3 presents statistics on the stocks handled by the agency since the launch of the FTLRP. The worsening domestic supply situation since 2002 is evident, although a spike in imports in 2005 and 2006 may have softened the adverse impact on households.

Since 2000, GMB has been affected by cash shortages, weak pricing structures, and transport and fuel shortages. In 2003, the GMB depot in Mwenezi was relocated from Sarahuru business centre in the old communal area (CA) to Rutenga Business Centre in the former commercial area (now Model A1 resettlement areas). The relocation of the GMB has made it less accessible to most households who turned to informal sources that sourced maize from South Africa and Botswana and accepted foreign currency in exchange for maize irrespective of government ban on dollar-denominated transactions. However, full dollarization of the economy is speculated to widen the gap between the have and the have-nots as sources of forex were mainly through remittances from relatives abroad or through cross-border trading among non-workers (FAO, 2009).

Due to inflation, cash trading of maize was very minimal among farmers except where such transactions were denominated in the South African rand. Most farmers preferred barter trading with livestock (goats, sheep, cattle, chicken, etc), clothes, household utensils, farm equipment (ploughs, scotch carts, hoes) or building materials. Such trade was meant to counteract the government's price control measures and gave the farmers platforms to bargain with buyers for better returns. The preferred barter trading system by farmers deprived the GMB of local grain supplies which consistently declined from 2007. Maize imports remained greater than locally procured maize, except for the 2004/05 and 2006/07 seasons. This also probably reflects the growing importance of the informal market in augmenting government procurement efforts.

Table 3. *National maize procurement statistics for GMB (Grain Marketing Board (GMB), Zimbabwe).*

Marketing year	Local intake/procurement (tonnes)	Imports (tonnes)
2001/02	154,847	88,656
2002/03	49,418	763,594
2003/04	244,187	375,198
2004/05	186,661	75,609
2005/06	181,219	685,983
2006/07	543,725	161,235
2007/08	194,331	401,285
2008/09	35,593	417,825
2009/10[a]	6,062	3,580

[a]Figures for the 2009/10 marketing year are as at week ending Friday July 10, 2009.

Emergence of new maize production areas

Cereal marketing in the formal markets of Zimbabwe has for the recent past been constrained by low production and formal market irregularities. The fast track land reform coincided with frequent droughts and hyper-inflationary environment in Zimbabwe, which caused uncertainties in the agricultural sector. Mwenezi District is inherently dry, with rainfall averaging 500mm/year. Prior to the land reform, cattle ranching and game farming were the dominant activities among large scale farmers. With the FTLRP, the cattle ranches were subdivided into small and medium sized farms parcelled out to beneficiaries of the land reform programme (the ex-combatants and party loyalists). This saw the introduction of crop farming in the area together with small scale cattle rearing at household levels.

4. Summary and conclusion

The study examined the trends in maize production and marketing in Zimbabwe associated with the fast track land reform programme beginning from 2000. The unique situation of Zimbabwe allows for a comparison of different modes of implementation of land reform within one generation and broad governance arrangement or political system. It is clear that the broad equity and productivity goals of land reform were achieved in the first phase of the land resettlement programme that lasted up to the mid-1990s. Efforts to raise funds to sustain the momentum of the programme failed so that, up to 1999, there was little or no activity towards land re-distribution. In the meantime, discontents developed and turned into anger and frustration at the unmet expectations for a people who had suffered prolonged deprivation and could no longer wait (Groenewald, 1999).

In the event, the successor programme became haphazard and virtually directionless. At the same time, government's inability to finance broader development investments resulted in shortage of basic inputs, equipment and spares severely impaired agricultural support services which lowered agricultural productivity in general. With diminished fiscal capacity, cultivated areas also fell sharply leading to severe supply bottlenecks which have had far-reaching consequences on the nature of maize market transactions. With deepening supply bottlenecks in the face of a severe cash crunch, ordinary Zimbabweans reverted to ancient practices like barter-trading that imposed serious transactional hardships. The indication that malnutrition reached as high 45% suggests that consumer satisfaction was hardly achieved. In such a situation, it is hardly debatable that the standard goals of land reform to facilitate growth, promote equity, enhance tenure security, strengthen food security and reduce poverty were not realized.

It is therefore clear from the foregoing that proper planning is non-negotiable for a land reform programme to successfully deliver the benefits of equitable distribution of land and enhanced agricultural productivity. It is also clear that real marketing is impossible in the absence of goods and services and anything that chokes off supply of physical output is bound to weaken primary markets serving the poor. Policies to empower small farmers by re-distributing land in order to boost food production and link them to markets must undoubtedly be sensitive to these issues. The authorities in South Africa have already drawn immense lessons from the Zimbabwean experience in re-directing its own Land Reform Programme about a decade ago and the recent adoption of area-based planning to speed up land redistribution is clear indication of a determination to avoid repeating its neighbour's mistakes. The diversity of the Zimbabwean programme makes these results applicable to other countries embarking on even less complex programmes.

References

BBC-News (2010). Brown Says Too Early to Lift Sanctions Against Zim. British Broadcasting Corporation News, 5 March 2010.

Central Statistical Office (2008). Quarterly Bulletin 2008. Harare, Government of Zimbabwe.

Chirwa, E.W. (2004). Access to Land, Growth and Poverty Reduction in Malawi. Research Project on Macroeconomic Policy Choices for Growth and Poverty Reduction, North-South Institute, Canada.

FAO (2010). GIEWS Country Brief on Swaziland. Food and Agriculture Organisation of the United Nations (Global Information and Early Warning System), Rome, Italy.

Groenewald, J. (2003). Conditions for Successful Land Reform in Africa. Pre-IAAE Conference on African Agricultural Economics. University of the Free State, Bloemfontein, South Africa.

Jayne, T.S., Chisvo, M., Rukuni, M. and Masanganise, P. (2006). Zimbabwe's food insecurity paradox: hunger amid potential. In: M. Rukuni, P. Tawonezvi, and C. Eicher (eds.), Zimbabwe's Agricultural Revolution Revisited. University of Zimbabwe Publications, Zimbabwe.

Jayne, T.S., David L. and Tschirley, D.L. (2007). Food Crises and Food Markets: What has been learned in Southern Africa over the Past Decade? Paper prepared for the Workshop on Vulnerability to and Early Warning for Food Emergencies:Conceptual Issues and Practical Implementation, organized by the FAO Global Information and Early Warning System (GIEWS) on Food and Agriculture, Trade and Markets Division FAO Headquarters, Rome, Italy.

Joint UN Mission (2001). Special Report FAO/WFP. Crop and Food Supply Assessment. Mission to Lesotho 5 - 16 May.

Kinsey, B. (1999). Land Reform, Growth and Equity: Emerging Evidence from Zimbabwe's Resettlement Programme. Journal of Southern African Studies 25: 173-196.

Ministry of Agriculture, Mechanisation and Irrigation Development (2009). Second Round Crop and Livestock Assessment Report-April 2009. Zimbabwe.

Muchara, B. (2009). Implications of the Fast Track Land Reform Programme on Markets and Market Relationships for Livestock, Cotton and Maize in Mwenezi District of Zimbabwe. Department of Agricultural Economics and Extension, University of Fort Hare (mimeo), South Africa.

Mushunje, A. (2005). Farm Efficiency and Land Reform in Zimbabwe. University of Fort Hare, Alice, South Africa.

Richardson, C. (2004). The Collapse of Zimbabwe in the Wake of the 2000-2003 Land Reforms. Edwin Mellen Press, Lewiston, New York, NY, USA.

SADC (Southern African Development Community) (2008). Second Ruling of the SADC Tribunal (Case No. SADC - T2/08). Southern African Development Community Tribunal, Windhoek, Namibia.

Short, C. (1997). Letter to Zimbabwe Minister of Agriculture - Kumbirai Kangai.

The Economist (2002). Southern Africa's Food Shortage: with the wolf at the door. The Economist Newspapers Vol. 363, No. 8275, 1 June, 2002.

USDA (United States Department of Agriculture) (2009). 2009 Corn Area in Zimbabwe. Commodity Intelligence Report, United States Department of Agriculture.

WFP (World Food Programme) (2003). ODJ Regional Consolidated Report for Southern Africa. Issue No 2, 31 August, 2003.

Zikhali, P. (2008). Fast Track Land Reform and Agricultural Productivity in Zimbabwe. Discussion Paper Series, EfD DP 08-30, Environment for Development, Sweden.

Property rights, land markets and the efficiency of land use: an analysis in rural China

Franz Heidhues and Stephan Piotrowski

Land markets as instruments of efficient resource allocation require appropriate economic and institutional framework conditions. History and path dependency, ideology, social institutions, labor market constraints and lack of social security coverage, lead to market fragmentation and tend to inhibit an efficient functioning of the land rental market. Reform policies need to address these constraints if they are to establish more efficient land markets.

Abstract

The reform of the land property rights system and the establishment of a land and land rental market pose some of the most complex and controversial challenges for transformation countries. History, ideology, path dependency and institutional and social constraints compete with the intention to guide land use to its most productive purposes. Rural land in China is by law 'collectively owned', in practice this means it is common property of the village. Villagers Committees (VC) transfer to village households long-term use rights to equal shares of the village land. A great number of factors, such as power relationships, Party membership, rent seeking, distance from town/township or county, influence the land allocation process. As a result, extremely diverse land tenure arrangements can be observed today. Several factors constrain the land market. The need to actually farm the land in order to maintain land use rights inhibits off-farm employment and reduces land mobility. Also villages tend to restrict the renting out of land to members of the same village. Employees in urban areas generally are not covered by social security; to have a fall back in case of becoming unemployed or in old age they tend to keep their land in their village, often farmed by family members. The key to developing a more efficient land rental market in rural China would be to de-link land use rights from off-farm employment and establish a social safety net for those employed off-farm. Also opening land rental markets to non-village households would contribute to a more efficient land rental market.

Keywords: property rights, land markets, land reform, China

1. Introduction

In the transformation process from a centrally planned to a market oriented economic system, the reform of the land property rights system and the establishment of a land and land rental market pose some of the most complex and controversial challenges. History, ideology, path dependency and institutional and social constraints compete with the need and intention to raise economic incentives and to guide land use to its most productive purposes. In this paper, we intend to contribute to a better understanding of the land reform process in rural China by discussing the many factors that influence it and analyzing on the basis of an empirical research work the key driving forces and constraining hindrances for an efficient land market. The paper starts with a discussion of the land property right system and how it has evolved since the Cultural Revolution; it will present the formulation and implementation of land policies in rural China; and highlight issues and challenges ahead. In its second section it will present the results of an empirical analysis based on a survey of more than three hundred rural households in about twenty villages in three provinces of the North China Plain (NCP), detailing the role of economic, social and institutional factors in establishing a rural land rental market. In its third section we will conclude with a set of policy recommendations aimed at improving the functioning and efficiency of the land rental market.

2. Land property rights system in rural China

The guiding principle of land distribution in the transition from the 'People's Commune' era to the newly established Household Responsibility System, which was introduced in the early 1980s, was equality.

Rural land in China is by law 'collectively owned'. For practical purposes the collective is the village, and rural land can be characterized as common property of the village with the village representatives as 'management groups'. Individual households have long-term use rights to equal shares of the village land; they may be seen as 'co-owners' of the land. This system of collective ownership and privatized use rights is known as the two-tier land system (Chin, 2005). However, ultimate ownership rests with the state (Cai, 2003; Ho, 2001); and the constitution of the PRC stipulates that the state may requisition collectively owned land in the public interest (PRC, 2004: Art. 10). This interpretation of the de facto and ultimate ownership is, however, contested and the legal status of rural land is seen as ambiguous.

A second source of ambiguity stems from the question which administrative unit represents the 'village'. During the transformation of rural institutions in the early 1980s three types of 'villages' emerged (Figure 1): the natural village (or villagers group), formerly the production team; the administrative village, formerly the production brigade, and the township (or town), formerly the commune.

Originally, the natural village had in fact been recognized as the basic unit of the commune and thus as the legal owner of the land within its vicinity (Ho, 2001: 405). Over time its status became weaker and it is the administrative village that became the most important unit being in charge of implementing higher-level policies and determining their impact on individual farmers. However, its leading status in land rights is far from uniformly recognized. A great number of factors, such as power relationships, membership and influence of representatives in the Chinese Communist Party (CCP), rent seeking,

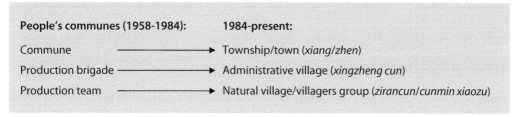

Figure 1. *Transformation of rural administrative institutions (Adapted from Choate (1997) and Ho (2001)).*

industrial activities, distance from town/township, county, prefecture or provincial centers, and others determine an administrative village's power in land right issues (Hsing, 2006; Zhang and Carter, 1997; Zhou and Yang, 2004).

Within villages, land affaires and other issues of common property are administered by villagers committees (VCs) whose members are partly elected by villagers, partly appointed by the local party branch. Often the village secretary of the CCP is the most influential member (Vermeer, 2004: 127). As a result of the multiplicity and variability of influencing arrangements and determining factors, extremely diverse land tenure arrangements can be observed today (Nee and Su, 1990: 20; Zhu and Jiang, 1993: 441).

Furthermore, land tenure differs according to rights and obligations associated with its land use. Table 1 summarizes the different types of tenure found in rural areas.

This system of subdividing land allocation by land use and by allowing land use right acquisition by an auction process implied abandoning the principle of egalitarian distribution of land and probably led to an even greater fragmentation of land allocation. The egalitarian principle moved increasingly into a conflict situation with the efficiency of land markets.

Table 1. *Rights and obligations associated with different types of land tenure in rural China (Chen and Brown, 2001; Li et al., 2000: 6; Lohmar, 2006; Rozelle et al., 2005).*

Chinese term	Common English translation	Definition, rights and obligations
Ziren tian	Responsibility land	Allocated to households on the basis of family members or number of laborers
Kouliang tian	Ration land	For household subsistence needs
	Self-sufficiency land	Usually not subject to taxation
	Consumption land	
Jidong di	Flexible land	Rented out by the village to households for a fee, often in a bidding process
	Mobile land	
	Reserve land	Land used to accommodate for reallocations and contingencies
		If reserve land is rented out to households it also is referred to as contract land (*chengbao tian*)
Chengbao tian	Contract land	Contracted to households in an open bidding within the Two field system
		Auctioned off or allocated by village leaders for a fee
Huang di	Unused land	Land of very poor quality that is auctioned off to households
	Waste land	
Ziliu di	Private plots	Small, backyard plots for growing vegetables etc. for meeting subsistence needs
		Very stable use rights

Of particular relevance is the setting aside of reserve land, by law restricted to 5% of a village's land, in fact however reported to reach in some cases 50% (Deininger *et al.*, 2006). The possibility of using reserve land for accommodating a growing village population and other necessary adjustments in land allocation has increased the sense of land tenure security. It has also been found that reserve land was allocated to married women who had not received land in their husbands' villages (Li and Xi, 2006).

Decisive for the development of a land rental market is the provision in the land law that households may transfer their use rights by subcontracting, exchanging, transferring and 'other means' (Art 32 of the Law on Land Contract in Rural Areas). While the law does not explicitly limit the transfer of land use rights to inhabitants of the same village, it does state that 'under equal conditions, members of the collective economic organization shall enjoy priority'. If land is contracted out to non-members of the village, two thirds of the villagers must approve. (Art 15 of the Land Administration Law)

3. Issues

As the land allocation system over time has evolved it is still facing unresolved issues for developing an efficient land rental market. While the law stipulates a 30-year use right period, not all villages adhere to it. Reallocations take place to restore an egalitarian land distribution, to accommodate changes in household size or establishing new households. While reallocations increase tenure insecurity, its impact on investments in land improvement, fertilizer use and productivity and off-farm employment is hard to substantiate (Piotrowski, 2009: 38).

A major constraint to developing a land rental market is the link between actual land use and land use rights. It is necessary to actually farm the land to maintain use rights to arable land; engaging in off-farm employment may lead to a loss of land rights. As land has an important function as a social safety net, farm households hesitate to give up farming completely with the consequence of low land mobility and a reduced supply elasticity for off-farm labor (Hertel and Fan, 2006).

4. Land rental markets in the North China plain: an empirical analysis in Henan, Hebei and Shandong provinces

As part of the International Research Training Group (IRTG) 'Sustainable Resource Use in North China', funded by the German Research Foundation (DFG) and the Ministry of Education of the People's Republic of China, a comprehensive survey of more than 300 households in 20 villages and 5 counties in the provinces of Henan, Hebei and Shandong, which constitute the largest part of the North China Plain (NCP), had been conducted in May 2005 (Piotrowski, 2009).

Main results of the module on the rural land rental markets are summarized in the following paragraphs. The study shows that in the total sample, only 9.5% of the households stated to have currently rented in at least one plot of land. This result is very much in line with other empirical studies that find that 5% to 10% of households participate in the nascent rental market for rural land use rights (Deininger and Jin, 2005; Lohmar *et al.*, 2001). There are numerous factors that influence land allocations. At the individual household level, with an increasing family size the amount of land allocated also increases, however with declining marginal rates. Also, with rising age the number of plots allocated to households seems to decline slightly. However, neither the amount of land nor the number of plots per household (fragmentation) showed a significant correlation with the land rental market. While there is much debate on the characteristics and motivations of renting-in households, there is consensus that off-farm income opportunities play a large role in activating the supply of land. There are marked differences in the intensity of land transactions between the three provinces in the sample and these conform in their order with findings of Schwarzwalder *et al.* (2002: 201) as shown in Table 2. Rental activity is highest in the prosperous coastal province of Shandong, which shows that overall economic development of a province is a good indicator for the intensity of land rental transactions. In fact, because of the close linkages between economic development and the land rental market, most studies on land rental activities concentrate on certain prosperous provinces, such as Zhejiang in South China (e.g. Wu, 2006; Zhang *et al.*, 2004).

A subsequent survey in one of the counties from this household survey confirmed also in an econometric model that there is a positive relation between land market activity in villages and the share of off-farm income in total income (Piotrowski, 2009). However, the relation appeared to be quadratic, implying that at very high shares of off-farm income, land rental market activity again decreases. This is plausible, since the survey also confirmed that rental arrangements are typically confined to members of the same community. In such a situation, a distinctly off-farm oriented village may have a high propensity to rent out land but at the same time a low demand for land within the community.

Apart from the legal restrictions outlined above, there are apparently a number of reasons for the low extent of trans-village rental arrangements. The most important ones are high transaction costs and possible social pressure on renting-out households. The latter may include dispossession of land in subsequent rounds of reallocations (Lohmar *et al.*, 2001).

Table 2. *Intensity of land renting in three provinces of the North China Plain.*

	% of households renting in		% of households renting out	
	Piotrowski (2009)	Schwarzwalder *et al.* (2002)	Piotrowski (2009)	Schwarzwalder *et al.* (2002)
Henan	5.9	12.0	0.7	8.4
Hebei	4.3	9.3	0.0	7.0
Shandong	15.8	21.4	6.8	18.6

5. Policy recommendations

To overcome in transformation countries the most complex and controversial issue, i.e., the reform of the land property rights system and the establishment of an efficient land and land rental market, social, institutional and economic constraints need to be addressed concomitantly. In rural China, the key to developing a more efficient land rental market would be to delink land use rights from off-farm employment and establish a social safety net for those employed off-farm. Concomitantly, agricultural productivity for small-scale farming would need to increase substantially to provide higher incentives for farming households to rent-in additional land. During the last two decades, China has moved cautiously in reforming rural policies, allowing experimentation, benefiting from learning by doing and subsequently legalizing successful local practice (Heberer and Schubert, 2006). This approach of piece wise experimentation with policy reforms and recognizing the value of well functioning local institutions has been reasonably successful and may well serve as an example for other countries. In China (and most likely in similar situations in other countries) the reform process can be supported by improving risk-reducing institutions, better market information systems and taking into account inter-linkages between land and labor markets.

References

Cai, Y. (2003). Collective ownership or cadres' ownership? The non-agricultural use of farmland in China. The China Quarterly 175: 662-680.

Chen, K. and Brown, C. (2001). Addressing shortcomings in the HRS: Empirical analysis of the Two-Farmland System in Shandong Province. China Economic Review 12: 280-292.

Chin, G.T. (2005). Securing a rural land market: Political economic determinants of institutional change in China's agriculture sector. Asian Perspective 29: 209-244.

Choate, A.C. (1997). Local governance in China: An assessment of villagers' committees. Working Paper Series, No. 1. The Asia Foundation.

Deininger, K. and Jin, S. (2005). The potential of land rental markets in the process of economic development: Evidence from China. Journal of Development Economics 78: 241-270.

Deininger, K., Jin, S. and Rozelle, S. (2006). Dynamics of legal change in a decentralized setting: Evidence from China's Rural Land Contracting Law. Paper presented at the Annual Meeting of the Allied Social Science Associations (ASSA), Boston, MA, USA.

Heberer, T. and Schubert, G. (2006). Political reform and regime legitimacy in contemporary China. Asien 99: 9-28.

Hertel, T. and Fan, Z. (2006). Labor market distortions, rural-urban inequality and the opening of China's economy. Economic Modelling 23: 76-109.

Ho, P. (2001). Who owns China's land? Policies, property rights, and deliberate institutional ambiguity. The China Quarterly, 166: 394-421.

Hsing, Y.-T. (2006). Brokering power and property in China's townships. The Pacific Review 19: 103-124.

Li, Y. and Xi, Y.-S. (2006). Married women's rights to land in China's traditional farming areas. Journal of Contemporary China 15: 621-636.

Li, G., Rozelle, S. and Huang, J. (2000). Land rights, farmer investment incentives and agricultural production in China. Working Paper, No. 00-024. University of California Davis, Davis, CA, USA.

Lohmar, B. (2006). Feeling for stones but not crossing the river: China's rural land tenure after twenty years of reform. The Chinese Economy 39: 85-102.

Lohmar, B., Zhang, Z. and Somwaru, A. (2001). Land rental market development and agricultural production in China. Paper presented at the Annual Meeting of the American Agricultural Economics Association, Chicago, IL, USA.

Nee, V. and Su, S. (1990). Institutional change and economic growth in China: The view from the villages. Journal of Asian Studies 49: 3-25.

Piotrowski, S. (2009): Land property rights and natural resource use: An analysis of household behavior in rural China. Development Economics and Policy Band 61, Peter Lang Verlag, Frankfurt am Main, Germany.

PRC (People's Republic of China) 2004. Constitution of the People's Republic of China. Foreign Languages Press, Beijing, China.

Rozelle, S., Brandt, L., Li, G. and Huang, J. (2005). Land tenure in China: Facts, fictions and issues. In: P. Ho (ed.), Developmental dilemmas: Land reform and institutional change in China. Routledge, London, UK.

Schwarzwalder, B., Prosterman, R., Ye, J., Riedinger, J. and Li, P. (2002). An update on China's rural land tenure reforms: Analysis and recommendations based on a seventeen-province survey. Columbia Journal of Asian Law 16: 142-225.

Vermeer, E.B. (2004). Egalitarianism and the land question in China - A survey of three thousand households in industrializing Wuxi and agricultural Baoding. China Information 28: 107-140.

Wu, Z. (2006). Land distributional and income effects of the Chinese land rental market. Paper presented at the International Association of Agricultural Economists Conference, Gold Coast, Australia.

Zhang, L., De Brauw, A. and Rozelle, S. (2004). China's rural labor market development and its gender implications. China Economic Review 15: 230- 247.

Zhang, B. and Carter, C.A. (1997). Reforms, the weather, and productivity growth in China's grain sector. American Journal of Agricultural Economics 79: 1266-1277.

Zhou, D. and Yang, X. (2004). Power sharing in rural China behind social transformation - traditional culture, town and village enterprises and social transformation. Chinese Sociology and Anthropology 36: 5-43.

Zhu, L. and Jiang, Z. (1993). From brigade to village community: The land tenure system and rural development in China. Cambridge Journal of Economics 17: 441-461.

Part 3.

Market access, value chains and institutions

Institutions and institutional arrangements

Understanding institutional arrangements for improved market access in Africa: how to explain seemingly irrational causes of success and failure

Guido Van Huylenbroeck, Marijke D'Haese, Divine Foundjem-Tita and Jacques Viaene

Institutions are needed to create incentives for people to invest, increase their knowledge and organize the markets they are involved in.

Abstract

Economists struggle with predicting what makes an institutional arrangement successful for market access in Africa. According to New Institutional Economics theory, the rational farmer will chose to engage in the institutional arrangement that is best performing in minimizing transaction costs, or that create order in the economy. Yet, failures have been reported of projects that typically had potential to reduce transaction costs such as contract farming, group farming, cooperatives and associations. In this essay we use two case studies (group markets for non timber forest products in Cameroon and sales of Nile perch from Lake Victoria in Kenya) to illustrate that in order to be successful, new institutional arrangements should address the particular challenges of the people concerned and the vicious poverty circles that many of them are caught in.

Keywords: market access, institutions, farmer decision making, transaction costs, group marketing, non timber forest products, Nile perch, case studies, Cameroon, Kenya, Africa

1. Introduction

Aad van Tilburg has focused a large part of his research career on studying how to improve the livelihoods of farmers in developing regions. His work has mainly focused on market institutions and how changes in market integration and market efficiency can improve the lives of farmers in the South. This is quite a challenging task in which Aad has made important contributions (Kambewa *et al.*, 2008; Kuiper *et al.*, 2003; Lutz *et al.*, 2007; Ruben *et al.*, 2007; Van Tilburg *et al.*, 2008). Aad was one of the first to understand that poverty alleviation is not a pure production problem but mainly a problem of functioning of markets and behavioral forces that influence success and failure of these markets. As we agree with this vision, we contribute to this book in honor of Aad with an essay that illustrates the importance of taking into account the specific conditions and challenges faced by African farmers when trying to explain the success or failure of market arrangements in Africa. This essay aims at confirming and illustrating the proposition that institutions are needed to create incentives for people to invest, increase their knowledge and organize the markets they are involved in.

In the next section we first argue how important market institutions are for poverty alleviation by referring to the New Institutional Economic theory. Next we give two examples to show the importance of external factors in understanding the attitude and behavior of African farmers towards such market institutions. One example is derived from our own research on a case of group marketing for non-timber forest products in Cameroon while the second is based on the work of Aad van Tilburg himself on Nile perch marketing channels in Kenya (Kambewa *et al.*, 2007). Section four ends with concluding remarks.

2. The importance of market institutions

Agricultural economists already struggle for decades to understand why apparently in other parts of the world successful recipes for poverty alleviation through agricultural growth do not or insufficiently work in Africa (World Bank, 2007). Government or NGO interventions for rural poverty alleviation that were mainly seeking to improve technology adoption and production improvements have not resulted in the expected outcome to increase income in Africa. Differently from Asia, the green revolution in Africa has not been able to upscale agricultural activities (World Bank, 2007).

Since the work of Schultz (1964) it is commonly accepted that smallholder farmers in Africa are poor but produce in an efficient way. Or in other words, the input-output relationship is similar in smallholder production systems as it is for larger producers. The major challenge is then to move the farmers' production systems to a higher input- output level. Arguably, better market integration for both inputs and outputs could break the vicious circle that keeps many poor farmers in their smallholder situation. Better physical and economic access to higher value markets for their produce, would increase the farmers' household income, yielding possibilities to improve technology, increase input use or change input mix. This could lead them to reach higher indifference curves, hence production curves and optimal production levels. On the medium term, one could envisage entrepreneurial famers to change type of production, to expand or to diversify activities outside agriculture. Yet, apart from a selected number of case studies, general statistics from sub-Sahara Africa show a rather disappointing success rate with exceptions in southern African countries (World Bank, 2007). Agriculture remains a livelihood system, but not a profitable business.

The reasons for these failures are multiple and complex. Yet, one particular explanation is the fact that we seem unable to fully understand or at least to explain theoretically the decision-making behavior of smallholder farmers under the Africa context. A potential explanation that we can derive from New Institutional Economics theory is the absence of governance, which would be the means by which order in the economy is created and transactions costs are lowered (Williamson, 2005). Such market arrangements should increase market access by lowering a number of entry barriers for smallholders and by creating opportunities for the rational small farmer to engage in better income-generating activities and as such to escape from poverty. But apparently this is not enough as literature also reports important challenges of potentially successful arrangements such as contract farming, group farming, cooperatives and associations when applied in Africa (Francesconi, 2007; World Bank, 2007 to cite a few). Sometimes it may seem that farmers in Africa are not interested to 'gain money' and simply refuse to engage in theoretically cost-efficient market arrangements. We argue that the often neglected challenge for these new institutional arrangements is that they need, certainly in an initial stage, to increase market access but without jeopardizing the other important goal of smallholder farming systems being food security and secondly that not only the decrease of global transaction costs is important but also the influence of the new arrangement on the division of transaction costs among transacting partners. This means that when developing such arrangements it is especially important to take into account the particular context in which farmers operate as well as the global consequences caused by new market arrangements. We try to illustrate this hypothesis in the next sections of this essay based on the two case studies mentioned.

3. Case studies

The economic behavior of farmers in Africa cannot be solely explained as that of income/profit/production maximizing agents. Decisions which may seem to be irrational can only be explained by taking into account the production and marketing environment farmers have to face in Africa. The production maximizing laws of neoclassical economics are defied by constraints in market access; market price signals and ways to reduce transaction costs are blurred by market failures, lack of infrastructure, market information, unkind natural environment, and a non supportive institutional environment. Reasonable choices may arguably be a reaction to constraints, problems or disasters famers have experienced in the past or by cultural heritage. The following paragraphs illustrate our arguments by discussing two case studies, namely an own study on group marketing for non-timber forest products in Cameroon and the Nile perch marketing channels in Kenya studied by Kambewa *et al.* (2007).

Case study 1: group marketing of non timber forest products in Cameroon

With financial support of NGOs, farmers/collectors and traders of kolanuts (*Cola anomala*) and njansang (*Ricinodendron heudelotii*) are proposed to join in associations in the forest zones of North-West and Centre regions of Cameroon. Through the associations, farmers and traders are brought together at a market place for group sales. For farmers the association and group sales are advantageous in increasing bargaining power, reducing marketing and transaction costs. Particularly transport and communication costs can be lowered for these products from remote areas. For traders, group marketing has advantages in generating enough liquidity to pay for the products to be bought and in reducing assembly and transportation cost. Individual traders seem to be unable to generate sufficient money to pay the farmers in cash when they bulk their harvest for group sales. Yet, as also shown in other case studies, the associations are only successful when they can consolidate efforts of their members and prove to be profitable. As shown by our results (Tita, 2009), the costs of organizing or/and institutionalizing the association should be sufficiently low. Although it may seem economic rational to join efforts in group or cooperative marketing, for farmers who have an arrangement with a local shopkeeper that they will repay for consumer goods by a share of their harvest, this is not as obvious. Also Kambewa *et al.* (2007) (see next paragraph) refer to the problem of interlocked arrangements for explaining the failure of seemingly rational market arrangements.

A second observation is that the nature of the product plays a role. In Cameroon, group sales are successful for njansang, but not for kolanuts. Group marketing of kolanuts was successful only twice, in nine attempts. The reason for failure was that the group of producers and traders were unable to conclude on a price that was acceptable for both parties. Farmers refused the price offered by the trader group after which both groups lost trust in each other. It is worth noting that kolanuts are more prone to quality losses due to weevil attacks that may not be visible at the time of trade. Traders try to assess kolanuts after visual inspection of samples and used the fear of future weevils attack to offer low prices that the farmers considered not just per their own judgment of the quality of their produce and efforts made to meet traders quality criteria. Yet this is a subject of hard negotiations in the absence of objective quality measuring standards. When trying out the collective marketing channel, farmers who brought the kolanuts to the marketing place over a long distance preferred to leave the fruits to rotten instead of selling these for a low price. Although taking the fruits back home was considered too expensive and the probability of finding other buyers was low, farmers seemed to fear that agreeing with a too low price would put them into a low bargaining position for subsequent sales. Their decision to walk away from the market with empty hands was perhaps not economically rational, but a result of a lack of rules on quality standards and on who should pay the costs of loss of quality during the transport, which in the traditional marketing channel is clearly faced by the trader as he buys at the farmers' place. This shows that in understanding market behavior it is important to look for the global picture and that indeed the fact that a new market arrangement may lead to a new division of transaction costs is an important element.

Case study 2: Nile perch (Lates niloticus) marketing channels at Lake Victoria in Kenya

In their case study on Nile perch (*Lates niloticus*) marketing channels at Lake Victoria in Kenya, Kambewa *et al.* (2007) give an example of a similar incidence of a disbanded trade arrangement between a beach management unit (comprising fishermen and traditional leaders) and middlemen over a price dispute. In this case, fish was ultimately sold hours later at a much lower price than was offered by the new arrangement. The fishermen are price takers because they are locked in informal contracts with the middlemen. In return for the provision of credit, fishing gear and equipment by the middlemen, fishermen promise exclusive sales to them. The conditions of these 'contracts' are particular unclear in terms of information sharing (especially price information) and repayment conditions. In absence of any other source for financing the purchase of boats, engines, nets and other fishing gear, and in absence of other employment or income opportunities, fishermen agree to these seemingly unfavorable conditions. The consequence of the interlocked credit fish market is that fishermen are not motivated to use good fishing gears, apply proper fishing practices (e.g., no catch of undersize fish) or to invest in adequate fish handling because they do not know whether they will be rewarded for doing so. To address the destructive fishing practices that are currently taking place in the lake, arrangements should be searched that deal with the interlocking market problem in this case input credit needs and output markets. This shows again that when developing new market institutions the global picture should be taken into account.

4. Concluding remarks

The above illustrations and recommendations bring us back to the proposition made that institutions are needed that create incentives for people to invest, increase their knowledge and organize the markets they are involved in. This is indeed true but the challenging task for the development of such institutions is that they must not only be based on economic rationality of output markets but that they also need to deal with other rationalities of producers or market players. Our examples clearly show the importance of taking into account the dependency of small producers of credit facilities given by local shops or traders. If new developed market institutions do not deal with this, they will not be accepted by local producers. The other problem illustrated is the one of the division of transaction costs. As illustrated by the Cameroon case it may well be that new arrangements decrease overall transaction costs but if this results in an unequal division of these transaction costs such arrangements will not be accepted by the trading parties with trade withdrawal as a result.

It remains a challenging task for policy makers and development economists to respectively create and study the institutional environment within which pro-poor institutional arrangements can be crafted benefiting to smallholder producers. It is hereby important as already stated by Nobel Prize winners Williamson (2000) and Ostrom (2005) that the institutions are embedded within the traditions, customs, values and religion of a particular community or country. It is furthermore important that the institutional arrangements address the particular challenges of the people concerned and the vicious poverty circles that many of them are caught in. It remains therefore an important topic for development economic research to understand decision making of small farmers and farmers' communities in complex production and market environments such as in Africa. The work of Aad van Tilburg in Kenya, Benin, South Africa and many other places provides us with examples which are certainly a source of knowledge, experience and inspiration for researchers in agricultural marketing to come up with proposals for reasonable institutional innovations that *create incentives for people to invest, increase their knowledge and organize the markets they are involved in.*

References

Francesconi, G.N. (2007). Promoting milk quality in smallholders' cooperatives: evidence from Ethiopia. In: R. Ruben, T. Van Boekel, A. van Tilburg and J. Trienekens (eds.), Tropical food chains, Governance regimes for quality management. Wageningen Academic Publishers, Wageningen, the Netherlands, pp. 159-166.

Kambewa, E., Ingenbleek, P. and Van Tilburg, A. (2008) Improving income positions of primary producers in international marketing channels: The Lake Victoria EU Nile perch case. Journal of Macromarketing 28: 53-67.

Kambewa, E., Van Tilburg, A. and Abila, R. (2007). The plight of small-scale primary producers in international Nile perch marketing channels. In: R. Ruben, T. Van Boekel, A. van Tilburg and J. Trienekens (eds.), Tropical food chains, Governance regimes for quality management. Wageningen Academic Publishers, Wageningen, the Netherlands, pp. 111-132.

Kuiper, W.E., Lutz, C. and Van Tilburg A. (2003). Vertical price leadership on local maize markets in Benin. Journal of Development Economics 71: 417-433.

Lutz, C., Kuiper, W.E. and Van Tilburg A. (2007). Maize market liberalisation in Benin: A case of hysteresis. Journal of African Economies 16: 102-133.

Ostrom, E. (2005). Doing Institutional Analysis. Digging Deeper than Markets and Hierarchies. In: Ménard, C. and Shirley, M.M. (eds.), Handbook of New Institutional Economics. Springer, Dordrecht, the Netherlands, pp. 819-848.

Ruben, R., Van Boekel, T., Van Tilburg, A. and Trienekens, J. (eds.) (2007). Tropical food chains. Governance regimes for quality management. Wageningen Academic Publishers, Wageningen, the Netherlands.

Schultz, T.W. (1964). Transforming traditional agriculture. Yale university press, New Haven, CT, US.

Tita, D.F. (2009). A transaction cost analysis of factors affecting market arrangements: in the agroforestry tree product value chain in Cameroon. Master Dissertation. Master of science in rural development, Ghent University, Belgium.

Van Tilburg, A., Kuiper, W.E. and Swinkels, R. (2008). Market performance of potato auctions in Bhutan. Journal of International Food and Agribusiness Marketing 20: 61-87.

Williamson, O.E. (2000). The new institutional economics: Taking stock, looking ahead. Journal of Economic Literature 38: 595-613.

Williamson, O.E. (2005). Transaction Cost Economics. In: C. Ménard and M.M. Shirley (eds.), Handbook of New Institutional Economics. Springer, Dordrecht, the Netherlands, pp. 41-65.

World Bank (2007). World Development Report 2008. Agriculture for Development. The World Bank, Oxford University Press, Washington DC, USA.

Value chain participant councils: a tool for improved market coordination and broad-based growth

John Staatz and Donald Ricks[12]

In the rapidly changing and uncertain environment facing participants in agricultural markets in both developing and industrial economies, purely individualistic competition among the various participants in agricultural value chains often leads to poor vertical coordination and ineffective market performance. Moreover, these coordination failures frequently result in growth patterns that tend to exclude or limit the participation of smaller farmers, marketers, and processors. In such situations, collective analyses, problem-solving, and planning for needed improvements by key participants in agricultural value chains, organized into value chain participant councils, can play a critical role in improving effective vertical coordination, thereby improving the capacity of agricultural markets to contribute to sustainable, broad-based economic development.

Abstract

Value chain participant councils are an important form of voluntary collective action by representatives of key participants in a vertical marketing chain. The goals of these councils are to improve economic coordination and promote effective and inclusive economic growth. They typically include representatives from farmer and trader organizations, processors, shippers, exporters, retailers, government agencies, and research and outreach organizations. The councils frequently provide key collective goods and services, such as analysis and diagnosis of system-wide problems that affect all participants in the value chain, and the development of workable plans to overcome these problems. The need for such participant council organizations to improve vertical coordination is becoming increasingly important, in both developing and industrialized countries, given the rapid changes transforming agricultural markets worldwide. This essay briefly describes what value chain participant councils are and what they do, and illustrates these points with examples both from Sub-Saharan Africa and from the United States. It then addresses four key design issues for these organizations: the need for an organizational entity that functions as an objective and well-accepted facilitator-coordinator and provider of empirical information; membership structure; financing; and continuity.

Keywords: vertical coordination, strategic planning, value chains, participant councils, marketing, Africa, North America

---

[12] The authors gratefully acknowledge insights into the issues discussed in this paper derived from discussions with our colleague Steve Haggblade.

1. Introduction

The pace of change in agricultural markets in both developing and industrialized countries is rapidly accelerating. Demands for product quality, including food safety, are becoming more stringent, requiring tighter vertical coordination of value chains; new competitors and pathogens arise as markets integrate globally; and new technologies in production and processing offer exciting opportunities to increase value-added. The growing concentration of processing and retailing worldwide, with the rise of large chains like Wal-Mart, has resulted in the spread of private grades and standards and the demands for large volumes of consistent production, which threaten to exclude small farmers from the rapidly growing agricultural markets of the 21st century (Weatherspoon and Reardon 2003). At the same time, with the spread of market reforms since the 1980s, many of the parastatals and other state-run marketing agencies that historically attempted to coordinate economic activity within specific value chains in developing countries have either been disbanded or are proving increasingly unsustainable (Rashid *et al.*, 2008).

This essay argues that *value chain participant councils*, which can also be described as subsector or industry councils, can play an important role in helping assure improved and more inclusive value chain coordination and development in this dynamic new environment. These councils offer an alternative way of enhancing performance rather than relying on either (a) top-down state-dominated organization of an industry or value chain or (b) purely private coordination through single-firm ownership of an entire vertical chain. The paper briefly describes what these councils are and what they do, and illustrates these points with examples both from Sub-Saharan Africa and from the United States. It then addresses four key design issues for these organizations: the need for an organizational entity that functions as an objective and well-accepted facilitator-coordinator and provider of empirical information; membership structure; financing; and continuity.

2. Value chain participant councils: what are they and what do they do?

Value chain participant councils (VCPCs) are voluntary organizations, typically organized along value chain lines, that engage in joint analyses and problem-solving planning by a broad spectrum of key participants in a specific value chain. Participants typically include representatives from individual firms, farmer and trader organizations, processors, shippers, exporters, retailers, other marketing firms, government agencies, input dealers, and research and outreach organizations, including agriculturally oriented universities. Such councils typically are created in response to either a set of perceived threats (e.g., increased competition from imports) or opportunities (e.g., a new technology that greatly expands production, raising the need to find profitable new market outlets) that individual participants in the value chain cannot address adequately by themselves. Thus, these participant councils arise because of perceived needs to take performance-enhancing actions that will benefit a broad array of stakeholders in the value chain, but which no individual participant can effectively or profitably undertake by itself. In other words, the basic motivation for such councils is the identification and creation of critical 'public goods,' which are essential for successful agricultural development (World Bank, 2007).

The organizing entity for such councils can be either a public or private entity. In some cases, the organizer is a 'channel captain': a participant that has a broad vision of the issues facing the value chain and is motivated to find a solution (Harrison *et al.*, 1987). The motivations can arise because an improved solution will benefit the participant individually (as well as other stakeholder participants) – as in the case of a large wholesaler – or because helping provide such solutions is part of the participant's mandate, as in the case of an agricultural research-outreach institute. Such councils are most often formed in response to a specific challenge or opportunity – e.g., the need to develop grades and standards that respond to end-users' demands in a new market – and hence in those cases may be termed 'task forces.' Our experience is that stakeholders often soon realize, however, that the challenges facing most value chains are continually changing, so that as one task is completed, several others are identified for attention. Hence, there are frequently incentives to transform these more temporary and narrowly focused task forces into ongoing councils, with subcommittees handling specific, time-limited issues as sub-task forces.

VCPCs, at their best, operate instruments for on-going value-chain or industry strategic planning and performance-enhancing action programs (Lyford *et al.*, 2002). Such strategic planning involves priority problem identification and analysis by the stakeholders, along with development of proposals for programs to improve value chain performance. In some cases, the councils can work with their members to implement the programs directly; in other cases, the proposals require government sanction and/or action, and the councils work via the political system to obtain that authorization and/or cooperation. In carrying out their problem identification, analysis, and design of proposals, the VCPCs address a number of fundamental problems inherent in developing effective solutions to improve vertical coordination within value chains that involve multiple and diverse participants. One of these fundamental problems is that the information needed to design a workable solution is dispersed among various participants within the value chain. Another fundamental problem is that the interests among the participants frequently conflict. The VCPC provides a structure for consultation and collaboration, pulling together the dispersed information held by various participants to come up with a consensual view of the nature of the challenges facing the value chain. In the process, participants learn more comprehensively about the perspectives and experiences of others in the chain, which can (but does not always!) lead to greater appreciation of the points of view of their 'rivals' in the system, thereby fostering greater cooperation. By working together, the VCPC can emphasize its members' common interests and the joint needs for improved chain performance. Then with the council's collective knowledge base of key aspects of the vertical chain, it can together, if astutely coordinated, develop workable sets of performance-improving program actions.

A few examples illustrate the range of activities such councils can undertake:
- In Zambia in 2005, the Agricultural Consultative Forum (ACF), an association that promotes information exchange among farm groups, agribusiness, and government, began a series of discussions on the potential for greatly expanded cassava production in central and southern Zambia, based on the spread of improved varieties that had earlier been introduced into the north of the country. The potential for rapidly expanding cassava production offered new income opportunities for farmers, processors, and agribusinesses if profitable new market outlets for the product could be developed. The ACF discussions led fairly rapidly to the creation of the Acceleration of Cassava Utilisation (ACU) Task Force. Between 2005 and 2009, the task force sponsored feeding trials to assess the suitability of substituting cassava chips for maize in livestock feed in Zambia, examined the market opportunities for exporting cassava chips to the Democratic Republic of the Congo (Zambia's neighbor to the north), evaluated consumer acceptability of composite flours that mix cassava flour with maize flour for the production of various products, such as bread and fritters (a popular fast-food snack in Zambia), and the development of proposed new grades and standards for cassava. The latter were subsequently endorsed and implemented by the Zambian Bureau of Standards throughout the country (Chitundu *et al.*, 2009). The ACU Task Force still exists in 2010, illustrating our point about 'task forces' frequently evolving into de facto ongoing value chain participant councils.

- Throughout Francophone West Africa, the cotton value chain has been undergoing radical restructuring since the early 2000s. Historically, this value chain was organized in each country through single-firm vertical integration (*filière*) run by national monopolies that were joint ventures between individual country governments and the French state-owned multi-national firm Dagris. The integrated system coordinated cotton research throughout francophone West Africa, provided farmers with inputs and credit, and marketed all their output. However, performance of the system, in terms of overall profitability and prices received by farmers, declined markedly beginning the late 1990s due to falling world prices, poor management (a frequent problem with monopolies, especially those subject to strong political influence), and the strong value of the local currency (the CFA franc, whose value is tied to the euro). In an attempt to regain competitiveness, the systems have begun to liberalize various market system functions, such as ginning. Yet as the competitiveness of individual components has increased, overall vertical coordination has declined. To help fill this vertical coordination inadequacy, stakeholders are fostering the creation of *interprofessions,* which are value-chain organizations involving representatives of growers, ginners, and cotton processors. The *interprofessions* aim to carry out the types of value chain strategic planning and coordination functions previously assured by the old integrated structures while still letting farmers benefit from the new, more competitive value-chain structure (Tschirley *et al.*, 2009). Thus, these *interprofessions* function as a type of value chain participant council.
- In the US, two illustrative examples of the VCPC approach have been the US Tart Cherry Industry Strategy Planning Council and the Michigan Apple Industry Strategic Planning Council. These councils have included representatives from growers, grower associations, processors, shippers, marketing cooperatives, processor and shipper associations, general farm organizations, university extension and research, and representatives from state and federal government agencies. Representatives from additional participant segments such as key input suppliers and other specific government agencies have also been temporarily involved when certain issues of special relevance are considered. Examples of issues these councils have addressed include grades and standards, market research on customer preferences and needs, pricing arrangements, technology research and adoption, industry-wide demand expansion programs for domestic and export markets, new product and new market development, research and subsequent information campaigns on health benefits of consuming these products, coordinating and balancing subsector supplies and demand, research and information on market cycles and fluctuations, development and use of superior varieties, modernization of facilities and orchards, and identification of needed government statistics and information for effective value-chain planning. These councils also work closely with various government agencies on needed government policy actions and coordination so that various relevant government policies and programs are based on, and are consistent with, the realities and complexities of the value chain.(Ricks *et al.*, 1999).

3. Key design issues

Numerous issues arise in the design, coordination, and functioning of effective VCPCs. Here we briefly mention four of these important issues.

Identifying an organizing entity

Because the interests among stakeholders in the value chain often conflict (as stakeholders are frequently competitors or in adversarial buyer-seller relations), it is critical that someone or a core group in the council (frequently the convener-coordinator) be perceived and accepted by the participants as an objective, impartial, and contributory organizing entity. The role of the organizing entity includes helping to frame the debates and, ideally, helping to provide unbiased information to illuminate the discussions, problems, and performance-enhancing alternatives. In Zambia, ACF played this role; in Mali, it has been the national agricultural research institute. In the US and in several other countries, staff members of agricultural universities, extension services, and public research institutes have played this role. If an effective organizing entity cannot be found or developed, experience shows that it will be very difficult for a VCPC approach to be successful.

Membership structure

The membership of the councils needs to include individuals who are acknowledged industry leaders, 'broad thinkers,' and those who are open to exploring possibilities for working with other value-chain participants for needed improvements. To the extent possible, it is important that these people also be leaders of stakeholder organizations within the value chain, such as farmer or processor associations. Including such participant organization leaders in the VCPCs allows these key individuals to link back to their memberships effectively, leading to broader discussion, input, and information into the issues the council is addressing and broadening the ownership and implementation of its proposed solutions.

Financing

A critical issue is whether the council should seek dedicated funding for its activities. While obtaining external 'core' funding for the activities of the council may allow it to act more quickly on key decisions (such as to undertake consumer testing of a new product), one possible disadvantage is that such funding may attract participants to the council who are mainly interested in gaining access to the funding for their personal benefit. In order to avoid this sort of rent seeking, it may be preferable (as was done with the ACU in Zambia and in the two above-mentioned US councils) to rely on in-kind contributions of time and resources by the council members for the council's main ongoing activities, complemented with applications for small grant funding for specific information-gathering or outreach activities (Chitundu *et al.*, 2009).

Continuity

Ultimately, how well a VCPC or task force performs and how long it continues will depend on its utility to stakeholders. Having a time-limited horizon for specific activities helps focus attention and avoid 'empire-building' by the council leaders. Because most value chains today are changing so rapidly in so many ways, however, we have observed that many VCPCs are often likely to continue well beyond the specific problems that led to their creation. The need for the type of broad-based value-chain information gathering, strategic planning and design of proposals for improved market performance that such councils can provide is ongoing and increasingly important in today's dynamic value chains. Hence this model, if successfully implemented, is likely to have a long life.

4. Conclusions

Given the dynamic and uncertain environment in which they operate and the increasing consumer and processor demands for consistent quality and other important performance aspects, agricultural value chains in both developing and industrialized economies face recurring problems related to inadequate vertical coordination. These coordination challenges are manifested in a number of ways including, for example, production of goods that do not adequately meet end-users needs (leading to low prices for producers) or missed opportunities for the development of profitable new markets. Value chain participant councils, a form of voluntary collective action, when carefully designed and implemented, have demonstrated their value as tools to improve such coordination and to promote more effective and inclusive economic growth. Successful councils can provide some of the important missing 'public goods' that are crucial to successful market development.

Yet numerous challenges can hamper the development of successful VCPCs. First, the potential participants need to perceive enough of a common opportunity or threat to overcome the centrifugal forces of rivalry and distrust that often keep them from cooperating effectively with one another. Identifying an appropriate convening and coordinating entity for the council, who is viewed as impartial and objective, is key to creating such a common vision and environment of trust among the participants with their varying perspectives. The convener-coordinator entity can help to frame the issues, foster an appropriate shared vision of challenges facing the participants, and provide empirical analysis to feed the council's discussions and development of solution alternatives. Fruitful discussions, problem analyses, and appropriate remedial actions will be enhanced if the participants have been carefully chosen to include those who have the knowledge and respect of the industry and the inclination to work collaboratively with others in the value chain for their joint benefits. In addition, developing a funding strategy that avoids incentives for rent-seeking but allows the council to undertake actions in a timely way is frequently an important aspect. If a VCPC is successful in achieving concrete results with respect to the initial challenges that prompted its creation, it has the potential to become an ongoing instrument that will continue to foster better vertical coordination and inclusive growth as the value chain faces the on-going changes that shape the evolution of the vertical system.

References

Chitundu, M., Droppelmann, K. and Haggblade, S. (2009). Intervening in Value Chains: Lessons from Zambia's Task Force on Acceleration of Cassava Utilisation. Journal of Development Studies 45: 593-620.

Harrison, K., Henley, D., Riley, H. and Shaffer, J. (1987). Improving Food Marketing Systems in Developing Countries: Experiences from Latin America. MSU International Development Working Papers Reprint no. 9. East Lansing, Michigan: Michigan State University Department of Agricultural Economics. Available at: http://aec.msu.edu/fs2/papers/older/idprp9.pdf. Accessed December 2009.

Lyford, C.P., Ricks, D.J., Peterson, H.C. and Sterns, J.A. (2002). A Framework for Effective Industry Strategic Planning. Journal of Agribusiness 20: 131-146.

Rashid, S., Gulati, A., and Cummings, J. (eds.) (2008). From Parastatals to Private Trade: Lessons from Asian Agriculture. Johns Hopkins University Press for the International Food Policy Institute, Baltimore, MA, USA.

Ricks, D., Woods, T. and Sterns, J. (1999). Supply Chain Management: Improving Vertical Coordination in Fruit Industries. Journal of Food Distribution Research XXX(3): 44-53.

Tschirley, D., Poulton, C. and Labaste, P. (eds.) (2009). Organization and Performance of Cotton Sectors in Africa: Learning from Reform Experience. World Bank, Washington DC, USA.

Weatherspoon, D. D. and Reardon, T. (2003). The Rise of Supermarkets in Africa: Implications for Agrifood Systems and the Rural Poor. Development Policy Review 21: 333-355.

World Bank (2007). World Development Report 2008: Agriculture for Development. World Bank, Washington DC, USA.

Certification and standards

The future of Fair Trade

Ruerd Ruben

While Fair Trade is helpful to assist smallholders' initial access to international markets, for maintaining long-term competitiveness private labels offer better prospects to enhance quality upgrading.

Abstract

After its start 25 years ago, the market for Fair Trade products has been rapidly expanding. In many developing countries, groups of smallholder producers received substantial support for their certification and a wide range of Fair Trade products reached the shelves of Western supermarkets. Southern producers benefitted from increased market access, stable prices, pre-financing arrangements and the distribution of a Fair Trade premium. Further growth of the Fair Trade market is currently challenged by several new marketing arrangements involving large agro-industrial firms that look for business-to-business (B2B) labelling (e.g. Utz Certified, Rainforest Alliance, CAFE Practices) and also engage into sector-wide agreements (e.g. Common Codes, Round Tables). This gradual shift from 'Fair Trade' to 'Responsible Trade' also marks a change from output-price support to the promotion of good agricultural practices (GAP) under market-conform pricing. This article reviews current adjustments in the coffee market, discusses the implication of the proliferation of private labels and outlines some major challenges for Southern producers. It is argued that the future of Fair Trade depends on its capacities to enhance scale and to reinforce quality upgrading.

Keywords: Fair Trade, responsible trade, smallholders, production standards, private labels, price, welfare, quality, upgrading, coffee, Uganda, Tanzania

1. Introduction

During the last few decades, numerous efforts have been made to introduce social justice and sustainability dimensions into international trade networks. After initial steps for labelling Fair Trade products taken under the initiative of civil society agencies, private companies are increasingly responding with efforts to include social, environmental and labour rights concerns into corporate business operations. Even while some critical voices fear that such corporate social responsibility (CSR) becomes merely 'window dressing' or 'green washing' of the company's image (Doane, 2005; Utting, 2005), with the acceptance and consistent enforcement of standards these CSR criteria became more effectively embedded within core activities and entrepreneurial values.

Coffee is one of the first commodities where collective efforts were made to develop process standards that address socioeconomic and sustainability concerns. The collapse of the International Coffee Agreement (ICA) in 1989 broadly coincided with reshaping of the power balance within the coffee sector due to the rapid transformation towards an increasingly buyer-driver supply chain (Kolk, 2005). Whereas 70% of coffee production is managed by smallholders and approximately 125 million people in developing countries are dependent on coffee, only five large toasters (Kraft, Nestle, Proctor & Gamble, Sara Lee and Tchibo) control more than half of the world market. While the value and prices of coffee in consuming countries increased, the income of coffee-producing farmers in the South strongly declined.

Increasing public awareness of this situation paved the way for fundamentally challenging the existing coffee market configuration. In several countries, alternative trade organizations started in the late 1980s to develop support systems and certification regimes to enhance direct smallholder access to the market, reducing the dependency on intermediaries and guaranteeing a minimum selling price that covers production costs and guarantees a decent livelihood. In addition, a premium is paid for investment in community activities. Fair Trade (FT) certified coffee has rapidly grown to volumes around 35,000 MT (metric tonnes) and represents roughly a quarter of all FT sales. However, Fair Trade coffee sales have levelled off in most countries to no more than 2-3% of the domestic market (Raynolds et al., 2007).

International coffee companies always maintained careful distance from Fair Trade, arguing that the guaranteed minimum price regime reduced the incentives for improving coffee production and should be interpreted as a market distortion. Recently, however, they show more openness towards certification regimes that support sustainable coffee production through the promotion of 'Good Agricultural Practices' (GAP) under social and environmental criteria. New standards, like Utz Certified and Rainforest Alliance, offer opportunities to both smallholder groups and plantations for mainstreaming coffee supplies that are delivered under market-conform conditions, but receive higher prices due to improved input efficiency and better quality performance. This marks a fundamental change from global output price support towards targeted input management. Similarly, market access is less perceives as the main problem, and attention is gradually shifting towards value chain upgrading.

While earlier experiences with standards appeared to act as significant barriers to trade in agricultural and food products, these private standards might have similar effects. Swinnen and Maertens (2007) provide consistent evidence that tight public and more demanding private standards can also be considered as effective incentives for improving smallholder efficiency and equity in value chain. Moreover, the trend towards collective private standards and the harmonisation and mutual recognition of standards across global markets suggests that these in fact facilitate trade. Indeed, there is evidence that the tendency and speed towards harmonisation of private food safety and quality standards far exceeds similar efforts in public spheres (Henson, 2006).

While the current proliferation of standards may easily lead to new dimensions of market segmentation, it can also be considered as a normal expression of the existing diversity and heterogeneity in production conditions. Different standards might be required to address specific binding constraints in the supply chain, and dynamic improvements of performance might be better supported through progressive regimes that enable farmers gradual upgrading of their production management practices (Van Beuningen and Knorringa, 2009). Moreover, given the increasing importance of speciality coffee markets, price conditions are intrinsically related to quality performance. Quality premiums are therefore considered a better incentive than stable guaranteed prices, since they stimulate continuous upgrading of supply chains and permit adjustments in production systems in line with market demands (Hobbs et al., 2002).

Empirical comparisons regarding the impact of trade standards on farmer's welfare could shed light on the feasibility of coexistence of different labelling regimes and the perceived benefits for smallholder producers. Muradian and Pelupessy (2005) argue that some voluntary certification schemes embrace weaker selection criteria and thus provide opportunities for large company's to 'green wash' their image (Renard, 2005). Other studies are rather doubtful about the possibilities of smallholders to comply with more stringent quality-based certification regimes (Lazaro *et al.*, 2008). Few empirical field studies are available to assess the micro-economic effects of private labels on production and farm-household welfare. We draw in this article on a recently conducted first comparative survey amongst Fair Trade and Utz Certified coffee producers in Uganda and Tanzania to explore major implications at farm-household and community level.

The remainder of this contribution is structured as follows. We start by discussing the proliferation of private standards and outline major differences between productions standards and company standards in coffee trade. Hereafter, empirical evidence regarding the welfare effects of Fair Trade and Utz Certified (Responsible Trade) is reviewed, focussing on the direct effects for production volumes and yields, as well as the indirect implications for quality upgrading and loyalty. Finally, we conclude with a discussion on future prospects of different production standards and options for further supporting smallholder involvement. Main attention is given to different roles of standards for both broadening market access and deepening market participation, and the requirements for tailoring private standards into a dynamic regime towards smallholder development.

2. Proliferation of standards

Globalization of international commodity trade is increasingly accompanied by standards and private procurement arrangements that aim to guarantee food safety, product quality and reliability of sourcing. Based on the establishment of long-term partnerships along the supply chain, these standards includes codes of behaviour for information sharing, service provision and trust building to support agency coordination and to reduce transaction costs (Reardon *et al.*, 2001).

During the last few decades, three major types of private standards have emerged in the coffee sector (see Table 1 for an overview of main characteristics):
1. *Production standards* to support practices of Fair Trade (FLO), organic production (IFOAM), responsible trade (UTZ Certified) and sustainable trade (Rainforest Alliance).
2. *Company standards*, like C.A.F.E. Practicas by Starbucks and Nespresso AAA by Nestle, that aim to guarantee sustainable sourcing under private label.
3. *Verification standards* like the Common Code for the Coffee Community (4C) agreed upon by national coffee associations, trade unions and NGOs, and key industry players to guarantee minimum sector-wide sustainability standards.

Production and company standards are based on detailed prescription of preferred production, processing and handling practices and involve independent verification. Some standards also include tracking and tracing regimes. To some extent, private standards have become the predominant basis for product differentiation in markets increasingly driven by quality-based competition. Standards take the form of technical specifications, terms for crop management and definitions and principles through which goods are categorized or included in product groupings. Thus, in the context of agricultural and food products

Table 1. *Comparison of major coffee standards (based on TCC, 2009).*

	Start	Volume (MT)	Characteristics
Production standards			
Fair Trade	1989	78,500	Minimum price + FLO premium + Pre-finance. Equitable trading arrangements for smallholders organized in democratic organizations (cooperatives).
Utz certified	1997	77,500	Market price + negotiable premium. Global decency standard for responsible coffee growing and sourcing; Protocol for Good Agricultural Practices (Global-GAP) and Worker welfare (ILO);Tracking & Tracing.
Rainforest Alliance	1993	62,000	Market price. Integrate productive agriculture: biodiversity conservation & maintenance of shade cover, protection and restoration of native forest reserves and human development.
Company standards			
C.A.F.E. practices	2004	120,500	Market price + contract terms. Scorecard for sustainably grown and processed coffee to assess economic, social and environmental aspects.
Nespresso AAA	2006	13,000	Market price + quality premium. Assessment of sustainable quality (for grand cru and gourmet coffee).
Verification standards			
4C	2007	27,000	Market price; Code of Conduct with baseline requirements for sustainable production, processing and trading of coffee. Elimination of unacceptable practices and guidance for dynamic improvement process.

FLO: Fairtrade Labelling Organization, MT: Metric tonnes.

they permit the production, identification and preservation of product and process characteristics through the supply chain in a consistent manner over time. This is most critical in the case of credence attributes that relate to the way in which products are produced and handled rather than the intrinsic characteristics of the product itself (Henson and Traill, 1993; Hobbs *et al.*, 2002). Indeed, private standards have arguably become a critical element of strategies to differentiate products and firms, that requires the consistent supply of food safety and quality attributes supported by branding and certification (Berges-Sennou *et al.*, 2004).

Production standards

Fair Trade (FT) emerged in the 1960s as an alternative marketing system, established to change existing trade relations dominated by large international buyers and to empower Southern producers (Renard, 2005). FT is usually presented as a trading partnership based on dialogue, transparency and respect, seeking greater equity in international trade. In practice, FT producers can sell their production at pre-defined and guaranteed minimum floor prices, receiving an additional premium for deliveries to FT market outlets which should be used for community purposes (Ruben, 2008). The Fairtrade Labelling Organizations International (FLO-Cert) is the independent organisation responsible for inspection and certification of producer organisations and traders. FT has certain requirements for producers that can become certified: they should be smallholder producers depending mainly on family labour and organized in cooperatives operating under democratic lines. FT further aims to eliminate the role of middlemen along the chain and create a kind of social conscience amongst retailers and consumers. Accordingly, the philosophy behind FT is based on significant ethical and solidarity dimensions that differ substantially from the neo-classical paradigm which considers minimum prices as a price distortion that affects well-functioning markets. This is often considered a major constraints for fully involving multinationals and supermarkets into FT programs.

Utz Certified – previously known as *Utz Kapeh* (meaning good coffee in a Maya language) – was developed by a foundation with its headquarters in the Netherlands and with support from global retailer Ahold (Farnsworth and Goodman, 2006). It is a market-based certification program focussed on how farms are managed and underlining aspects of farm efficiency and coffee traceability, while certified units are also demanded to perform well on social and environmental issues (Bitzer *et al.*, 2008). Utz has developed a set of standards for third party verification that is aligned with GlobalGap certification system for the sourcing of fruit and vegetables led by European retailers (Muradian and Pelupessy, 2005). Unlike FT, Utz does not require that a producer cooperative acts as a medium and is open to a wider range of producers (Tallontire and Vorley, 2005). Another difference with FT is that Utz does not embrace the concept of minimum prices but offers a flexible, negotiable price premium (Bitzer *et al.*, 2008). Utz claims to offer stability to preferred suppliers and aims to move beyond the FT-niche by mainstreaming certified responsible coffee.

FT and organic coffee occupy a niche market that is on average less than two percent of consumption in the more developed markets (Bitzer *et al.*, 2008). Experts assume that especially FT coffee may have hit a glass ceiling unable to grow beyond a socially conscious but limited consumer base (Giovannucci and Koekoek 2003). Consequently, FT has remained an option available to only a limited number of producers. In contrast, Utz is the fasted growing certification initiative in the world (Lazaro *et al.*, 2008). In practice, it should be noted that many farmers sell their coffee via multiple markets, i.e. dividing their produce over the FT, Utz and conventional outlets. Multi-certification presents itself as a strategy for diversifying sales to different buyers with differing quality and delivery requirements. Otherwise, Giovannucci and Ponte (2005) express concerns that certification can become a de facto market requirement and simultaneously raise market entry barriers for coffee growers.

Rainforest Alliance (RFA) started in the late 1990s a coffee certification program with support from the Nations Development Programme (UNDP) and the Global Environment Facility (GEF). It aims to integrate productive agriculture, biodiversity conservation and human development, certifying both large and smallholder coffee producers in tropical countries. RFA farmers should avoid child labour, maintain non-discriminatory hiring practices and must pay legal minimum wages. Sustainability criteria are developed with partners in the Sustainable Agriculture Network (SAN) to help conserve biodiversity and labour standards intend to improve local people's lives. RFA coffee farms must have plans to maintain or restore natural forest cover to achieve minimum shade coverage (i.e. at least 70 trees per hectare) and maintain native species. Moreover, farmers are not allowed to alter natural water courses, and when using chemicals buffer zones of natural vegetation between the crop areas and areas used by humans should be maintained. Standards also prohibit such activities as trafficking in wild animals, destruction of ecosystems, dumping untreated wastewater, and other harmful practices.

Company standards

Recently, the number of private labels for producing and delivering sustainable and responsible coffee trade has further increased. Starbucks started a programme in 2004 under the title C.A.F.E. (Coffee and Farmer Equity) Practices to evaluate, recognize, and reward producers of high-quality sustainably grown coffee. C.A.F.E. Practices involves a coffee sourcing guideline developed in collaboration with the NGO Conservation International and implemented through Scientific Certification Systems (SCS), a third-party evaluation and certification firm. C.A.F.E. Practices seeks to ensure that Starbucks sources sustainably grown and processed coffee by evaluating the economic, social and environmental aspects of coffee production against a defined set of criteria. Starbucks defines sustainability as an economically viable model that addresses the social and environmental needs of all the participants in the supply chain from farmer to consumer. Currently, almost 185,000 producers participate in the C.A.F.E. Practices program.

In a similar vein, the Nespresso AAA Sustainable Quality Program of Nestlé has been developed with a focus on high quality (AA = coffee quality and the third A stands for sustainability). The compliance with the standard is verified by Rainforest Alliance. It features social and environmental practices of coffee that is mainly purchased from Latin-America, and some farms in Africa and Asia. Nespresso makes no distinction in terms of a premium for meeting the AAA standard, but claims that the eligible producers receive well above the market price for a combination of quality and sustainability.

Sector-wide standards

The German Coffee Association and the German government's international development agency (GTZ) initiated the Common Code for the Coffee Comunity (4C). It aims to foster sustainability in the 'mainstream' green coffee chain and to increase the quantities of coffee meeting basic sustainability criteria. Participating in the initiative are producers, represented mainly by national coffee associations, trade union representatives and NGOs, as well as key industry players, including Nestlé, Sara Lee/Douwe Egberts, Tchibo and Kraft. 4C builds on basic good agricultural and management practices. Its code of conduct intends to eliminate the most unacceptable practices and encourage ongoing improvement.

The 4C distinguishes itself from Fairtrade, Rainforest Alliance and UTZ Certified by relying on 'verification' rather than 'certification' of standards compliance. 4C hopes to achieve a baseline benchmark for coffee production across mainstream industry. Verification entails an internal monitoring system incorporated within the corporate business model rather than relying on external verifiers and/or third party guarantees. During its launch in 2007, the 4C Association stated to only verify 'virgin' coffee, which is coffee that has not been verified or certified by any other production standard in the coffee market. In its first operational year, the 2007/2008 coffee harvest 4.5 million coffee bags of green coffee complying with the 4C criteria were verified in 21 countries. Figures presented by 4C maintain some confusion about the existing overlaps with other initiatives. Although broad support and commitment of various stakeholders organised in the 4C association is promising, only a fraction of the available verified 4C coffee has actually been purchased by its members. About 10% of the total volume – 475,000 bags of coffee – have been actually traded as 4C coffee in 2007/2008 (Available at: http://www.teacoffeecocoa. org/tcc/Commodities/Coffee/4C).

3. Comparison of welfare effects

Field studies that compare the effectiveness and implications of different standards are scarce. Most attention is given to the verification of compliance, whereas sound impact analyses are notably absent. This is partly due to the fact that different standards target specific categories of producers, implying that self-selection is in place. Reliable base line studies conducted before the start of certification are mostly absent, making a sound assessment of the effects after some period of implementation extremely difficult. Moreover, each standard relies on different sets of criteria and pursues specific objectives, and therefore trade-offs between socio-economic and environmental sustainability indicators are likely to occur.

For a sound comparison of the welfare effects of different standard regimes, attention should be focuses on both socio-economic and behavioural dimensions. Ruben (2008) distinguishes five major aspects of farm-household welfare: (1) direct effects on production and prices, (2) indirect effects on farm management, labour conditions and quality performance, (3) changes in the structure of household income and expenditures, (4) wealth implications related to asset accumulation and access to finance, and (5) adjustments in attitudes and behaviour. Earlier studies indicate that Fair Trade standards only lead to modest changes in farm production and household income, but that the increased certainty regarding prices and market outlets have important effects on household expenditures, access to finance and investment attitudes. Fair Trade farmers can rely on delivery contracts that provide access to finance, consistently invest more in education and house upgrading, and also appear to be significantly less risk-averse. On the other hand, new standards for responsible and sustainable trade focus more attention on the indirect effects of improved farm management practices and quality upgrading as major strategies for improving farm-household welfare. This also implies that knowledge dimensions that guarantee compliance with technical standards, and loyalty with the producer organization tend to become more relevant.

The Centre for International Development Issues (CIDIN) at Radboud University Nijmegen, the Netherlands, conducted explorative field surveys in Uganda and Tanzania to compare the production and welfare effect as well as the behavioural implications of Fair Trade and Utz Certified coffee produced in likewise rural cooperatives (Regts, 2009; Verkaart, 2009). The comparison involves Utz certified (=treatment) and conventional producers (=control) in Uganda, and multi-certified (= treatment: FT + Utz) with only FT-certified farmers (= control) in Tanzania (see Table 2). Farm-household and wealth characteristics are broadly similar, thus enabling a balanced comparison between both categories of producers.

The field results indicate that Utz-certified farms use substantially more inputs with similar amounts of labour, and outperform conventional coffee production in terms of labour productivity (as shown in the Uganda case), whereas Utz farms' labour productivity is still lower compared to farms with only Fair Trade certification (in Tanzania). This is partly due to lower tree density (and sometimes older trees) on Utz farms. However, no significant differences in land productivity are registered, despite the higher input intensity.

Quality performance on Utz-certified farms in Uganda and Tanzania is generally better, as demonstrated by the lower percentage of defects and the larger average size of beans. This is mainly due to reliance on improved practices for drying that require more labour use. In addition, quality is positively influenced by participation in training events and more prolonged cooperative membership. In countries with free

Table 2. *Comparative assessment of coffee standards (Uganda and Tanzania) (CIDIN Field Survey (2009)).*

Variables	Uganda (N=81)			Tanzania (N=86)		
	Utz certified	Conventional producers	Significance	Utz+FT	FT	Significance
Coffee production						
Coffee area (acres)	4.70	3.20	***	1.20	1.75	**
Coffee production (kg)	1,370	1,008	*	197	379	**
Coffee price (US$/kg)	0,72	0.61		0.56	0.73	***
Tree density (trees/acre)	337	472	*	281	384	*
Labour input (hours/week)	38	38		23	23	
Land productivity (kg/tree)	306	389		218	242	
Labour productivity (kg/labour)	38	20	*	9	26	*
Input use (US$/year)	175	56	***	19	5	***
Quality performance						
Defects (%)	15	22	**	13	17	
Fruit size (1-3 scale)	2.2	1.3	***	1.9	1.6	***
Labour conditions						
Fringe benefits (#)	3.9	3.3	***	2.9	3.3	**
Job satisfaction (1-5 scale)	4.4	4.2	**	3.9	3.6	***
Job safety (1-5 scale)	4.0	3.2	***	2.8	2.4	**
Behaviour						
Participation (1-5 scale)	4.4	4.3		2.9	3.3	**
Knowledge (1-5 scale)	3.9	3.6	***	2.6	2.5	
Loyalty (% side sales)	28	50	**	10	18	**
Economic performance						
Coffee income (US$)	1,330	1,042		343	219	*
Total household income (US$)	2,475	2,240		1,153	714	*
Household assets (US$)	1,058	987		181	394	*
Amount of credit (US$)	157	58	*	35	2	

*Significant at 10%, **Significant at 5%, ***Significant at 1%.

market regimes (Uganda) the Utz quality advantage is directly translated into price, whereas under more regulated price conditions (Tanzania) this is still less the case.

Social indicators reveal significantly higher job satisfaction and better job safety conditions on Utz-certified farms in Uganda (compared to conventional producers), which is confirmed in the case of Tanzania (comparing with only Fair Trade certification). Similar differences are registered with respect to the amount of fringe benefits that are received from the cooperative. Especially in the area of participation in cooperative affairs, Fair Trade farmers proved to be far more involved. However, this is not translated into greater loyalty towards the cooperative channel, which seems to be better guaranteed on Utz-certified (and multi-certified) farms.

Direct economic benefits of the Utz label are hardly registered. Utz-certified farms in Uganda perform slightly better than conventional farmers, but the difference is not statistically significant. Access to credit by Utz farmers is significantly better, thus enabling more input purchase and the application of improved crop management practices. In Tanzania, multi-certification with Utz and FT labels clearly outperforms farms with only the FT label in terms of coffee returns and household income. This is even the case when the latter possess more land and fixed assets.

In summary, farmers with Utz-certified coffee production tend to focus more on input intensification and quality upgrading, and are abler to reap better return particularly under conditions of broad market competition. Investments in knowledge and improved cropping practices are critical to remain competitive in the long run. Multi-certification can thus be useful to enable farmers to make the transition from the 'protected' Fair Trade segment towards more demanding 'responsible trade' markets.

4. Outlook

With the proliferation of private standards in coffee production and trade, the landscape of marketing channels and outlets has become increasingly complex. In addition to consumer-oriented labels, new standards are increasingly oriented towards the regulation of production and trade practices within business-to-business arrangements. Almost all standards rely on independent inspection and certification (except the 4C initiative) and claim that participating producers are able to reap substantial welfare benefits. Empirical evidence regarding the comparative performance of each of these standards is, however, still rather scarce.

The gradual shift from Fair Trade towards responsible and sustainable trade marks a more significant change from strictly value-based to more control-based standards. While the former focus on shared principles, open dialogue and wide stakeholder participation, the latter ask for clear rules and procedures that protect brands from loss of reputation. The regime of Fair Trade proves to be especially suitable to assist local farmers' organizations in getting initial access to the market, but incentives for further upgrading of production systems and quality performance appear to be rather restricted. In fact, cooperatives with long engagement in Fair Trade tend to become over-specialised in coffee and neglect investments in upgrading (Ruben, 2008). Therefore, in subsequent phases further alignment with private brands might be a useful step to guarantee sustained market participation and an increased capacity to adapt to increasing stringent market demands. The price premium may then disappear and can be replaced by a quality performance premium.

We can thus outline some likely tendencies for the future structure of producers' affiliation with different types of coffee standards. While Fair Trade is helpful to assist smallholders initial access to international markets, for maintaining long-term competitiveness private labels offer better prospects to enhance quality upgrading. Recently established farmers cooperatives might initially benefit from the stability provided by Fair Trade labels, whereas more consolidated groups can readily switch to more demanding (and potentially also more rewarding) Responsible or Sustainable trade standards. It is therefore to be expected that the affiliation of farmers with distinct standard regimes follows a kind of life cycle, where Fair Trade provides the financial base for subsequent investments in performance and quality upgrading. Some farmers may still prefer multi-certification that enables simultaneous relationships with different market outlets.

A critical condition for further dovetailing of the different coffee standard regimes would be to include the expansion of capacities and explicit learning objectives into the standard-setting and verification procedures. This will enable smallholder farmers to switch attention from objectives of volume and scale towards criteria of quality and reliability, and is likely to reinforce also internal organization and loyalty. Such progress standards can substantially reduce market imperfections and will provide useful incentives to producers to remain competitive in a highly dynamic market environment.

References

Berges-Sennou, F. Bontems, P. and Requillart, V. (2004). Economics of Private Labels: A Survey of Literature. Journal of Agricultural and food Industrial Organization 2: 1-23.

Bitzer, V., Francken, M. and Glasbergen, P. (2008). Intersectoral partnerships for a sustainable coffee chain: Really addressing sustainability or just picking (coffee) cherries? Global Environmental Change 18: 271-284.

Doane D. (2005). Beyond corporate social responsibility: minnows, mammoths and markets. Futures 27: 215-229.

Farnworth, C. and Goodman, M. (2006). Growing Ethical Networks: the Fair Trade Market for Raw and Processed Agricultural Products. Background paper for the World Development Report 2008, available at: http://www.rimisp. org/getdoc.php?docid=6442. Accessed November 2009.

Giovannucci, D.S. and Ponte, S. (2005). Standards as a new form of social contract? Sustainability initiatives in the coffee industry. Food Policy 30: 284-301.

Giovannucci, D.S. and Koekoek, F.J. (2003). The State of Sustainable Coffee: A study of twelve major markets. International Coffee Organization. International Institute of Sustainable Development, London, UK.

Henson, S. (2006). The Role of Public and Private Standards in Regulating International Food Markets. Paper IATRC Summer symposium 'Food Regulation and Trade: Institutional Framework, Concepts of Analysis and Empirical Evidence'. May 28-30, Bonn, Germany.

Henson, S.J. and Traill, W.B. (1993). Economics of Food Safety. Food Policy 18: 152-162.

Hobbs, J.E., Fearne, A. and Spiggs, J. (2002). Incentive Structures for Food Safety and Quality Assurance: An International Comparison. Food Control 13: 77-81.

Kolk, A. (2005). Corporate social responsibility in the coffee sector: the dynamics of MNC responses and code development. European Management Journal 23: 228-236.

Lazaro, E., Makindara, J. and Kilima, F.T.M. (2008). Sustainability standards and coffee exports from Tanzania. Copenhagen: DIIS Working paper.

Muradian, R. and Pelupessy, W. (2005). Governing the coffee chain: The role of voluntary regulatory Systems. World Development 33: 2029-2044.

Raynolds, L.T., Murray, D.L. and Wilkinson, J. (2007). Fair Trade: The Challenges of Transforming Globalization. Routledge, London/New York.

Reardon, T., Codron, J.M., Busch, L., Bingen, J. and Harris, C. (2001). Global Change in Agri-Food Grades and Standards: Agribusiness Strategic Responses in Developing Countries. International Food and Agribusiness Management Review 2: 421-435.

Regts, N. (2009). The Impact of Knowledge and Participation on Cooperative Loyalty in Uganda and Tanzania: Does Certification Matter? Thesis, CIDIN, Nijmegen, the Netherlands.

Renard, M.C. (2003). Fair trade: quality, market and conventions. Journal of Rural Studies 19: 87-96.

Ruben, R, Ed. (2008). The Impact of Fair Trade. Wageningen Academic Publishers, Wageningen, the Netherlands.

Swinnen, J.F.M., (ed.) (2007). Global Supply Chains, Standards and the Poor. CABI, Wallingford, UK.

Tallontire, A. and Vorley, B. (2005). Achieving fairness in trading between supermarkets and their agrifood supply chains. UK Food Group, London, UK, available at: http://www.ukfg.org.uk/docs/ UKFG_Briefing_Fairness_in_Trade_Sept_2005.pdf. Accessed July 2009.

TCC (2009). Coffee Barometer 2009. Tropical Commodity Coalition, Amsterdam, the Netherlands.

Verkaart, S. (2009). Effects of Utz Certified and Fair Trade on coffee producers in Uganda and Tanzania: Certification and the People and Profit Dimensions of Corporate Social Responsibility. CIDIN, Nijmegen, the Netherlands.

Utting, P. (2005). Corporate responsibility and the movement of business. Development in Practice 15: 375-388.

Van Beuningen, C. and Knorringa, P. (2009). Inclusive Improvement: Standards and Smallholders. ISS & HIVOS, The Hague, the Netherlands.

Value adding through certification? Insights from the coffee sector in Nicaragua

Tina Beuchelt, Anna Kiemen and Manfred Zeller

In certified coffee value chains, the added value evaporates at the cost of the primary producer due to long chain structures in consuming countries, causing high transaction costs, information asymmetry and bad governance in intermediating cooperatives.

Abstract

Although certification schemes are widely applied and promoted in coffee value chains, research seldomly addresses the added value of certification by different chain actors and the relative benefits of producers. Based on the value chain concept, we selected several conventional and Organic-Fair Trade value chains and investigated prices, income shares, information flows and governance structures. Quantitative and qualitative data was collected from small-scale coffee producers in Nicaragua as well as from their cooperatives, exporters, importers and roasters. Results show that the structure of the value chain and conventional coffee prices have a major influence on the benefits for certified farmers. The share of producers' price on the final retail price is substantially lower in certified than in conventional chains. Differences in final farm income, transparency and information flows also depend on the cooperative's structure and management. Using certification to add value is not benefiting producers as expected due to information asymmetry, governance issues in cooperatives and long chain structures in consuming countries causing high transaction costs. In order to improve farmer's livelihoods in Nicaragua, policy measures should rather address business knowledge of producers and cooperatives as well as access to credits and extension in order to increase productivity of the coffee production.

Keywords: coffee, cooperative, governance, income share, information, Nicaragua, Organic-Fair Trade, smallholders, value chain analysis

1. Introduction

Many coffee producers have increased participation in certification schemes to add more value to their product – 'coffee' – as governments, NGOs and donors see this as a possible way to reduce poverty at farm level (IFOAM, 2006; Kilian *et al.*, 2006; Neilson, 2008). These market niches are based on standards for production and processing related to environmental and socio-economic criteria (Ponte, 2002). While some research on quality and certification has shown price premiums at producer levels (Bacon, 2005; Wollni and Zeller, 2007), other research has found negligible benefits for farmers (Kilian *et al.*, 2006; Neilson, 2008; Valkila, 2009).

In coffee producing countries the value captured for production and primary processing varies, depending on the year, between 10-20% of the final retail value (Daviron and Ponte, 2005; Fitter and Kaplinsky, 2001). In coffee consuming countries the import and trade activity adds up to 40% of the final retail price, whereas roasting adds a further 20%. The major value adding is realized in branding and retailing (Daviron and Ponte, 2005). Product differentiation and thus value adding becomes increasingly important to gain competitive advantage. Investing in certification enables upgrading of production processes and access to niche markets.

In contrast to claims by Fair Trade initiatives and organic lobbyers (IFOAM, 2006; Osterhaus, 2006), the few existing studies of certified value chains indicate that certified coffee producers do not necessarily benefit more than conventional producers, while at the same time certified coffees enable chain actors in the roasting and retail levels to create economic rents (Mendoza and Bastiaensen, 2003).

The question is not only how much, but also what share of the final retail price producers receive, how power is distributed and what information is communicated. The different existing business models as well as the determining factors for a successful integration of producers in the value chain – like power and information (Gereffi *et al.*, 2005; Talbot, 2002) – are often overlooked in research on certified value chains (Tallontire, 2009). Thus, our study addresses the added value producers achieve when applying certification as an upgrading strategy. This knowledge is needed to support policy decisions which aim at a better market integration and increasing benefits to small-scale producers.

2. Methodology

Based on the value chain concept, this research selected several conventional and Organic-Fair Trade value chains and investigated prices, information flows among chain actors, governance structures and upgrading strategies.

The field research was conducted in Nicaragua where coffee is one of the most important national level export sectors with a 25% share of total exports. Data collection took place in 2007 and 2008 in three important coffee producing provinces: Matagalpa, Madriz and Nueva Segovia.

Three business models, one conventional and two Organic-Fair Trade certified cooperatives, were analyzed. Qualitative research methods, especially semi-structured interviews, were chosen. Interviews were conducted with 34 small-scale coffee producers in 22 communities, as well as with 7 presidents of grassroots cooperatives, 5 cooperative staff members, a coffee exporter as well as with German and American importers and roasters. Additionally, three focus group workshops were conducted with farmers and cooperative staff in each cooperative.

3. Upgrading through certification

One of the greatest motivations for producers and cooperatives to participate in certified markets is the promise of a high coffee price. Table 1 shows the prices paid at all levels of the three business models in the coffee value chains as well as the shares on the final retail price for producers and cooperatives for the production year 2007/08.

Producers do not necessarily receive higher prices for being members of a Fair Trade certified cooperative. The conventional producers in Fair Trade cooperative B even received a lower price than their non-certified colleagues. The farmers indicated that in the last two years they were only paid the local market price. Double certification, Organic-Fair Trade, is also no guarantee for better prices. According to Fair Trade standards, an organic premium of 0.15 US$/lb must be paid in addition to the market price, but as the farm-gate price for cooperative B shows, there is only a very small difference to the conventional price (0.01 US$/lb)[13].

Interesting is also the high coffee price difference of 0.23 US$/lb between the Organic-Fair Trade certified producers in cooperative A (1.31 US$/lb) and B (1.08 US$/lb). The cooperative B stated that it was not able to distribute a premium due to missing gains from export. The cooperative only sells 40% of the coffee to fairtrade markets and cannot market all organic coffee as organic, which partly explains the low price. The reason for the low market shares is not exactly clear and may be due to a lack of access to certified markets, low management skills or low quality coffee. In contrast, cooperative A sold all coffee

Table 1. *Prices in the different coffee value chains of the three business models for 2007/08 (based on interviews, 2008; data on conventional retail price (2007) from ICO (2009)).*

	Farm gate price in US$/lb[1]	FOB price in US$/lb[1]	Retail price in US$/lb[2]	Share of farm-gate price at retail price (%)
Conventional				
Cooperative - Exporter - Retail Germany	1.07	1.31	3.94	27.15
Cooperative - Exporter - Retail US	1.07	1.31	2.92	36.69
Fairtrade - Conventional				
Cooperative B - Importer - Roaster in USA	0.94	1.58	11.41	8.24
Fairtrade - Organic				
Cooperative B - Importer - Roaster in USA	1.08	1.84	11.41	9.46
Cooperative A - Importer - Roaster in USA	1.31	1.87	11.41	11.48
Cooperative B - Importer/Distributor I in Germany	1.08	1.84	10.52	10.27
Cooperative A - Importer/Distributor I in Germany	1.31	1.78	10.52	12.45
Cooperative A - Importer - Distributor in Germany	1.31	1.78	8.47	15.47

[1]Converted to green exportable coffee. [2]Green coffee equivalent price. Conversion factor for roasted/green coffee=0.84, VAT included.
FOB: free on board.

---

[13]From June 2008 onwards, the fair trade minimum prices and the social premium were raised. The farm-gate price is lower than the FOB price as costs for processing, export and administration are subtracted. The cooperative's management and the product's quality further determine how much can be sold as certified coffee.

with the double certification. Yet, even in this cooperative many producers indicated that daily life remains a struggle for survival. This may be due to low coffee yield levels.

The price data show that farmers in the conventional chain receive a much higher share of the final retail price in the USA (37%) and Germany (27%), than farmers in the certified chains. In the fairtrade chains, conventional producers have a share of the final retail price of 8%, organic producers of 9-15%. Other studies show lower shares (10-20%) for conventional producers but do not include recent developments on the coffee market (Daviron and Ponte, 2005; Fitter and Kaplinsky, 2001). Several aspects may explain the differences regarding the producer's share of final retail price:

- First, the cooperatives' management indicated in the interviews that recovering world market prices has led to lower price differences for organic and fairtrade coffees over conventional coffees. This was also shown by Valkila (2009) and Kilian *et al.* (2006). Thus, competition in periods of good international prices, like in the production 2007/08 year, is very high for the fairtrade certified cooperatives. Producers are increasingly selling to local intermediaries who do not require as stringent quality parameters as the cooperatives do.
- Second, cooperatives are not always able to market all their coffee as certified coffee. In part this is due to the increased international competition, the relatively low demand for certified coffees in relation to world coffee demand, and the varying capacity of the cooperatives' management. Highly-educated and committed managers are scarce.
- Third, large distribution channels in the conventional market, e.g. the big importing and roasting companies in the retail market in Germany, can realize economies of scale which are not likely to be reached in the alternative trading and retail models of world shops and organic food stores.

4. Governance and information flows in the three value chains

The coffee value chain is buyer-driven which means that buyers determine minimum quality standards and price (Daviron and Ponte, 2005). The manager of the conventional cooperative stated having no bargaining power on prices as they sell only to one exporter who sets the price. However, by increasing her management skills through higher education and the long-term relationship based on high trust between the cooperative and the exporter, the cooperative manager indicated potential for bargaining. The exporter supports the cooperative with stable credits and pre-financing conditions as well as the idea to pursue certifications. The producers' position in price negotiation and product definition is not better in certified chains than in the conventional chain because the amount of premiums is determined by the buyers and cooperatives. At the cooperative level in the certified chains, roasters and importers demand a defined quality and therefore cooperatives can participate in the price bargaining process. The slightly better bargaining position of the Fair Trade cooperatives is likely to be due to their produced quality. They have also long term relations with actors in consuming countries. Cooperative staff indicated that quality is not automatically paid for. In part this may relate to the small size of some buyers and/or the complex chains of certified coffee with many actors in consuming countries where different enterprises control the importing, roasting and marketing, thus increasing transaction costs.

In terms of communication, producers in the conventional chain are in contact with staff from the cooperative through farm-based technical support, and visits to the cooperative office for credit facilitation. The cooperative management is in frequent contact with the exporter to communicate on production and credits. However, almost no information on the chain regarding prices, product attributes, and destinations for conventional coffee is released to consumers or producers.

In the certified chains, information for producers about coffee, quality issues, and pricing is communicated at the annual general assembly, in monthly group meetings, and monthly on-farm visits. Additionally, monthly meetings are organized by the grassroots cooperatives to facilitate dialogue with the second order cooperative management. Organic certified farmers in these chains are better informed on standards and the value chain than the conventional producers. While the system of Fair Trade remains unclear to nearly all producers and even to leaders of the grassroots cooperatives, knowledge on the standards for organic production is better. The quality and frequency of information flows strongly varies in the two investigated chains. In certified chain A there is a high trust relationship between the individual producer and the cooperative staff. In certified chain B, producers and presidents of grassroots cooperatives stated that they are not satisfied with the relationship and do not trust their second order cooperative, mainly because lack of transparency in terms of the management of processing, payment and relevant marketing information. The good information flows in chain A may be related to the small size of the cooperative (only 400 members), while the 2,000 members in chain B may increase communication logistics and costs and thus hinder information flows. This enables the manager of the second order cooperative in chain A to have direct contact with most of the producers and maintain personal relationships with members. In chain B, only the extension workers and the grassroot cooperative staff have direct contact with the producers.

5. Conclusions

Results show that coffee prices as well as the governance structure of the value chain and information flows influence the benefits of individual farmers and their integration in certified value chains. Farmers and their cooperatives are found to have no bargaining power over prices irrespective of the value chain. Organic-Fair Trade coffee prices can be higher than conventional prices but the difference depends strongly on the cooperative. The share of producers' prices on the final retail price is substantially lower in the certified chains than in the conventional chain. This low share may in part be due to the small amounts handled and the many actors involved in the consuming countries raising transaction costs. Certified coffees may offer benefits to farmers in periods of low coffee prices while high coffee prices make certification much less attractive. This especially relates to conventional Fair Trade coffee producers.

Due to many chain actors in consuming countries causing high transaction costs in certified chains, information asymmetry and bad governance in intermediating cooperatives the value added through certification evaporates at the cost of the primary producer. In order to improve farmer's livelihoods in Nicaragua, policy measures should rather address access to credits and extension in order to increase productivity of the coffee production. On the cooperative side, training to further improve organizational and marketing skills is recommended.

References

Bacon, C. (2005). Confronting the coffee crisis: Can fair trade, organic and specialty coffees reduce small-scale farmer vulnerability in northern Nicaragua? World Development 33: 497-511.

Daviron, B. and Ponte, S. (2005). The coffee paradox. Global markets, commodity trade and the elusive promise of development. Zed Books, London and New York.

Fitter, R. and Kaplinsky, R. (2001). Who gains from product rents as the coffee market becomes more differentiated? A value-chain analysis. IDS Bulletin 32: 69-82.

Gereffi, G., Humphrey, J. and Sturgeon, T. (2005). The governance of global value chains. Review of International Political Economy 12: 78-104.

IFOAM (2006). Organic agriculture and rural development. Available at: http://www.ifoam.org/organic_facts/politics/pdfs/Rural_Development_Leaflet.pdf. Accessed July 2006.

Kilian, B., Jones, C., Pratt, L. and Villalobos, A. (2006). Is sustainable agriculture a viable strategy to improve farm income in Central America? A case study on coffee. Journal of Business Research 59: 322-30.

Mendoza, R. and Bastiaensen, J. (2003). Fair trade and the coffee crisis in the Nicaraguan Segovias. Small Enterprise Development 14: 36-47.

Neilson, J. (2008). Global private regulation and value-chain restructuring in Indonesian smallholder coffee systems. World Development 36: 1607-22.

Osterhaus, A. (ed.) (2006). Business unusual. Successes and challenges of fair trade. Newcastle-upon-Tyne: FLO (Fairtrade Labeling Organizations International), IFAT (International Fair Trade Association), NEWS! (Network of European Worldshops) and EFTA (European Fair Trade Association).

Ponte, S. (2002). Standards, trade and equity: Lessons from the specialty coffee industry. CDR Working Paper 2: 1-43.

Talbot, J.M. (2002). Tropical commodity chains, forward integration strategies and international inequality: Coffee, cocoa and tea. Review of International Political Economy 9: 701-34.

Tallontire, A. (2009). Top heavy? Governance issues and policy decisions for the fair trade movement. Journal of International Development 21: 1004-14.

Valkila, J. (2009). Fair trade organic coffee production in Nicaragua - sustainable development or a poverty trap? Ecological Economics 68: 3018-25.

Wollni, M. and Zeller, M. (2007). Do farmers benefit from participating in specialty markets and cooperatives? The case of coffee marketing in Costa Rica. Agricultural Economics 37: 243-48.

Technological impact on chains and markets

The impact of telecommunications on agricultural incomes in developing countries

Hans Jansen, Grahame Dixie and Máximo Torero

In rural areas investments in telecommunications have the highest impact on welfare but governments have largely missed the boat so the private sector has taken over. However, governments still have an important role to play in generating public content and optimizing the complementarities of infrastructure investments.

Abstract

Improving information services through telecommunications technology has a proven positive impact on rural incomes. Access to public telephones and especially individual mobile phones improves agricultural productivity, increases market access and expands marketing options for rural producers. This essay provides examples of both qualitative and quantitative evidence regarding the impact of telecommunications on rural welfare, citing examples from India, China, Africa and Central America. In most developing countries the telecommunications revolution in rural areas is driven by the private sector. However, this does not mean that there is no role for the public sector. On the contrary, penetration of the use of telecommunication technology in developing countries is far from complete implying a huge remaining potential for further increases in rural incomes. In order for telecommunications to have their maximum impact on rural welfare, complementary investments in public goods such as infrastructure and services are required. In this way the public sector can help in leveraging the potential of telecommunications even further leading to improved market efficiency and economic opportunities in both the farm and non-farm rural sectors.

Keywords: developing countries, market efficiency, market information, mobile phones, public investment, qualitative evidence, quantitative evidence, rural income, telecommunications

1. Introduction

Improved market access for smallholders has been identified as one of the most important prerequisites for increasing agriculture-based growth and reducing rural poverty in developing countries (Von Braun, 2009). Improving information services in rural areas in developing countries is a crucial element in ensuring better market access through the reduction in marketing costs[14] and telecommunications technology (public telephones and especially individual mobile phones) plays an increasingly important role in this respect.

---

[14] For example, in Sub Saharan Africa marketing costs account for up to 70 percent of crop retail values, thus reducing the effective price farmers receive for their products (Fafchamps and Hill, 2005).

Indeed the development and application of telecommunications in developing countries have increased at exponential speed during the past few years. There exists plenty of anecdotal evidence that the provision of relevant, reliable and cost-effective information in rural areas via telephones can have a significant impact on the welfare of rural farm households. These increases in welfare occur mainly via improvements in agricultural productivity, improved market access and marketing opportunities leading to higher farm-gate prices, and changes in cropping patterns towards higher-value crops. The types of information demanded by farmers range from seasonal weather forecasts, help with sourcing better inputs such as quality seeds and fertilizer (where and which types), farm management issues such as improved cultivation practices, pest and disease management, and marketing including price discovery (see also Figure 1). Information provided by telephones can not only increase agricultural productivity but also reduce transaction costs through better matching buyers and sellers of agricultural produce and commodities. This is particularly important for small producers who typically face higher transaction costs. In this way access to telecommunications may not only improve agricultural productivity but also increase market efficiency which may lower price levels and price variation while reducing marketing margins.

Compared to the wide body of qualitative evidence which may be more or less anecdotal in nature, there exist relatively few quantitative studies that rigorously measure the impact of telecommunications on rural welfare. But knowledge regarding such impact is important given the substantial opportunity costs of investing in telecommunications and the need for adequate prioritization of public investments. Both private and public investors need to compare the benefits of providing access to telecommunications among rural households against the costs of establishing and operating the necessary infrastructure. From a private investor's point of view the necessary investments have to be compared to the income generating potential from user charges levied, whereas the costs of public investments in telecommunication have to be assessed against their impact on rural incomes and subsequently compared with the welfare impacts of alternative public investments (e.g. roads, electricity etc.). Because in general market information is a 'product' that is difficult to sell (the buyer does not know its value until after it is 'purchased') and easy to reproduce (making it hard for the 'producer' to recover costs), the private-sector supply of information

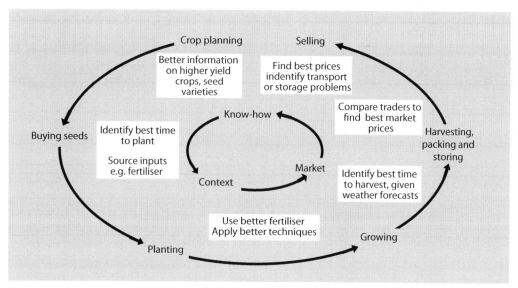

Figure 1. *Information requirements through the agricultural cycle (Mittal et al., 2010).*

may be suboptimal, implying a role for governments and international organizations in facilitating the flow of market information. This is particularly true in the case of agricultural markets in developing countries, whose performance is a key determinant of the incomes of the rural poor.

Provision of land-line based telecom services in developing countries is dominated by the public sector because it is widely believed that subsidies are necessary especially in rural areas. In this paper we will provide some evidence that shows that investments in public telephones in rural areas can yield high returns, implying that the often poor performance of public telecommunication utilities is not necessarily due to lack of inherent economic profitability. Perhaps because of the poor performance of many of these utilities, in most developing countries the fast adoption of mobile telecoms has been largely driven by the private sector. Where the public sector has engaged in mobile telephony, the experience is mixed: for example in Ethiopia the government-run mobile telephone monopoly has a penetration rate of only 3.5% but in Costa Rica the telecommunications monopoly has achieved virtually 100% penetration.

2. Selected qualitative evidence

In India, Reuters Market Light (RML) in June 2009 started providing a text-based service to 125,000 users who pay 1.40 US$ per month for local weather and price information. Tata Consultancy Services offers a service called mKrishi which allows farmers to send queries and receive personalized advice in agriculture. The MS Swaminathan Research Foundation in cooperation with Tata Teleservices and Qualcomm is piloting a mobile information service model for fishermen called Fisher Friend following earlier findings by Jensen (2007) who showed that mobile phones among fishermen reduced price dispersion and wastage. Nokia launched another information service in India around the same time called Nokia Life Tools which includes agricultural information and crop price data at a cost of between 0.65 US$ and 1.30 US$ per month. IFFCO Kisan Sanchar Ltd. offers mobile services similar to RML.

Mittal *et al.* (2010) used focus groups and interviews among farmers to assess the impact of these types of telecommunications services. They show that mobile phone services indeed contribute to increased agricultural productivity in India, in the order of 10-40% leading to income increases ranging between 5-25% or 15-75 US$ per month. Farmers identified seed information, market prices, plant protection and fertilizer application, weather, and machinery/tractor prices and subsidies (in that order) as the types of information that they value most. In comparison, unpublished Reuters Market Research suggests the following order of prioritization of information needs among farmers in India: accurate local weather forecasts, technical information, input sources and production costs, and market information. However, these priorities would change over the production season. For example, during the monsoon season, farmers in the Punjab value rainfall forecast information most.

In addition to Reuters Market Research, unpublished information obtained from RML for India indicates increased interest in cash crops as farmers are keen to move towards commercialization and diversification of their crops. In parallel farmers simultaneously seek information about new varieties of traditional crops: particularly in the case of Basmati rice there has been consistent demand for information about improved varieties. Farmers have also articulated an appetite for entirely new types of information. For example, in the case of vegetables they have requested RML to provide price information for different grades separately and they see clear opportunities for mobile phones to help them access new markets, e.g. in neighboring states or even foreign markets in Dubai and the US. Some banana and flower farmers have been demanding the inclusion of wind speed in weather information given the sensitivity of their crops. Farmers have also expressed interest in knowing weather forecasts for 3-4 days in advance in order to enable them to plan their activities accordingly. Timeliness of the information provided is crucial: e.g. as most auctions for vegetables and fruits happen in the early morning, farmers want the information of vegetable and fruit prices sent to their phones latest by 10:00 AM. In tube well irrigated areas, electricity schedules are in high demand, and in case of canal irrigation, farmers highly appreciate the water release schedules published by RML. Besides crop information, RML now also provides livestock-related information which is also in high demand with farmers especially seeking information about quail and live chicken prices. Finally, the RML experience in India strongly suggests that farmers prefer getting the SMS messages in their own vernacular language.

Farmers indicate that the main advantages provided by telecommunications that lead to the productivity impact include easy accessibility and customized content, mobility benefits and improved convenience and time savings in accessing information. But currently only 40% of all farmers in India access information about agricultural technologies and inputs. Leveraging the full potential of information for smallholder producers will require significant improvements in the supporting infrastructure (especially access to roads, irrigation and other inputs) and in capacity building to farmers in order for them to better interpret and use the information provided.

Whereas the extension of mobile phone-based information among farmers in India is entirely based on private sector-led initiatives and is growing fast, telecommunications geared towards farmers are currently most developed in China under a public-private partnership (PPP) where China Mobile has teamed up with the Department of Agriculture. This PPP offers a service called Nong Xin Tong that provides weather information and details of farming-related public policies. Nong Xin Tong currently has 50 million users and is growing fast.

Whereas in general terms telecommunications penetration has advanced much more in Asia than in Africa, the latter is catching up. For example in Uganda, a joint venture between MTN (Africa's largest mobile phone operator), Google and the Grameen Foundation's 'Application Laboratory' launched a range of phone-based services under the name of 'Farmer's Friend' which is similar to India's mKrishi. These services include seasonal weather forecasts, advice in agriculture and market information. Google also operates a service that matches buyers and sellers of agricultural commodities called Google Trader. Whereas provision of these kinds of information services is more complicated than providing simple phone services, the Uganda example shows that it can be done by working closely with local partners and 'community knowledge workers' who provide and interpret location-specific information while accounting for cultural differences.

3. Selected quantitative evidence

Public telecom enterprises may often have performed poorly but this is not due to lack of inherent profitability of telecommunications investments. In the context of a wider study regarding the impact of the Central America Free Trade Agreement (CAFTA) on agriculture and the rural sector in five Central American countries, Torero *et al.* (2007) used propensity score matching techniques combined with GIS-based access information and market chain survey data to analyze how improved access to public telephones could help to maximize the benefits or minimize the costs that rural producers would face as a result of CAFTA. The results are summarized in Jansen *et al.* (2007) and suggest that compared to alternative public investments in rural roads or electricity, investment in public telephones had by far the largest impact on rural incomes, generating per capita net present values of 399 US$, 105 US$ and 456 US$ in respectively Honduras, Guatemala and El Salvador; or 1.5 times to 20 times higher than alternative public investments in rural roads or electricity. In all three countries, public telecommunication investments have a particularly high pay-off in livestock producing areas. In the case of private investments in the use of telecommunication services for providing information to farmers, the rapid spread of such services throughout the world itself is witness to its profitability, despite the relatively low user fees of most of these services. Chong *et al.* (2009) investigated the direct impact of telecommunications on rural incomes in Peru using a quasi-natural experiment using propensity score matching methods. In this particular experiment a privatized telecommunications company was required by the government to randomly install and operate public pay phones in small rural towns throughout the country. The findings suggest that most characteristics of public telephone use are positively linked with both farm income and non-farm rural income. Not only do the findings hold when using instrumental variables but they are further confirmed when using propensity scores matching methods.

Goyal (2008) analyzed the effect on farmer prices of increased availability of market price information delivered over the internet to public access points. Her study compared the farmer price in the regulated market (so-called Mandi markets[15]) for soya beans in two areas of the state of Madhya Pradesh (MP) in India. In one area multiple so-called e-choupals[16] were in operation while the other area had only Mandis (see Figure 2). The results indicate that market prices, as disseminated by the e-choupals were widely known and understood among farmers. On the other hand in other areas with few if any e-choupals, soya price information was less available and market information asymmetries were more evident. Goyal's results convincingly show that farmers obtain better prices when they have access to wider market information, leading to price increases in the range of 1-3%, with an average of 1.7% which is statistically significant at the 1% level (Figure 3). The additional farm income from soya beans in MP (which may well be in the order of 20 million US$ per year) can be largely considered as a transfer from traders to producers[17] as the former were forced to reduce malpractices in order to compete with direct purchases by the agri-business firm who set up the e-choupals.

Similarly, Aker (2008) in her study in Niger exploits the fact that between 2001 and 2006 mobile phone service was phased in throughout the country, providing an alternative and cheaper search technology to grain traders and other market actors. The author constructs a novel theoretical model of sequential search in which traders engage in optimal search for the maximum sales price, net of transport costs. The model predicts that mobile phones increase traders' reservation sales prices and the number of markets over which they search, leading to a reduction in price dispersion across markets. To test the predictions of the

---

[15] Mandi markets refer to traditional wholesale market yards that are part of a wider government-regulated marketing system defined by the Agricultural Produce Marketing Acts. Even though the mandi system is auction-based and was originally set up to protect farmers from unscrupulous buyers outside the mandis, it is now increasing consensus that mandis are inefficient, lack integration, and are plagued by trader collusion and high levels of physical wastage (Minten *et al.*, 2009).

[16] An E-choupal (choupal means 'village gathering place' in Hindi) is an internet kiosk manned by a local farmer who acts as an agent for an agri-business firm and where farmers can access price information from a wide range of mandis as well as obtain the price paid by the agri-business firm for direct purchases by the firm at one of its hubs. Other types of information (weather forecasts, farming techniques etc) are also usually available.

[17] Formally a relatively small part (less than 7%) of the total income gain to farmers is welfare gain of deadweight loss under monopsony, implying that about 93% represents a redistribution of surplus away from traders to farmers.

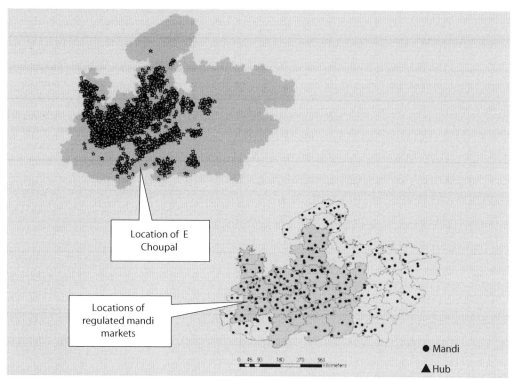

Figure 2. *Location of E-Choupals and Mandi markets in Madhya Pradesh, India (Goyal, 2010).*

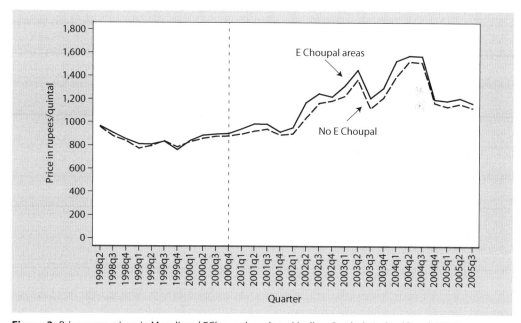

Figure 3. *Price comparison in Mandi and EChoupal markets, Madhya Pradesh, India. (Goyal, 2010).*

theoretical model, Aker uses a unique market and trader dataset that combines data on prices, transport costs, rainfall and grain production with mobile phone access and trader behavior. The results provide evidence that mobile phones reduce grain price dispersion across markets by at least 6.4% and intra-annual price variation by 10%. Mobile phones have a greater impact on price dispersion for market pairs that are farther away, and for those with lower road quality. This effect becomes larger as a higher percentage of markets obtain mobile phone coverage. The primary mechanism by which mobile phones affect market-level outcomes appears to be a reduction in search costs, as grain traders operating in markets with mobile phone coverage search over a greater number of markets and sell in more markets.

4. Complementarities with other types of infrastructure increase the impact of telephones

The qualitative and quantitative discussion of the experiences above points to the importance of investments in other, complementary infrastructure and services in order for telecommunications to have their maximum impact on rural welfare. Whereas these interaction effects have not been quantified as yet in many countries, the research by Torero *et al.* (2007) for Central America, as well as a number of other studies (see e.g. Jansen *et al.* (2006) for Honduras, Escobal and Torero (2005) for Peru, and Torero and Chowdhury (2006) for Bangladesh) suggest that while access to one type of infrastructure has a limited impact on household incomes, the effects of access to three or more types of infrastructure simultaneously are very significant. Moreover there is some evidence that suggests that simultaneous access to different types of infrastructure especially benefits women. Thus, removing barriers to raising agricultural productivity and rural incomes goes far beyond communications access alone and the latter needs therefore to be regarded as an essential building block in a much wider range of policies and investments. India again provides a good illustration in this respect. Mittal *et al.* (2009) report that in farmer focus groups the most important constraint to higher productivity and better incomes identified was the difficulty of sourcing quality and reliable inputs. This problem was highlighted twice as frequently as the next most important bottleneck: lack of irrigation facilities. Sub-standard or outright counterfeit agricultural inputs are a serious problem throughout South Asia: for example, spurious and substandard pesticides alone are estimated to result in a loss of income of about 1 billion US$ per year in India alone.

5. Conclusions

The provision of farmer information through improved access to telecommunications can have a significant impact on rural incomes mainly through increases in productivity and reducing market inefficiencies. But in order to fully exploit this potential, three things need to happen. First, complementary investments in other types of complementary infrastructure are necessary. This is clearly shown by countries such as China and South Korea which, in comparison to most African countries but also India not only have very high penetration rates but also much stronger systems of input delivery, wider road networks, better physical market infrastructure etc. Second, the debate regarding telecommunications needs to go beyond access and move towards how individuals can leverage the capabilities of telecommunications to fully exploit economic development opportunities. This would include transformations in rural livelihoods towards more profitable occupations both within and outside agriculture. And last but not least and related to the previous point, since it is the private sector that has pulled the telecommunications cart in most countries which have achieved success, it is crucial that developing country governments do not stand in the way and provide a legal and regulatory environment that fosters healthy competition in which private entrepreneurs can take full advantage of the opportunities as they present themselves to further build on and expand the telecommunications revolution.

References

Aker, J.C. (2008). Does Digital Divide or Provide? The Impact of Cell Phones on Grain Markets in Niger. Mimeographed. University of California at Berkeley, CA, USA.

Chong, A., Galdo, V. and M. Torero (2009). Access to Telephone and Household Income in Poor Rural Areas using a Quasi-Natural Experiment. Economica 76: 623-648.

Escobal, J. and Torero, M. (2005). Measuring the Impact of Asset Complementarities: The Case of Rural Peru. Cuadernos de Economia 42: 1-26.

Fafchamps, M. and Vargas Hill, R. (2005). Selling at the Farmgate or Traveling to Market. American Journal of Agricultural Economics 87: 717-734.

Goyal, A (2010). Information, Direct Access to Farmers, and Rural Market Performance in Central India. American Economic Journal: Applied Economics (in press).

Jansen, H.G.P., Pender, J., Damon, A. and Schipper, R. (2006). Rural Development Policies and Sustainable Land Use in the Hillside Areas of Honduras: A Quantitative Livelihoods Approach. IFPRI Research Report No. 147, Washington DC, USA.

Jansen, H.G.P., Morley, S. and Torero, M. (2007). The Impact of the Central America Free Trade Agreement on Agriculture in Five Central American Countries. Working Paper No. 26, Regional Unit for Technical Assistance (RUTA), San José, Costa Rica.

Jensen, R. (2007). The Digital Provide: Information Technology, Market Performance and Welfare in the South Indian Fisheries Sector. The Quarterly Journal of Economics CXXII: 979-924.

Minten, B., Reardon, T. and Vandeplas, A. (2009). Linking Urban Consumers and Rural Farmers in India: A Comparison between Traditional and Modern Food Supply Chains. IFPRI Discussion Paper 00883. International Food Policy Research Institute, New Delhi, India.

Mittal, S., Gandhi, S. and Tripathi, G. (2009). Socio-Economic Impact of Mobile Phones on Indian Agriculture. Working Paper No. 246, Indian Council for Research on International Economic Relations (ICRIER), New Delhi, India.

Torero, M. and Chowdhury, S. (2006). Impact of Infrastructure on Rural Households in Bangladesh: An Empirical Investigation. Mimeographed, International Food Policy Research Institute (IFPRI), Washington, DC., USA.

Torero, M., Benza, M., Nakasone, E. and Jansen, H.G.P. (2007). Priorizando Inversión Pública en Infraestructura para Optimizar los Impactos del CAFTA (Prioritizing Public Investments to Optimize the Impacts of CAFTA). Unpublished manuscript, International Food Policy Research Institute (IFPRI) and Regional Unit for Technical Assistance (RUTA). Washington DC, USA and San José, Costa Rica.

Von Braun, J. (2009). The Way Forward on Food and Nutrition Security. Statement Prepared for the World Summit on Food Security November 16, 2009.

Food technology and marketing in the developing world: two of a kind

Martinus van Boekel

Food technology and marketing are complementary in improving the quality of food and the position of smallholders in developing countries.

Abstract

This essay addresses the role of food technology in food supply chains with respect to quality performance. A very important constraint of foods is that they are highly perishable, and so the quality of most foods declines over time quickly after harvesting. Food technology is basically a battle against this deterioration. Food technology can help in preserving food, to improve nutritional quality, to improve food safety, to prolong shelf life, to make food attractive. It is argued that food science knowledge can help in alleviating quality problems on the product level by improving food availability, by strengthening the position of smallholders in trade relationships because of a better quality product and by increasing local employment in food processing. Then it is argued that interaction with marketing is essential to make the connection between consumers' wishes and product properties and to help overcome problems related to chain governance and institutional barriers. By putting this marketing-food technology interaction in practice, local, regional and even international markets should become more accessible for smallholders in developing countries. This could lead to better food security as well as poverty reduction.

Keywords: food quality, marketing channels, consumer wishes, smallholders, food technology, market access

1. Introduction

In discussing the problem of supplying the world with enough food, the keywords are *food security* (is there enough food), *food safety* (is the available food safe to consume), and *food quality* (is the food of such a quality that it can fulfil the need of the consumer). While food security and safety are universally valid, the concept of quality is a more difficult one. In the context of this essay, it is interesting to keep in mind that quality requirements for local consumption may be quite different from those in international trade relationships. In principle, enough food can be produced for the whole world population, in other words, food security can be realized (Koning *et al.*, 2008). In practice, however, this appears not to be possible due to socio-economic and political problems, such as putting up institutional barriers in international trade, infrastructural problems, ignoring or neglecting agricultural issues by governments. In the Western world, food security as well as food safety and quality have improved tremendously over the past 50-100 years. However, on a global scale food security and food quality are not realized at all. In developing countries, food security is still an important issue and we are, in fact, faced with tremendous challenges to feed the world population in the near future (Hubert *et al.*, 2010). In this essay, I would like to explore how food technology and marketing can play a role to mitigate the problem by increasing food security, food safety and food quality from the perspective of the supply chain. In a recent book (Ruben *et al.*, 2007) a theoretical framework was proposed for supply chains in which channel choice and governance regime pertain to the *structure* of the supply chain while quality performance and value added distribution pertain to supply chain *performance*. Identified linkages between structure and performance were such aspects as subcontracting or outsourcing (integral quality control), quality assurance and certification, co-innovation and co-operation, standards, labels and branding. In this essay, I would like to focus on how food technology relates to chain performance in developing countries, acknowledging the fact that there are differences in local and global supply chains. I then argue how food technology should be connected to marketing issues to improve the chain structure as well as the chain performance.

2. Food technology

Let me start with a small anecdote. My first experience as a food technologist in developing countries was in West Africa some 15 years ago and we started by bringing a courtesy visit to the local Dutch embassy. I encountered an almost hostile attitude towards the fact that I came as a food technologist. The ambassador's opinion was that the country did not need technology at all to improve the food situation. The country needed agronomists to help in increasing crop production and nutritionists to evaluate the nutritional problems, but that technology could mean anything useful was beyond comprehension. That was rather shocking for me because I was (and still am) of the opinion that food technology is essential in improving the food situation, both on the local level for small scale food processing as well as in relation to foods produced for international trade. What I learned from this is that food technology apparently evokes wrong associations. So let me first describe briefly what the role of food technology is in the food chain.

The following points are important to consider. The first activity of producing food is basically the production of raw materials in agriculture, horticulture, animal husbandry and aquatic production systems. This is essentially a food quantity issue relevant to both food security and poverty reduction The main scientific disciplines involved are plant and animal breeding, agronomy, soil science, water management, phytopathology, and related disciplines. The main actors involved are farmers, seed companies, fertilizer and pesticides producers. The second activity is about the processing of raw materials into food, i.e., food technology, where the focus is on ensuring food safety (by removing hazards such as micro-organisms and toxins) and increasing food quality (by increasing shelf life, improving nutritional quality, enhancing attractiveness, etc.). This is all very necessary because foods tend to spoil very quickly and by applying food technology principles we can delay this decay effectively and efficiently. This activity starts after harvesting and 4 sub activities can be distinguished (Van Boekel, 1998): stabilization, transformation, production of ingredients, and production of fabricated foods. *Stabilization* implies that measures are taken to prevent spoilage. The most important cause of spoilage is microbial activity; this is even dangerous as the micro-organisms may be pathogenic and are a threat to human health. This concerns the very important aspect of food safety relevant to both food security and compliance with international trade requirements. Hence, many food technology activities are directed towards the prevention, or at least inhibition of microbial growth. When microbial growth is prevented, chemical and biochemical reactions are the next cause of spoilage. This implies oxidation reactions and the so-called Maillard reaction (leading to desired changes such as browning and flavour compounds, and undesired changes such as loss of nutritive value and toxicological suspect compounds). Biochemical changes occur as a result of enzyme activity; this can lead to colour, flavour, taste and texture problems. By knowing the action of enzymes this opens up possibilities to influence this enzymatic activity, notably by manipulating temperature but also by changing the gas composition around the food, so that the rate of deterioration can be slowed down, for instance, by delaying ripening of fruits until the moment of consumption. *Transformation* implies that raw materials are changed into something different, for instance, milk into cheese, wheat into bread, barley into beer, pineapple into pineapple juice, etc. This can be done on a very small scale at the local level as well as on industrial scale and it is a way to preserve raw materials that would otherwise be lost, and, in addition, the resulting products can be potentially of high quality. In other words, this is a way of realizing added value in supply chains and can be a boost for the local economy and may help in poverty reduction. *Production of ingredients* is self-evident: sugar can be extracted from sugar beets and sugar cane, protein and oil from soybeans; this activity can also imply production with the help of micro-organisms or enzymes. This activity can be done at the local level and on a small scale and can be quite useful in reducing poverty, provided that the resulting product is of sufficient quality. Finally, production of *fabricated foods* implies that foods are composed/designed from several raw materials (bread, sauces, desserts, pastry are some examples). Disciplines involved are food science and technology and nutrition, actors involved are processors (artisanal as well as industrial). *Packaging and distribution* follows immediately after transformation (though sometimes packaging is already needed directly after harvesting to avoid immediate quality loss). The author would actually consider packaging to be part of processing. In any case, packaging is an essential element of food technology as it protects the food against all kinds of threats from the environment (micro-organisms, insects, water, oxygen, physical damage). Also, packaging technology can nowadays be actively used to preserve foods by applying controlled atmosphere and modified atmosphere. This implies that the gas atmosphere influences metabolic reactions of the food (such as the above mentioned enzymatic activity in ripening) as well as of the micro-organisms present in a desired direction. Furthermore, packaging can also function as information carrier for the consumer, such as nutritive value, presence of possible allergens, and any other relevant information, including advertising. Disciplines involved are food science, logistics, marketing, actors are food processors, middlemen, retailers. Then, finally the last activity is about *retailing and consumption*. Retailers have quite some power these days, as they are able to influence the consumer directly by determining what to offer to consumers. They seem to have appreciable governance in the food chain, and this also can have consequences for smallholders in developing countries through the quality requirements they have to meet. Increasingly, globalizing markets are becoming important, that is to say that foods from all over the world may end up at the consumer's plate. While this is not a bad development as such, this phenomenon has several institutional implications, such as access to markets and a strong effect of rules and regulations that make it sometimes difficult for developing countries to comply with this (Ruben *et al.*, 2007). It is proposed here that the discipline of food technology can help primary producers and local processors to gain access to these international markets. Global developments in food production also raise the question whether or not sustainability problems are enhanced. Actors involved are food processors, marketers, retailers and consumers, and governments to some extent when it is about regulation.

3. On the role of food technology in improving food security, safety and quality

Because of the natural decay of fresh food products, it is stated here that food technology plays a key role in helping to alleviate many of the problems related to food security. First of all, knowledge of what causes post-harvest losses will help to tackle this problem. It is estimated that 30-40% losses occur in developing countries, and therefore measures to avoid this will have a big effect on food security as well as on food safety. One of the problems with post-harvest spoilage is that micro-organisms produce toxins (such as the carcinogenic compound aflatoxin) that are really very dangerous to human health. Prevention of this would definitely help increase food security as well as safety.

Second, when raw materials are processed into foods, desired and undesired things happen. Desired effects are increased digestibility, increased food safety because of elimination of pathogens, increased shelf life. Undesired effects are destruction of essential nutrients, and losses of resources (excessive waste). Since lack of micronutrients is a serious problem in the developing world, making micronutrients more bio available, possibly by adding them to food, and preventing losses of these compounds during processing, would make a major contribution to alleviate inadequate nutrition.

Third, if food processing of local crops can be connected to demand of urban consumers, i.e., by aligning food processing to consumers' wishes, this would offer the opportunity to raise income and earn a living for the local processors and producers. In doing so, it is essential that food safety and quality can be guaranteed. Food technology can help in realizing this. An example that I recently experienced in Benin is the disappearance of a local dish made with cowpeas, even though consumers like it. The reason it is disappearing is that it is very time consuming to prepare and requires a lot of firewood. By applying some basic technological principles it should be possible to reduce the preparation time considerably, while improving nutritional quality as well as safety, so that local producers could fulfil a market need for consumers that do not want to prepare the dish themselves.

Fourth, institutional barriers to access markets (regionally and internationally) could be tackled by investing in quality and safety by technological measures, and to have knowledge about the products produced so that real safety problems can be distinguished from trade barriers in disguise. It is undeniable that in some cases the microbial contamination of tropical products is so high that they are indeed unsafe to consume. However, measures can be taken to reduce this contamination, and it would give developing countries much more power if they are equipped with food science knowledge, so that they can take the right measures on the one hand, but also can argue with stakeholders about the validity of norms and standards.

A very important aspect with all preservation technologies is to prolong storage by using the right way of packaging. A package forms the barrier between the food and its environment, it can protect the food from recontamination and other undesired influences from the environment (such as oxygen). Packaging has therefore a large effect on food quality as well as on food safety. Food technology can help in adjusting packaging technology to what is needed for a particular food. In doing so, the position of smallholders (farmers, local processors) could be strengthened considerably because then they can offer foods with a defined shelf life to market channels.

4. Food technology and trade

Above it has been argued several times that food technology offers powerful tools that can be applied in the supply change to realize food security, food safety and food quality. The basic characteristic of foods is that they are highly perishable and vulnerable. Food technology offers ways to turn them into higher quality products that have an acceptable shelf life. Although there are all kinds of barriers to realize this situation in developing countries (lack of infrastructure, financial barriers, lack of cooperation within the supply chain, lack of food science knowledge, etc.), I am convinced that with basic knowledge about what happens in foods in the supply chain, and with basic, simple processing operations, the bargaining position of smallholders can be improved considerably. The key is that they find ways to turn perishable products into attractive, less perishable and safe products under the conditions in which they have to work. These conditions are definitely not favorable in all respects, but based on my experience in developing countries I am convinced that much can be improved. In that way, smallholders would have a much stronger negotiation power, for instance, with respect to middlemen, and this would definitely help in poverty reduction. The question then becomes how to realize this. Although I do not have a blueprint, I think that it is essential that in considering policies on poverty reduction it should not be neglected that food technology can play an important role, and therefore, that investments should be made in this respect. If that can be realized, I can go back proudly as a food technologist to Dutch embassies to tell a success story.

5. On the link between food technology and marketing

I have argued above that food technology can be used to prevent losses, to preserve foods by increasing the shelf life, and by improving safety and quality. In other words, food technology offers tools to realize quality performance in the food chain. Where then is the link with marketing? Well, a potential problem arises when there is no alignment between the products delivered by the food chain and the consumers of these products. Quality ultimately means: satisfying the needs of the consumer. At this point, it is important to realize that local and international markets are different. The supply chain is short for local markets (short in time and distance), while it is long in international markets. Moreover, quality demands are increasingly regulated for international markets. This has consequences in view of the rapid quality deterioration of foods. It raises the question whether or not a market differentiation should be made in the supply chain in the sense that the unavoidable variation in quality is actually exploited to serve the various markets, rather than to see quality variation as a burden. In any case, the important issue is to find out how quality can be realized by connecting product quality to consumers' needs. While this problem also exists in developed countries, it is worse in developing countries because it is mostly unclear for smallholders what their customers actually want, and even if they would know this, they face the problem that they do not have much control over the quality delivered. The same is true for actors downstream in the chain. As a result, the variation in quality is usually very large, and seemingly uncontrollable, when the product reaches the consumer. There are these institutional barriers mentioned above hindering access to the various marketing channels, expressed in demands and standards for food safety (residues of pesticides and toxins, micro-organisms) and quality (damaged products, over ripened fruits and vegetables, etc.). So, in my view, the connection between marketing and food technology is on two levels:
1. Identifying and, most importantly, specifying what quality actually means to the various actors in the chain, i.e., customers (value chain stakeholders) and consumers on local markets.
2. Identifying the relation between actors in the chain, as well as possible institutional barriers, in relation to market access.

By specifying quality on the product as well as on the market level, it becomes possible to work on improvement of quality performance by applying food science knowledge and taking appropriate technological measures at the critical control points in the chain where quality is most affected. This approach has been named QACCP (Quality Analysis Critical Control Points, Verkerk *et al.*, 2007). For instance, if the problem is about shelf life, measures can be taken to improve quality by changing the temperature in the chain, by using certain gas conditions, by applying the right packaging, etc. Of course, not all possible measures are immediately applicable in developing countries, but it becomes clear where quality can be controlled and improved. By disclosing chain governance and institutional barriers, it becomes possible to tailor activities in the chain as long as it is about product quality to meet certain standards and demands. For instance, if a product does not comply with certain food safety standards, then food technology knowledge can be used to reduce or eliminate the hazards.

6. Conclusion

This essay has addressed briefly the role of food technology in the food supply chain and then discussed how such knowledge can be integrated with knowledge on market channels and chain governance to gain access to markets, locally, regionally and globally. By making such connections, several important goals may be realized at the same time. Better food of higher quality and safety becomes available, which is beneficial for consumers, while this should also result in better market access for smallholders. If it is possible to realize such a development, it should ultimately be possible to reduce poverty by connecting urban food demand in developing countries to local food production, as well as by connecting to global food chains with products of acceptable quality.

References

Hubert, B., Rosegrand, M., Van Boekel, M.A.J.S. and Ortiz, R. (2010). The Future of Food: Scenarios for 2050. Crop Science 50: S33-S50.

Koning, N.B.J., Van Ittersum, M.K., Beckx, G.A., Van Boekel, M.A.J.S., Brandenburg, W.A., Van den Broek, J.A., Goudriaan J., Van Hofwegen, G., Jongeneel, R.A., Schiere, J.B. and Smies, M. (2008). Long-term global availability of food: continued abundance or new scarcity? NJAS Wageningen Journal of Life Sciences 55: 229-292.

Ruben, R., Van Boekel, M., Van Tilburg, A. and Trienekens, J. (eds.) (2007). Tropical Food chains. Governance regimes for quality management. Wageningen Academic Publishers, Wageningen, the Netherlands.

Van Boekel, M.A.J.S. (1998). Developments in technologies for food production. In: W.M.F. Jongen and M.T.G. Meulenberg (eds.). Innovation of food production systems. Wageningen Academic Publishers, Wageningen, the Netherlands.

Verkerk, R., Linnemann, A.R. and Van Boekel, M.A.J.S. (2007). Quality Analysis Critical Control Points in consumer-oriented agro-food chains. In: Ruben, R., Van Boekel, M., Van Tilburg, A. and Trienekens, J. (eds.), Tropical Food chains. Governance regimes for quality management. Wageningen Academic Publishers, Wageningen, the Netherlands.

Financial institutions

The financial crisis and microfinance

Sascha Huijsman, Robert Lensink and Erwin Bulte

The current financial crisis adversely affects microfinance institutions (MFIs), and the extent of the adverse impact depends on the funding structure of MFIs.

Abstract

We use detailed panel data to demonstrate that the current economic and financial crisis raises MFIs financing costs, reduces the availability of funding, changed demand for loans and implies a deterioration of clients' repayment behavior. We search for structural breaks in the times series of MFI performance indicators related to profitability, growth and portfolio quality. All performance indicators experience a negative shift. The timing of these shifts differs across the performance indicators and there are important geographical differences. Importantly, the extent of the impact depends on the funding structure of MFIs. MFIs attracting savings are significantly less affected.

Keywords: crisis, MFIs, micro credit, loan repayment

1. Introduction

Microfinance provides small entrepreneurs who do not have access to formal financial markets with financial services. It is built on the premise that it will create a more inclusive financial sector, increasing the efficiency and professionalism in delivering financial services to the poor. Microfinance is by many perceived as one of the most effective tools to fight poverty as it promotes the economic development of the poor presumably leading to a higher standard of living. It is estimated that there are approximately 10,000 microfinance institutions (MFIs) worldwide serving more than 155 million clients (Microfinance Summit Campaign, 2009).

We focus on the impact of the current financial and economic crisis on microfinance institutions. Some expected microfinance to be highly resilient to the current crisis (Microcapital, 2008) based on the idea that the performance of MFIs exhibits little correlation with performance of formal financial and economic markets. Empirical studies partly support this latter assumption, but results are ambiguous (Hermes and Meesters, 2009: unpublished working paper). The few available case studies specifically focusing on MFI performance during times of economic distress show that most MFIs are not immune to regional and domestic financial and economic crises (e.g., Marconi and Mosley, 2006).

Insight into the exposure of MFIs to adverse market shocks has become more relevant due to the growing importance of microfinance as part of local financial systems of developing countries (Gonzalez, 2007: unpublished working paper) and the increased involvement of commercial investors in the microfinance sector in recent years. The latter are often more concerned about the risk of investments than traditional non-profit microfinance investors.

The current financial crisis provides an opportunity to test the resilience of MFI performance during a period of global market distress and to investigate the linkages through which today's microfinance sector is integrated into formal economies and financial systems. We empirically analyze a panel of monthly financial data of 57 MFIs worldwide covering the period from January 2007 through August 2009. Fixed effects regressions are used to study so-called 'structural breaks' in MFI performance indicators related to profitability, growth and portfolio quality. This analysis is complemented with the results of a survey among 82 MFI managers to explore the effects of the crisis on MFIs. It attempts to grasp the mechanisms through which the financial crisis affects MFI performance. We also examine whether the impact differs across MFIs in different regions and with different characteristics.

2. Background

Muhammad Yunus, perceived as 'the founder' of microfinance and winner of the Nobel Prize in 2005, stated that 'despite the turmoil on financial markets, microfinance still works' (Microcapital, 2008). This statement confirms the common understanding that MFIs exhibit little correlation with formal markets which is considered to be one of the reasons why commercial investors have been increasingly attracted to investments in microfinance (Deutsche Bank Research, 2007) and why equity of microfinance institutions should deserve a premium over traditional finance (J.P. Morgan, 2009).

There are several reasons for the common assumption of a low exposure of MFI performance to financial- and economic market movements. First, MFIs were traditionally capitalized through social funding provided by institutions such as government agencies, development banks and NGOs. Availability and cost of this type of funding has a lower correlation with business cycles and provides MFIs with continuous access to funding (e.g., Fonseca, 2004; Walter and Krauss, 2009). Second, the typical short maturities of microfinance loans in combination with the generally long maturities of MFIs' liabilities creates a favorable maturity mismatch (J.P. Morgan, 2009). This positive mismatch gives MFIs the flexibility to adjust in times of tight liquidity. Also when interest costs increase, MFIs can quickly adapt lending terms of outstanding loans. Third, the low financial and operational leverage of MFIs, compared to that of mainstream banks, results in low fixed costs. Operations can be scaled back at a low cost in times of economic downturn or tight liquidity. Fourth, MFIs' portfolio quality is often assumed to be resilient to adverse market shocks. This may be because MFIs can early signal bad repayment behavior, and because microfinance clients have high incentives to repay. Moreover, microfinance clients are considered to be quick adapters to changed conditions, and are often relatively isolated from the state of the formal economy. Indeed, demand for products from microenterprises may flourish in times of economic recession as consumers possibly buy domestically-produced cheaper products to substitute for luxury imported goods.

On the other hand, as Hermes and Meesters (2009: unpublished working paper) point out, macroeconomic conditions may affect clients in many different ways. During times of economic recession overall lower demand for products could also reduce business opportunities for small enterprises, in its turn diminishing demand for microfinance loans and deteriorating repayment capacity of borrowers. The net effect of a crisis is therefore an open empirical question, and the few academic studies focusing on the relation between MFI performance and performance of formal markets show mixed results. Some studies support the assumption of low exposure of MFI performance to international markets (Walter and Krauss, 2009) and domestic macroeconomic markets (Gonzalez, 2007: unpublished working paper). However, other studies reject the latter and find significant relationships (Ahlin, 2006: unpublished working paper; Hermes and Meesters, 2009: unpublished working paper). Nevertheless, these studies do not test for periods of distress on economic and financial markets. Case studies which did investigate this often show MFIs to be negatively affected. However, the impact differs across types of MFIs and some MFIs do indeed show resilience to adverse macroeconomic shocks (Patten *et al.*, 2001).

Microfinance today

The current era implies extra challenges for the MFI sector. Not only is the current crisis more severe and widespread than earlier downturns, there is also evidence that social funding sources have to deal with budget squeezes. Moreover, today's microfinance sector is changing. The sector has evolved in recent years, and has increased its integration into formal markets. The funding landscape of the microfinance industry changed, and many private and institutional investors have become interested in investing in lending to MFIs. During the period 2005-2008 the stake of these investors in microfinance increased from 14% to 41%. Commercial funding has made a major contribution to the recent growth and to the professionalization of the microfinance sector, but its involvement may have its downsides as well. Next to the concern that the involvement of commercially oriented investors will lead to mission drift, the increased integration of MFIs in formal domestic and international financial markets is expected to diminish the advantages of stable funding sources as the cost and availability of commercial funding is subject to business cycles and to investor attitudes towards microfinance. Moreover, the abundance of available capital and the eagerness of MFIs to grow may have relaxed risk management of liabilities, increasing average leverage ratios and foreign currency funding in recent years.

In addition, typical microfinance practices and characteristics on which many of the explanations behind the low exposure of MFIs to downside market risk are based, are rapidly changing (think of group lending, the provision of short term loans and serving clients whose business activities are decoupled from the formal economy). Increasingly MFIs serve higher segments with larger individual loans and lend to small and medium enterprises (SMEs). While microfinance was always known for its excellent portfolio quality, concerns are nowadays raised about the deterioration of this quality due to policies in favor of fast growth. Hence, many of the premises on which the assumed resilience of the microfinance sector was based may no longer be true in the current context.

3. Theoretical framework

Figure 1 reflects the channels through which the current crisis may have an impact on MFIs. It describes the causes and effects from the origin of the crisis to the potential impact on MFIs. For a detailed discussion of the various effects, refer to the M.Sc thesis of Huijsman (2010).

Profitability

Net interest margins, net operating income, non operating income and the loan loss provisioning expense are the determinants of the profitability of financial institutions. The crisis affects all these components. For example, the most important driver of MFI profitability is the net interest margin (or the difference between interest revenue and interest expense divided by total assets). Higher interest costs facing MFIs during the current crisis in combination with the inability (due to regulation) or reluctance (in conflict

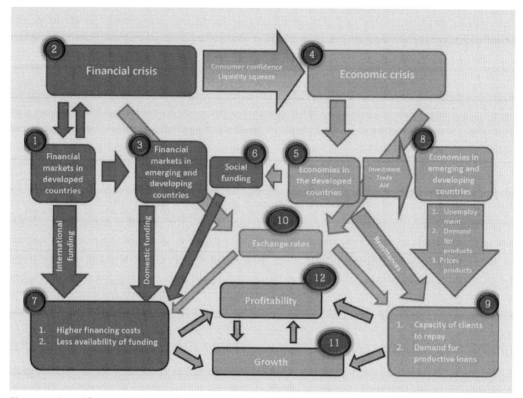

Figure 1. *Broad framework impact financial and economic crisis on microfinance institution performance.*

with social mission of MFIs) to pass these higher costs on to clients, implies MFIs' net interest margins come under pressure.

Portfolio quality

The repayment capacity of microfinance clients is probably negatively affected through a decline in remittances (thanks to contraction of economies in advanced countries). Moreover, we expect a negative impact on microfinance clients' income from business activities due to the increased integration of microfinance assets into formal markets and due to the nature of the current crisis.

Growth

Growth will be affected through an impact on both the demand for and the supply of loans. This constrains MFIs ability to expand its loan portfolio and client base. In addition, demand for loans is affected.

Across regions

Depending on how much the region is affected by the crisis (in its turn depending on the extent its financial sector and economy is integrated into the global economy); MFIs in different regions are expected to be affected to different extents by the crisis. We expect Eastern Europe & Russia to be most affected due to the direct impact on Russia and the features of the microfinance sector in this region.

Across MFIs

Institution specific characteristics, such as funding structure and lending practices, vary widely among MFIs. Based on these differences we expect the exposure of MFI performance to the crisis to differ. We expect MFIs attracting savings and being not very dependent on commercial funding to be less affected. Savings are considered to be a stable funding source, whereas commercial funding is expected to be most directly affected by the financial crisis. The impact of the crisis on repayment rates may also depend on the type of clients the MFI serves, sectors in which clients are employed, lending techniques used and loan products provided. These characteristics determine the extent to which clients are integrated into formal markets or incentives to repay.

4. Data and methodology

We investigated the impact of the current financial and economic crisis on MFIs' performance through two studies: (1) a survey among 82 MFI managers (a perception survey) and (2) a quantitative analysis of financial data of 57 MFIs (a financial performance study). The two studies are complementary: the empirical analysis of the financial data investigates whether performance of MFIs significantly changed during the current financial and economic crisis, while the survey among MFI managers enables us to analyze how the financial crisis is perceived to affect MFI performance.

Perception survey

The sample investigated in this part of the study is derived from the databases of SNS Asset Management, Developing World Markets and Triple Jump. We approached 160 MFI managers of which 84 responded. However, 2 MFIs returned the survey twice and hence 2 responses were eliminated leaving 82 MFIs for the analysis. It contains MFIs from all regions where microfinance plays a significant role. The questionnaire contains 47 questions motivated by earlier studies. The questionnaire was sent by e-mail in April 2009. Participants could take as much time as they needed. Most questions were multiple choice questions. The following categories were distinguished: general effects of the crisis, funding problems and effects on growth, operational expense ratio, loan loss ratio and net interest margins. The survey results are analyzed by computing respondents positively answering to a particular answer as a percentage of the total number of respondents or as a percentage of a certain subgroup. Moreover, we performed cross-tab analysis for some variables to analyze whether a significant relationship existed between effects felt by MFIs and particular characteristics of MFIs.

Financial performance study

We work with a panel of monthly data from 57 microfinance institutions which is part of the SNS Institutional Microfinance Fund (SIMF) and covers the period January 2007 until August 2009. We used profitability, asset quality and growth as performance indicators; all ratios so that we do not have to worry about currency differences. To analyze the impact of the crisis on the MFIs' financial performance, structural breaks in the time series of performance indicators over the period of study were identified. Fixed effects regressions were performed allowing the intercept in the regression model to differ cross-sectionally but not over time. Since it is not evident when the crisis started to have an impact, the structural break has been determined endogenously by performing regressions on all possible breaks (so-called rolling regressions). After we determined the structural breaks for all the performance indicators of interest we investigated whether the impact differed across regions, which we measured by generating interaction effects between the crisis-dummy and region dummies. Similarly, to explore whether MFIs with certain characteristics are more resistant (or more vulnerable) to economic or financial crises than others, we include an interaction term for the crisis dummy and different types of characteristics (as well as a regular characteristics variable).

5. Results

A large proportion (90%) of the 82 survey respondents reports to be affected by the current financial and economic crisis in some way. This is confirmed by the financial performance study. For all performance indicators a significant structural break is found. The signs of the coefficients, positive for portfolio quality and negative for profitability and growth, all point at an adverse effect in the period after the structural break. The timing of these breaks differ somewhat. They all occur in the period November 2008-March 2009, with the exception of the write-off ratio, of which the structural break does not occur until August 2009. Figure 2 presents the proportions of MFIs participating in our survey, which actually perceived their institutions to be affected by the main expected effects of the current financial crisis for MFIs.

Only a minority reported to have experienced direct funding problems, such as refinancing problems (16%) or problems to meet debt obligations (4%). The creation of emergency funds by development banks and governments provides financial support to MFIs with severe liquidity problems and is comparable to government support provided to banks in advanced economies. 7% used such a fund and another 8% expects to apply for emergency funding in 2009.

All MFIs experiencing negative effects of the financial crisis, took measures to limit the impact. Ninety-three per cent of MFIs increased their focus on portfolio quality which supports the notion that the crisis might offer an opportunity for MFIs to regain their focus on quality. To reduce risks, 55% focuses on the diversification of the outstanding loan portfolio. In contrast, some MFIs started to focus on particular types of loans which they perceive to be less risky, such as small loans and group loans and others focus on particular segments (such as clients employed in agriculture). Survey respondents are concerned about

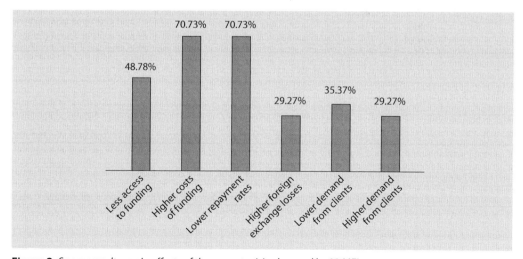

Figure 2. *Survey results: main effects of the current crisis observed by 82 MFIs.*

the risks of their liabilities as well. Sixty-two per cent reports to takes steps to increase diversification of their funding sources, and 35% to reduce the exposure to foreign exchange risk.

A more detailed analysis reveals that the financial crisis has had a clear negative impact on all performance measures for portfolio quality, growth and profitability. A structural negative shift of growth and profitability occurs in the last quarter of 2008. Results of our survey show that lower net interest margins, higher foreign exchange losses and the deterioration of repayment rates (through its impact on the loan loss provisioning expense) are putting pressure on profitability rates. Growth is in particular restricted by less availability of funding, a stricter lending policy and by lower loan demand from clients, although the impact on the latter is not unambiguous. Repayment rates experience an adverse impact of the crisis, becoming visible in November 2008, through the impact on the earliest indicator of portfolio quality followed by structural shifts in the time series of the other indicators of portfolio risk in March 2009 and of actual loan losses in August 2009. Survey respondents report the current macroeconomic situation, declined employment and lower remittances to be the main causes of the current deterioration of repayment rates. The significant adverse impact on all performance indicators and the underlying reasons provided by MFIs participating in the survey, demonstrate that on average MFI performance is substantially negatively affected by the current financial crisis.

Across regions

The impact of the crisis differs significantly across regions. Our financial performance study show MFIs from Eastern Europe & Russia to be most affected, which was not unexpected due to the direct impact of the current financial crisis on this region and due to the nature of the microfinance sector in this region. Also MFI performance in Central Asia & the Caucasus and Central America & the Caribbean was highly affected by the financial and economic crisis which could be explained by the geographical proximity of these regions to the affected economies of Russia and the United States. Performance of MFIs in South America is highly resilient. Portfolio quality of MFIs in this region may be controlled by the acute measures taken by South American MFIs in anticipation to the expected negative impact of the economic crisis on their clients' repayment behavior. Also MFIs in South- and South East Asia seem to feel a relative low impact from the crises possibly due to the quick revival of economies in this region.

Across MFIs

Our most pronounced finding is that savings make MFIs' portfolio quality more resilient to the impact of the current crisis, possibly by providing a financial cushion to microfinance clients in this economic difficult time. Moreover, MFIs most often perceive commercial funding to have become harder to obtain and to have become more expensive suggesting that MFIs relying on this type of funding suffer most. MFIs experiencing refinancing problems indeed rely all heavily on commercial funding, but an adverse impact on profitability of MFIs does not seem to increase in the dependence of the MFIs on commercial funding. Results show that a higher proportion of female clients reduces the impact at the early stages of the crisis whereas a high proportion of urban clients seems to increase the impact. However, these effects disappear if we look at later indicators of credit risk, implying that repayment rates of different types of clients are similarly affected in the course of the crisis. Lending through village banks seems to reduce the negative impact of the financial crisis on write-offs suggesting that eventual loan recovery through village banks is less affected in times of crisis. Lastly, survey respondents facing more than 10 competitors significantly more often report lower repayment rates due to the crisis than other MFIs.

6. Conclusions

Our main finding is that the microfinance sector is not as disconnected from formal markets as commonly assumed before the onset of the current financial crisis. Although microfinance institutions were not involved in the practices leading to the crisis, they are not insulated from its impact. Fixed effects regressions show that these effects became visible in the fourth quarter of 2008 when MFIs' profitability and monthly growth rates of loan portfolio and client base experienced a significant downward shift and when the first signs of a negative impact on portfolio quality started to occur. Our survey among 82 MFI managers confirms that the current financial crisis is perceived as the main influence putting pressure on MFIs' performance since 2008. The impact of the crisis manifested itself in higher funding costs, less availability of funding, an adverse impact on clients' repayment behavior and an impact on loan demand from clients. The impact differs highly across regions. Performance of MFIs in Eastern Europe & Russia is overall most affected whereas performance of MFIs in South America seems to be least affected. In addition, results indicate that a high proportion of savings reduces the exposure of portfolio quality to the impact of the crisis, providing evidence for the importance of savings for both clients and MFIs in times of market shocks.

A positive consequence of the crisis is that MFIs are now taking measures to enhance risk management on the liability side as well as on the asset side. This may imply that after the rapid growth experienced by MFIs during the past years, MFIs are in the process of restoring the good portfolio quality by which the sector was always characterized.

References

Deutsche Bank Research (2007). Microfinance an emerging investment opportunity:Uniting social investment and financial return. Available at: www.dbresearch.com. Accessed June 2009.

Huijsman, S., (2010). The impact of the current economic and financial crisis on microfinance, Msc. Thesis Corporate Finance, University of Groningen, the Netherlands.

Fonseca, D. (2004). Facing the Music: How to Survive in the Midst of Crisis. Microenterprise Americas. Available at: www.iadb.org. Accessed June 2009.

J.P. Morgan (2009). Shedding light on microfinance equity valuation: Past and Present. J.P. Morgan Global Research and CGAP. Available at: www.jpmorgan.com. Accessed August 2009.

Marconi, R. and Mosley, P. (2006). Bolivia During the Global Crisis 1998-2004: Towards a 'Macroeconomics of Microfinance'. Journal of Institutional Development 18: 237-261.

Microcapital (2008). Microcapital story: The Global Financial Crisis and Microfinance. Available at www.microcapital.org. Accessed July 2009.

Microcredit Summit Campaign (2009) State of the microcredit summit campaign report 2009. Available at: www.microcreditsummit.org. Accessed July 2009.

Patten, R.H., Rosengard, J.K. and Johnston D. (2001). Microfinance Success Amidst Macroeconomic Failure: The Experience of Bank Rakyat Indonesia During the East Asian Crisis. Preview. World Development 29: 1057-1069.

SNS Asset Management (2007). Overview 2007: Managing Abundant Growth. Annual Report SNS Institutional Microfinance Fund 2007.

Walter, I. and Krauss, N. (2009). Can Microfinance Reduce Portfolio Volatility? Economic Development and Cultural Change 58: 85-110.

Commodity futures markets as drivers of agriculture and agribusinesses in developing countries: what needs to be done?

Joost Pennings

Without futures contracts rooted in the least developed countries (LDCs), a sustainable development of efficient agricultural marketing channels in LDCs that create value for all channel members is impossible. A road map is needed that provides the necessary and sufficient conditions for successful commodity futures exchanges in LDCs.

Abstract

Price volatility in commodities translates more then ever into financial distress for producers in Least Developed Countries (LDCs). While risk management instruments, such as commodity futures contracts, exist for many commodities, these futures are unable to effectively reduce the risk for producers in LDCs. Here, a road map is proposed for developing commodity futures rooted in LDCs that ensures a sustainable development of efficient agricultural marketing channels in LDCs that create value for all channel members. The road map proposed uses a Marketing-Finance Approach that provides the necessary and sufficient conditions for successful commodity futures exchanges in LDCs.

Keywords: commodities, futures, hedging, poverty, least developed countries, risk

1. Introduction

Price volatility is the most important issue that farmers and agribusiness companies face in LDCs (Sapsford and Morgan, 1994). The reason is that, at the micro level, producers in LDCs have a relatively weak balance sheet. Hence, price risk translates quickly into financial risk (e.g., the chance of default). At the macro level, LDCs often rely on several commodities for their export earnings, making their national economy vulnerable to commodity price volatility.

Markets for agricultural products have become more globalized. The effects of agricultural market globalization on price volatility and the stability of income can be ambiguous. Globalization can cause prices to be less volatile in local markets that become linked through effective arbitrage, which reduces price differentials to transfer costs across space and time. In aggregate, this implies for farm incomes that quantity variations are compensated less by opposite price differences. On the other hand, integrated markets can reduce spatial diversification and heighten the implied market hedge between price and local yield. Price and income risk in agriculture are related to price and revenue risk in upstream and downstream industries. As supply chains become more important, the question arises where most of the price and income risk is located (Pennings *et al.*, 2010). This is particularly important for producers in

LDCs. Producers in LDCs have, on average, a low equity position; hence, their capacity to absorb price risk is limited. Pennings and Garcia (2005) show that the interaction between the individual's innovativeness and the time preference rate is crucial to begin understanding poverty. Investment in innovation can only be secured if profit risk is reduced and hence the risk-adjusted cost of capital. The time preference rate can be influenced when uncertainty about future (price) developments can be reduced. Both investments in (agricultural) innovation and time preference rates can be enhanced when channel members in the agricultural sector can manage their market risk effectively. The welfare effects are substantial, not only at the producer level but throughout the agribusiness sector. Since the agricultural sector is so important for LDCs, developing risk-management tools that fit the needs of producers in LDCs seems particularly important.

The importance of mitigating commodity price volatility in LDCs has been recognized by academic researchers as well as policy makers. Policies designed to reduce price risk have been in place since the 1930s, often in the form intervention programs. For example, Keynes (1938) suggested international buffer stocks to compensate for the low level of private storage in commodity markets. The establishment of 'buffer stock intervention' organizations (BSIO) was reinforced by International Commodity Agreements (e.g., Gordon-Ashworth, 1984). In the beginning (pre-World War II), the objective of BSIOs was to generate higher price levels for producers. Risk management in terms of reduced price volatility was merely a derived objective. In the 1960's -1970's, BSIOs focused more on reducing price volatility.

Nevertheless, BSIOs have not proven successful. Gilbert (1996) identified two main reasons for the death of BSIOs: (1) it proved to be impossible to set price ranges and to update these ranges over time in response to changes in the market place; (2) BSIOs were unable to secure sufficient funds to keep prices within the specified range. The question then arises which risk-management instruments might facilitate producers in LDCs to manage risk. Various authors (Morgan *et al.*, 1999; Petzel, 1985) have suggested that producers use futures contracts. However, successful futures exchanges that list commodity futures in LDCs are virtually non-existent.

In this paper, I will argue that commodity futures contracts can be interesting risk-management instruments for LDC producers. However, in order for producers in LDCs to benefit, futures contracts must be developed that provide a high level of hedging effectiveness (Pennings and Meulenberg 1997). The current futures contract listed in Developed Market Economies (DMEs) are not providing sufficient levels of hedging effectiveness (i.e., the spot risk reduction capacity of these futures contracts is relatively low). This paper addresses the issue of developing successful commodity futures contracts for LDCs. In addition to hedging effectiveness, the market microstructure of the commodity futures exchange, the financial- and transportation infrastructure, and the market advisory structure, amongst others, are key to the success of futures exchanges in LDCs. Furthermore, recognition is required that futures contracts are relatively complex financial instruments, the adoption of which by producers is not straightforward. This paper provides some guidance in establishing successful commodity futures contracts in LDCs that producers and agribusinesses can use to effectively manage their risk. First, I will explain how futures can be used to manage price risk. Subsequently, the risks that futures themselves introduce are discussed. In particular, basis risk and market-depth risk will be elaborated on. Futures will only be successful if producers adopt them as tool in their toolbox; hence, I will discuss the adoption process of producers of futures contracts and the role of market advisory services (MAS).

2. Commodity futures contracts: hedging effectiveness

A futures contract is a legally binding standardized agreement between two parties to buy or sell a predetermined quantity of a commodity during a specified delivery month at a price (the futures price) determined when a producer enters into the contract. The producer can reduce price risk by using the futures contract since a fall (rise) in the spot market will be partially offset by a rise (fall) in the value of the futures market position (compensation effect). Taking a position in the futures market to reduce spot market risk is referred to as hedging. There are two types of hedges: a short hedge and a long hedge. A short hedge is the selling of a futures contract to protect the sales price of a commodity in the future. A long hedge is the buying of a futures contract to protect the purchase price of a commodity in the future. In most cases farmers will liquidate the futures market position at the time they enter the spot market. The net price received (paid) is, in an ideal world, the price for which the farmer entered the futures market (because of the aforementioned compensation effect). Most farmers are able to liquidate or offset contracts prior to delivery. For instance, a grain producer can offset a short hedge by subsequently purchasing a contract with the same delivery month. While most contracts thus do not result in delivery, delivery for many agricultural contracts is possible and serves the purpose of keeping the prices of futures contracts in alignment with their underlying spot market, thus ensuring an effective hedge (i.e., high risk-reduction capacity). For a numerical example, please refer to Pennings *et al.* (2010) and Leuthold *et al.* (1989).

A futures contract will only be successful if it can be used to effectively reduce spot price risk. This so-called hedging effectiveness (the risk-reduction capacity of the futures contract) is driven by, amongst others, basis risk and market-depth risk. The fact that there will be a basis (i.e., the spot price minus the futures price at a particular point in time) at maturity of the futures contract is not necessarily a problem as long as it can be predicted. Unpredictability of the basis is referred to as basis risk, which reduces the hedging effectiveness of the futures contract, thus hampering success. To minimize the basis at maturity and to increase hedging effectiveness, market participants must be able to make or accept physical delivery at maturity, or the futures contract must be cash settled against a price that closely mimics the spot price at maturity (see Pennings and Meulenberg, 1997; Pennings *et al.*, 1998). In LDCs, basis risk is a challenge as the spot price in a particular location and for a particular grade may not always be known and, of utmost importance, arbitrage between spot and futures market may not be possible due to transportation problems (the spatial dimension of the basis). Hence, while futures markets are primarily 'paper markets' in which only a small percentage will be actually delivered, the fact that arbitrage is possible ensures low basis risk and thus high hedging effectiveness. Investments in transportation infrastructure are crucial to having futures contracts that truly reduce the spatial dimension of basis risk for LDCs producers and agribusiness companies. In addition, hedging effectiveness is influenced by liquidity (also referred to as slippage, e.g., Marsh *et al.*, 2007). Liquidity plays a crucial role when developing a futures contract and has many dimensions (e.g., Pennings *et al.*, 1998). Here, we focus on market depth: the extent to which market participants can buy (go long) or sell (go short) without changing the equilibrium price. Market-depth costs, the costs that a market participant faces because (s)he cannot trade all his futures against the equilibrium price, are a serious issue in newly developed futures contracts. Pennings *et al.* (1998) modeled market depth by examining the price path due to order imbalances and derived a two-dimensional market-depth measure. The first dimension represents the distance between the upper and lower bounds, i.e. how far prices fall (rise) due to a lack of market depth. The second dimension indicates the rate at which prices fall or rise. The market microstructure (the structure of the futures market itself) influences both dimensions of market depth and deals with the process and outcomes of exchanging commodity futures under a specific set of rules. These rules refer to, for example, trading hours, (daily) price limits, and types of market participants allowed to trade (insiders versus speculators). Financial regulation at the national level and the level of the exchange is crucial for market depth and hence hedging effectiveness.

3. Risk management needs and behavior

So far, we have discussed so-called financial factors regarding the development of commodity futures contracts. While these financial factors provide us with the necessary conditions for successful commodity futures contracts, these are not sufficient conditions. To obtain a sufficient set of conditions for success, a marketing approach is required as well. The marketing approach tries to provide an answer to the question whether the hedging services as provided by the futures exchange are able to satisfy the needs of potential customers. Since alternative products or services are usually available to the producer, marketing devotes much of its attention to the customer's decision-making process. Knowing how producers reach a decision and why they decide as they do provides clues on how to market the hedging service. Since needs constitute the starting point in marketing, let us first elaborate on the need for hedging.

The total set of producers (i.e., potential hedgers) needs with respect to a futures contract can be differentiated into instrumental needs and convenience needs. The producer will choose that 'risk-reduction service' (futures, options, cash forwards, etc.) which best satisfies his or her total set of needs, both instrumental and convenience, at an acceptable price. *Instrumental needs* are hedgers' needs for price risk reduction. Hedgers wish to reduce, or, if possible, eliminate portfolio risks at low cost. There are several different ways of managing price risks. The instrumental needs are related to the *core service* of the futures market, which consists of reducing price variability to producers. These instrumental needs express themselves through hedgers taking a hedge position in the futures market. For example, a farmer who is highly risk-averse may satisfy this need by hedging systematically all products that carry risk (therewith choosing a hedge ratio of 1). Not only do producers wish to reduce price risk, they also want to use the core service provided by the exchange with relative ease. This includes needs such as flexibility in doing business and an efficient clearing system, the so-called *convenience needs*. The service offering is therefore not restricted to the core service but is complemented by so-called peripheral services. These core plus peripheral services constitute the augmented service offering. An example of a futures market's peripheral service is the efficient and correct conclusion of transactions.

Both types of needs must be met for the futures market to be successful. In order to indicate which futures market division mainly satisfies the instrumental needs and which the convenience needs, I will first briefly review the business organization of the futures market. The futures market can be divided into two identities, namely: the 'floor' and the 'clearing house'. The 'floor' is where the actual transactions take place. Note that the term 'floor' should no longer be taken literally as there are floorless futures markets these days, where the traditional trading floor has been replaced with an electronic trading system. On the floor, the brokers execute customers' orders. Therefore, the floor can be seen as the place where mainly instrumental needs are being met. After all, the execution of an order means a hedge position has been taken in the futures market, which reduces the customer's price risk. After the execution has taken place, the clearing house takes care of the financial settlement and, in the case of actual delivery, makes sure that the commodities delivered meet the contract specifications. Therefore, the clearing house can be said mainly to meet convenience needs.

To understand how to meet these needs by introducing commodity futures, it is necessary to know *how* farmers choose between risk management alternatives and how the attributes of futures contracts and the market microstructure of the exchange are valued by farmers. Hence, a deep understanding of the adoption process of futures by farmers is needed. Pennings and Leuthold (2000) showed that the revealed adoption process of futures is a two-stage procedure. In the first stage, producers consider whether futures are a part of their toolbox (the so-called evoked set). During this stage, risk attitude, perceived ease of use, and the price-risk reduction capacity of futures contracts (i.e., hedging effectiveness) play an important role in addition to the opinion of the producer's advisors (e.g., accountant and/or banker) (Pennings and Garcia, 2010). In the second stage, after futures have been established as an element of the producer's toolbox, the producer decides whether to initiate a position in the futures market. In this stage, risk attitude, the producer's reference price, i.e., the price in the producer's memory that serves as a benchmark for judging and comparing prices (e.g., Pennings, 2002) and the futures price play dominant roles (Pennings and Leuthold, 2000).

4. The role of the decision making unit of producers in LDCs

Knowledge of the futures market's risks, of hedging effectiveness, and of its drivers is crucial. Here too, producers in LDCs should actively look for this knowledge and researchers should actively reach out to share new insights. Agricultural organizations, banks, ministries of agriculture, and particularly MAS all have a facilitating role in this process. In order to assume that role, however, these organizations will have to acquire this knowledge first. Moreover, knowledge alone is not sufficient: farmers should also be capable of actually implementing their own risk-management strategies. To this end, financial service providers, futures markets and banks should offer them an infrastructure, starting with the design of futures contracts with a high hedging effectiveness.

The successful development of new risk-management instruments, such as futures contracts, should be initiated by LDCs as futures exchanges often remain passive regarding the development of new futures in the agricultural complex. Due to a lack of domain-specific knowledge, they often find it difficult to determine the existing needs and develop contract specifications that maximize hedging effectiveness. In short, exchanges tend to be tentative: only when a sector indicates an interest in futures trade, does the exchange start developing a product.

In order to develop successful futures contracts, the following parties should cooperate closely: agriculture, the liquidity providers (i.e., market makers), brokers and the exchange. Each party should have its own role in the cooperation: the exchange offers the trading platform and financial clearing; the market makers ensure a market where bid and ask prices are not too far apart, thus contributing to a higher degree of liquidity; and the brokers collect the different orders and market the 'product', i.e., the futures contract, to its potential users. The most important role, however, is played by the agricultural sector: it identifies the needs and, based on these needs and knowledge of the spot market, it subsequently develops a contract specification which, among others, minimizes basis risk.

Finally, an infrastructure needs to be in place which offers farmers the opportunity to actually use risk-management instruments, where the results of these transactions are directly linked to the other financial results of that farmer. Laying this infrastructure is difficult in many LDCs since the banking infrastructure itself still requires much effort. Also, many bankers are as yet unfamiliar with agricultural risk-management instruments and are deterred by the risks they may generate when not well designed and or not properly used.

5. Complexity of futures contracts: the need for market advisory services in LDCs

Several researchers identified a trend towards outsourcing and have indicated increased firm reliance on external consultants in operational capacities (Henderson, 1990; Venkatesan, 1992). In the context of risk management in LDCs, Marketing Advisory Services (MAS) are crucial (Ortmann *et al.*, 1993). MAS are specialized companies that provide producers with recommendations regarding selling their crops. Their recommendations include when to sell and how to sell, for instance, selling crops forward by means of futures and options or in the spot market. Farmers in the US are known to place a high value on market advisory services as a source of price-risk management information and advice.

Market advisory services first began to emerge in the U.S. in the mid-1970s, following the steep increase in commodity prices due to several extreme and highly unusual developments that contributed to historic market volatility. The first companies geared toward giving specific marketing advice emerged. The early MAS were created in order to provide farmers with marketing information in an environment of increased market volatility. Since the incipient phase, MAS have generally gone through four evolutionary stages:
- *Stage I:* providing fundamental and technical market information, newsletters, and marketing tool seminars;
- *Stage II:* providing specific marketing recommendations in addition to stage I services;
- *Stage III:* providing electronic access, and;
- *Stage IV:* providing individual electronic access via e-mail and the Internet, as well as offering 'customized' marketing recommendations for individual clients (e.g., Isengildina *et al.*, 2006).

Overall, MAS may be described as firms whose primary business is to provide marketing information to farmers in order to help them decide how, when, and where to market their crops and livestock. As noted above, the central focus of advisory services is on providing market information, analysis, and specific marketing recommendations to subscribers. Related services often provided by such firms include market and government policy information, seminars on marketing tools and techniques, and, in some cases, speculative futures and options trading advice. Marketing recommendations range from the relatively simple (e.g., sell 50% of 2010 soybean production today in the cash market) to the highly complex (e.g., spot, futures and options strategies).

Today, the market advisory service industry in the DMEs (e.g., U.S) is approaching maturity For example, in a rating of seventeen risk-management information sources, Patrick and Ullerich (1996) reported that MAS were outranked only by farm records and computerized information services. Schroeder *et al.* (1998) found that a sample of Kansas farmers ranked MAS as the number one source of information for developing price expectations. Davis and Patrick (2000) reported that marketing consultants had the largest impact on the use of forward pricing by US soybean producers. Norvell and Lattz (1999) found that, in a list of seven, marketing consultants tied with accountants as likely to be most important to Illinois farmers in the future.

For LDCs, MAS are even more important than in DME since the knowledge infrastructure is less developed in LDCs. Stimulating the development of (commercial) MAS in LDCs is crucial for the adoption of futures by producers or producer groups (e.g., cooperatives).

6. Concluding thoughts

The welfare effect of futures contracts and futures exchanges that serve LDCs' agriculture must not be underestimated. Futures contracts may positively impact two of the key drivers of poverty as identified by Pennings and Garcia (2005), innovativeness and time-preference rate. In addition, the establishment of a futures exchange has positive spill-over effects to the overall economy. Powers and Tosini (1977) argued that commodity exchanges in LDCs serve as multiplier-type institutions that provide linkages useful to the development of an economy. For example, a commodity exchange contributes to the savings-investment flow and the capital stock (e.g., the clearing house effect) and reinforces bank structures. The success of futures contracts is, amongst others, driven by their hedging effectiveness, i.e., their risk-reduction capacity. To obtain high hedging effectiveness, basis risk and market-depth risk need to be small. The design of the futures contract and the microstructure of the market are crucial in this respect. Moreover, the choice behavior of all market participants regarding the attributes of the futures contract needs to be understood. In addition, the physical transportation system must be in place to ensure arbitrage possibilities between the spot and futures market. Powers and Toshini (1977) also indicate the importance of a fast and efficient communication network, grades, standards and quality control, a financial system capable of supporting capital transfer, and a legal system that recognizes and enforces the rights and duties embodied in contracts.

Future contracts are able to reduce risk in agricultural marketing channels and as such decreases the risk adjusted cost of capital at a channel level (Kuwornu *et al.*, 2009). It is important that futures contracts are rooted in least developed countries to obtain a sustainable development of efficient agricultural marketing channels in LDCs that create value for all channel members. Within LDCs, producers, banks, market makers, and government must work together to further develop and execute a road map that provides the necessary and sufficient conditions for successful commodity futures exchanges in LDCs. They can only work together if the knowledge gap that currently exists with these stakeholders is eliminated. In this context, supra-governmental bodies (e.g., the World Bank and the IMF) as well as commercial MAS have important roles to play in the future.

References

Davis, T.D. and Patrick, G.F. (2000). Forward Marketing Behavior of Soybean Producers. Selected paper presented at the American Agricultural Economics Association annual meetings, July 30-August 2, Tampa, Florida.

Gilbert, C.J. (1996). International Commodity Agreements: An Obituary Notice. World Development 24: 1-19.

Gordon-Ashworth, F. (1984). International Commodity Control: A Contemporary History and Appraisal. Croom Helm, Beckenham, UK.

Henderson, J.C. (1990). Plugging into strategic partnerships: The critical IS connection. Sloan Management Review 31: 7-18.

Isengildina, O., Pennings, J. M.E., Irwin, S.H. and Good, D.L. (2006). U.S. Crop Farmers' Use of Market Advisory Services. Journal of International Food & Agribusiness Marketing 18: 65-84.

Keynes, J.M. (1938). The Policy of Government Storage of Food-Stuffs and Raw Materials. The Economic Journal 48: 449-460.

Kuwornu, J.K.M., Kuiper, W.E. and Pennings, J.M.E. (2009). Agency Problem and Hedging in Agri-Food Chains: Model and Application. Journal of Marketing Channels (special issue: Managing Risks and Disruptions in Global Supply Chains) 16: 265-289.

Leuthold, R.M., Cordier, J.E. and Junkus, J.C. (1989). The Theory and Practice of Futures Markets. Lexington Books, Lanham, MD, USA.

Marsh, J.W., Pennings, J.M.E. and Garcia, P. (2007). Perceptions of Futures Market Liquidity: An Empirical Study of CBOT and CME Traders. Chapter 8. In: B.A. Goss (ed.), Debt, Risk and Liquidity in Futures Markets. Routledge, London and New York, pp. 171-190.

Morgan, C.W., Rayner, A.J. and Vaillant, C. (1999). Agricultural futures markets in LDCs: a policy response to price volatility? Journal of International Development 11: 893-910.

Norvell, J.M. and Lattz, D.H. (1999). Value-Added Crops, GPS Technology and Consultant Survey: Summary of a 1998 Survey to Illinois Farmers. University of Illinois, College of Agricultural, Consumer and Environmental Sciences, Working Paper, July 1999.

Ortmann, G.F., Patrick, G.F, Musser, W.N. and Doster, D.H. (1993). Use of private consultants and other sources of information by large cornbelt farmers. Agribusiness: An International Journal 9: 391-402.

Patrick, G.F. and Ullerich, S. (1996). Information Sources and Risk Attitudes of Large-Scale Farmers, Farm Managers, and Agricultural Bankers. Agribusiness: an International Journal 12: 461-471.

Pennings, J.M.E. (2002). Pulling the Trigger or Not: Factors Affecting Behavior of Initiating a Position in Derivatives Markets. Journal of Economic Psychology 23: 263-278.

Pennings, J.M.E. and Garcia, P. (2005). The Poverty Challenge: How Individual Decision-Making Behavior Influences Poverty. Economics Letters 88: 115-119.

Pennings, J.M.E. and Garcia, P. (2010). Risk & Hedging Behavior: The Role and Determinants of Latent Heterogeneity. Journal of Financial Research (in press).

Pennings, J.M.E., Garcia, P. and Oskam, A.J. (2010). Private Market and Price Stabilization Methods. In: A.J. Oskam, G. Meester and H. Silvis (eds.), EU Policy for Agriculture, Food and Rural Areas. Wageningen Academic Publishers, Wageningen, the Netherlands, pp. 181-187.

Pennings, J.M.E., Kuiper, W.E , Ter Hofstede, F. and Meulenberg, M.T.G. (1998). The Price Path Due to Order Imbalances: Evidence from the Amsterdam Agricultural Futures Exchange. European Financial Management 4: 47-64.

Pennings, J.M.E. and Leuthold, R.M. (2000). The Role of Farmers' Behavioral Attitudes and Heterogeneity in Futures Contracts Usage. American Journal of Agricultural Economics 82: 908-919.

Pennings, J.M.E. and Meulenberg, M.T.G. (1997). Hedging Efficiency: A Futures Exchange Management Approach. Journal of Futures Markets 17: 599-615.

Petzel, T.E. (1985). International Use of U.S. Futures Markets: Discussion. American Journal of Agricultural Economics 67: 999-1001.

Powers, M.J. and Toshini, P. (1977). Commodity Futures Exchanges and the North-South Dialogue. American Journal of Agricultural Economics 59: 977-985.

Sapsford, D. and Morgan, C.W. (1994). The Economics of Primary Commodities. Edward Elgar, Aldershot, UK.

Schroeder, T.C., Parcell, J.L., Kastens, T. and Dhuyvetter, K.C. (1998). Perceptions of Marketing Strategies: Farmers Versus Extension Economists. Journal of Agricultural and Resource Economics 23: 279-293.

Venkatesan, J. (1992). Strategic Sourcing: To Make or Not to Make. Harvard Business Review 70: 98-107.

Part 4.

The role of marketing research: past, present and future

Marketing's promise to development

Paul Ingenbleek

Marketing can provide a unique contribution to development thinking. Recent developments in marketing theory help to remember that marketing is inherently part of the solution rather than part of the problem.

'In the "underdeveloped" countries of the world ... marketing is treated with neglect, if not with contempt. ... It is generally the most backward of all areas of economic life. Marketing is also the most effective engine of economic development, particularly in its ability rapidly to develop entrepreneurs and managers.'

Peter F. Drucker, 1958.

Abstract

Marketing is often associated with negative side effects that may be detrimental for development, like price pressure and unfair distributions of rents. The marketing concept as it was developed shortly after the Second World War, however, holds a promise to development: marketing enables entrepreneurs to efficiently make use of all available purchasing power by segmenting consumers on the basis of their wants and needs. Because mainstream marketing research has over the past two decades strengthened its connections with the marketing concept, it is increasingly useful as a source of inspiration for development research. Marketing research may help to increase the understanding of responsiveness to customer wants and needs on consumer and business markets. Responsiveness can be studied at the level of individual entrepreneurs, the level of value chains that connect producers to final consumers, and on the level of marketing systems that also include institutions, NGOs, standard-formulating organizations, governments, and other third parties. Specific directions for research are suggested on each of these levels.

Keywords: marketing, market integration, market access, value chains, supply chains, consumers, corporate social responsibility, standards, certification, niche marketing

1. Introduction

Following in Aad van Tilburg's footsteps means following in footsteps that left their prints in many countries. Most of these countries have in common that they were relatively poor and that at least some part of underdevelopment was attributed to weak functioning markets. In his contribution to this book, Van Tilburg describes the developments over the past three decades in the theories and approaches that he and his colleagues applied to better understand development issues. The chapter makes clear that marketing theory and development were not always easy to connect. It required creativity and an exploration of theories to provide meaningful contributions as a marketing researcher to development issues.

Development is an interdisciplinary field of study consisting of among others development economists, rural sociologists, food technologists, macro economists, agronomists, and ecologists. Marketing researchers have traditionally played a minor role in this field (Ingenbleek and Van Tilburg 2009). It is not unlikely that the Marketing and Consumer Behavior Group in Wageningen is the only marketing research group with a permanent staff position that is for the greater part dedicated to development. The contribution of marketing research, therefore, cannot be taken for granted. Sooner or later marketing researchers will be confronted with the question what marketing's unique contribution is to development.

More than one answer exists to this question. The marketing discipline has changed over the past decades and I believe that these developments have also changed the potential contribution of marketing to the development field. Therefore, I would like to use this essay to discuss the proposition that marketing, as an academic discipline, has the potential to make a unique contribution to development and that the momentum is now to do so. In the following, I will refer to marketing as an academic discipline, as marketing research. Marketing research should not be confused with marketing as a business function or with market research, which is applied research on customers and competitors.

In the following, I will first describe some of the significant changes in marketing and their implications for the relation between marketing and development. Next, I will describe directions in which marketing research may make contributions to development thinking over the next years. The essay finishes with a brief conclusion.

2. Marketing: from part of the problem to part of the solution

The first association that many people have with marketing and development is that marketing is detrimental to development. Likewise, not everything that marketing research has to offer is equally useful for development purposes. Especially in the 1950s to 1980s, the greater share of marketing research followed a marketing management approach with behavioral and quantitative sciences as keys to knowledge development (see Wilkie (2005) for a more elaborate description of the development of marketing research). Researchers studied, for example, the optimal use of marketing instruments such as the four P's (Products, Price, Place and Promotion) that intended to push products through distribution channels meanwhile creating a pull on consumer markets through promotion and price actions. The focus of these studies was almost exclusively on marketing in North America and Western Europe. The research fitted a business landscape that was characterized by large divisional enterprises that considered their external environment as hostile and therefore tried to keep as many activities as they could within the boundaries of their own firms (Jones, 1996).

Through these push and pull strategies, marketing's contribution to society was often considered to be negative. Marketing was seen as a force that makes people's short-term wants and needs more salient, even at the expense of their long-term interests. The anti-globalist movement accused marketing among others of generating low prices that didn't cover all social and environmental costs for primary producers, of wasting resources for package material, of creating demand for products that are not in the interest of consumers (think for example of eating consumption disorders like obesity), and of pushing the Western consumption culture to non-Western societies (Witkowski, 2005).

In this context, marketing in the developing world was fundamentally different from marketing in Western markets. And most of the work on marketing in Western countries was probably of little use to marketing researchers in developing countries. The situation started however to change in the 1990s. The business landscape changed after former Communist countries opened up their markets, and with the emergence of new information and communication technologies. Confronted with intensified competition and international trade, companies returned to their core business. International business changed into a complex network in which the origin of products and the circumstances under which they were produced was often difficult to trace (Jones, 1996).

Academic marketing research responded to these developments by paying more attention to specific fields like business-to-business marketing and services marketing. The field fragmented and from the fragmentation, researchers started to search for new generalizations on the success factors of marketing. New concepts like relationship marketing and market orientation were seen as drivers of the creation of customer value. Customer value, in turn, was seen as the basis for customer satisfaction, which leads to market behaviors like repurchase, loyalty, and positive word of mouth. These behaviors subsequently yield superior financial performance (and shareholder value). From these 'home grown' ideas, new marketing perspectives and theories emerged, like resource-advantage theory (Hunt and Morgan, 1995) and service-dominant logic (Vargo and Lusch, 2004).

Returning to the marketing concept

Most of these new concepts and theories can be traced back to the marketing concept. The marketing concept, merely developed in the 1930s to 1950s, can be seen as the foundation of the marketing discipline. It holds that companies should develop a deep and accurate understanding of customer wants and needs. For example, a manufacturer of fruit juices is from a marketing perspective not in the business of making juice, but rather in the business of providing solutions to thirst, indulgence and maybe health.

Peter Drucker was a major contributor to the marketing concept. He was among others the author of 39 books (most of them management books, but also two novels, a biography and a co-authored book on Japanese painting), professor, consultant, columnist for the Wall Street Journal, and maker of 8 educational management films. In 1957, he received a prestigious award from the American Marketing Association for his contribution to the marketing field. His acceptance speech was entirely devoted to the role of marketing in development. The speech was subsequently published in the Journal of Marketing because of (as the editor formulated), 'the great significance of Mr. Drucker's remarks.'

Drucker (1958) expressed his concerns with regard to the increasing 'international and interracial inequality' as he called it. Whereas in earlier times, economic inequality was predominantly present within countries, Drucker recognized an emerging divide between countries that were becoming richer and countries that became poorer. He approached poverty as a consequence of poorly functioning economic systems, and marketing, he believed, was the key function to improve the economic system.

Drucker claims that developing countries have, like any other country, a demand that is characterized by different customer preferences. Marketing can unlock this latent demand by offering more differentiated products catered to more specific wants and needs. Once this gets organized in a marketing system, organic growth starts because the available purchasing power is used more effectively. This function of marketing 'cannot, by itself, create purchasing power. But it can uncover and channel all purchasing power that exists.

It can, therefore, create rapidly the conditions for a much higher level of economic activity than existed before, can create the opportunities for the entrepreneur' (Drucker, 1958: 156).

As Drucker pointed out, the marketing concept predicts an inherent positive contribution of marketing to development. Being related to the marketing concept, much of the research that is currently carried out in marketing is therefore easier to connect to development than it was in the past. In fact, the theories, concepts, and research techniques that are nowadays developed in mainstream marketing may be a source of inspiration to further examine the interconnections between marketing and development.

Unlocking demand from local, regional, and foreign high-income markets stimulates development only if marketing systems, and in particular, entrepreneurs in these systems are responsive to that demand. Marketing researchers can make a contribution to development by enhancing our understanding of responsiveness to customer wants and needs. Specifically, marketing research can contribute to (1) responsiveness of individual actors like entrepreneurs, managers or other decision-makers, (2), responsiveness of value chains, and (3) responsiveness of the marketing system as a whole, including the effectiveness of institutions that may support or inhibit responsiveness.

3. Entrepreneurial responsiveness

In the development discussion, there is a growing attention for the integration of producers from developing countries with high income markets. Market integration is hoped to support development because revenues are expected to flow in the direction of primary producers, enabling them to hire workers, invest in quality, and pay for consumer goods and their children's education. On a macro level, this will lead to a stronger connection of developing countries to export markets, which will make hard foreign currencies flow into the countries. Primary producers entering value chains that are oriented to high income markets, however enter a market where they might compete on a global scale and that often requires specific investments. Whether integration with international markets is the best option for primary producers in the longer term, is still an open question.

On the level of the entrepreneur, marketing can make a meaningful contribution to market integration thinking. Market integration, is frequently conceptualized as the amount of agricultural produce that is commercialized versus the amount that is consumed by the farmer's household. Market integration does not, however, tap the degree to which producers respond to new insights in customer wants and needs through innovation and specialization. This is where market orientation may come in. Kohli and Jaworski (1990), for example, define market orientation as the organization-wide acquisition, dissemination of and responsiveness to market intelligence pertaining to current and potential customers and competitors. A meta-analysis on over 200 correlations between market orientation constructs and business performance measures shows that overall, market orientation has a positive and significant impact on business performance (Kirca *et al.*, 2005). A key question is whether this concept is applicable to developing countries. If it is applicable, it would be interesting to test the hypothesis that market integration leads to better livelihoods of primary producers under the condition that producers and other actors in the system are sufficiently market oriented.

4. Chain responsiveness

Responsiveness to markets is not limited to the level of entrepreneurs or companies. Value chains connect producers in developing countries with the wants and needs and purchasing power of consumers. As interlinked sets of subsequent actors, value chains may make it more difficult to unlock purchasing power for development, because market feedback may get distorted or lost in the communication and negotiations between chain members. Traditionally, marketing research has contributed to the understanding of value chain responsiveness by studying the functioning of local markets and applying theories like transaction cost economics to chain relationships. These approaches help to explain why chains fail to respond to the opportunities that consumers in principle offer them. Whereas such work remains relevant, it can be complemented by two other directions of research on chain responsiveness.

First, marketing researchers can contribute more recent theories and concepts that help to understand the functioning of local and regional marketing systems, such as customer satisfaction, relationship marketing and word of mouth. Because these concepts are relatively generic, they seem to apply reasonably well to daily practices at markets in developing countries. Many entrepreneurs in developing countries have established relationships of trust and commitment with suppliers or customers, and may have found that these may help to achieve customer satisfaction, repurchase, loyalty, and good reputations that eventually help to improve livelihoods. These concepts may, among others, be helpful to understand how and when innovations in governance mechanisms help to improve chain responsiveness (see for example Kambewa, 2007).

Second, marketing researchers may contribute market research methods and techniques that help to uncover wants and needs in chains. The potential of these studies is not limited to consumer markets, because customers on business markets (like traders, processors, and retailers) often have additional wants and needs with regard to product specifications that help them to fulfill their roles in the system (think for example of freshness to increase shelf-life or firmness to decrease damage during transportation). They are also not limited to high income export markets. Developing local and regional markets may be an interesting option for producers in developing countries because these markets generally have lower entry barriers than most foreign markets and the available purchasing power on local and regional markets is in many cases not yet maximized in favor of the local or regional economy. Market research techniques as they are used in high income countries can be adapted to the context of developing countries so that they become less dependent on, for examples, formal sampling frames, educated respondents, and single languages.

5. Responsiveness of marketing systems

There is a growing interest of development researchers for the larger systems in which primary producers from developing countries are embedded. Rather than studying the individual decisions of primary producers only, attention focuses increasingly on the interrelationships within an entire system consisting of primary producers, other private parties, like traders, processors and exporters, as well as public actors like governments, NGOs, and organizations that are constellations of different stakeholders themselves, like certifiers and standard-formulating organizations (Ingenbleek and Immink, 2010).

These perspectives further complicate the understanding of responsiveness to markets, because they imply that responsiveness is not only the result of the market orientation of the individual value chain members and relationships between the members, but it depends also on the interactions between the institutions and value chain members. Marketing research can contribute to the responsiveness of such systems to the market, beyond the contributions to the responsiveness of entrepreneurs and chains. More specifically, I distinguish three additional directions of research: (1) the effectiveness of institutions, (2) the design of systems that connect niche segments of consumers from high income countries to producers from developing countries, and (3) corporate social responsibility.

The role of institutions

Entrepreneurial and chain responses to consumers' wants and needs cannot be generated in developing countries, without also paying close attention to the institutional environment. Traditionally, the development literature pays substantial attention to absence and failure of institutions (Fafchamps, 2004). The institutional landscape is however changing rapidly. The traditional focus on Governments' institutions that accompanied or replaced indigenous (like clan-based) institutions, is now accompanied by a focus on international business as a force that implements institutions. The new institutions are, for example, standards, farmer field schools, trainings, and workshops. The total sets of institutions that have been created by all these groups to help entrepreneurs and other decision-makers may have contradictory effects on development. Institutions may be overlapping, they may be rudimentary responses to social pressures that no longer exist, and they may have negative side effects such as making entrepreneurs more similar rather than more responsive (so called 'isomorphism'). As a result, they may guide entrepreneurs in conflicting or wrong directions. Marketing research may help to investigate the effectiveness of (combinations of) existing and new institutions in enhancing entrepreneurs' responsiveness to customers' wants and needs.

Consumer niche markets

Marketing research may help systems to respond to new opportunities that emerge from increasing transparency. With the intensification of globalization and increasing transparency, barriers are removed to move goods and money between developing countries and high income markets, to inform consumers about the origins of products, and to create an understanding of consumer wants and needs among producers. This creates new opportunities for development. Specific market segments of consumers in high income markets are interested in information about the origins of products and are willing to pay higher prices for products with origins that they prefer. Unlocking the demand from these market niches requires a systems approach, rather than a chain approach. Two of these groups are 'Diaspora' consumers and ethically concerned consumers.

'Diaspora' consumers are emigrants from developing countries who have moved abroad, generally seeking or responding to new opportunities. With the intensification of globalization, this trend has become more significant. In many cases, these consumers still have strong emotional, cultural, and social ties with their home country. This is expressed in their wants and needs, characterized by a preference for products from their home countries, and a continuation of cultural habits in consumption patterns that may last for many generations. Especially the people that moved to high income economies and managed to climb up to middle and high income classes of these societies are an opportunity for development. Marketing research can examine the preferences of these consumers to design systems that connect consumers to producers, and unlock the demand in favor of poverty reduction and sustainable development.

Ethically motivated consumers do not necessarily have ties with a country of origin, but feel an intrinsic motivation to express their concerns with regard to environmental and social sustainability in purchase decisions. These consumers typically have preferences for Fair Trade and Organic products. A study in the US has shown that a small percentage of consumers are susceptible to such positive claims on social responsibility (Sen and Bhattacharya, 2001). Most of these market segments have reached their natural growth limits in terms of size, but marketing research can still contribute to maintain this demand by examining how consumer loyalty can be strengthened when responsible brands are confronted with mainstream competitors that also start using Fair Trade and Organic ingredients. Part of the solution may be the development of systems in which consumers can make a more transparent contribution at the forefront of sustainable development than consumers of mainstream brands. The organic sector has, for example, experimented with strategies in which consumers could 'adopt' apple trees and chicken, and then later collect the apples or eggs. Because the boundaries between donations and consumption are fading in these initiatives, the development of these strategies requires a systems approach rather than a chain approach.

Corporate social responsibility

Beyond the specific market segments described above, most consumers are unlikely to actively search for information about the origins of products. However, also systems oriented to mainstream market segments that are catered by major brands and retailers, can benefit from increasing transparency. Because nearly all consumers are susceptible no negative information on social responsibility (Sen and Bhattacharya, 2001), they are likely to respond to unfair or unsustainable practices. The consequences of these responses may hit hard on the reputation of the companies in which consumers put their trust. When firms no longer control the information flow about themselves and their brands, companies increasingly allocate budgets for Corporate Social Responsibility (CSR) projects not in *reaction to*, but *to prevent* reputation damage. Rather than being dependent on incidental project budgets, CSR activities now receive structural support from the marketing and communication budgets in companies, suddenly creating a new opportunity for development.

The increase of CSR budgets has given a boost to standard-formulation and certification processes and led to new connections between companies, standard-formulating organizations, certifiers, and primary producers. Marketing research may help to understand the strategies that organizations pursue in the evolving systems and the impact of these strategies on actors in developing countries. The sharp increase in demand for certified produce puts pressure on the system. As a consequence, new risks of institutional failures emerge, like noncompliance, corruption, and other unforeseen negative side effects. If these risks result in actual scandals they may backfire on the companies that invested their CSR budgets in certification. Marketing research may contribute to minimize these risks by conducting consumer studies that examine how 'forgiving' consumers are with respect to specific potential risks and which precautionary measures may prevent reputation damage in case of institutional failures.

6. Conclusion

Although marketing is often associated with negative side effects that may be detrimental for development, the marketing concept holds a promise to development, i.e. that differentiated wants and needs of consumers provide opportunities for entrepreneurs and companies. Marketing research may support development by creating a better understanding on how marketing systems (including producers, other entrepreneurs and companies, as well as supporting institutions) can respond more effectively to customer wants and needs. Because mainstream marketing research has recently strengthened its connections with the marketing concept, it may increasingly function as a source of inspiration to development research.

In the years to come, I intend to make contributions that marketing research promises to development. I look forward to build on and extend the numerous relationships that my predecessor has built to this respect and like to collaborate with many of his contacts in order to further advance our understanding on the relationship between marketing and development. In doing so, I am happy that I do not have to start from scratch but can stand on someone's shoulders. Thank you Aad, for developing the field this far and for your trust in me as your successor.

References

Drucker, P.F. (1958). Marketing and Economic Development. Journal of Marketing 22: 252-259.

Fafchamps, M. (2004). Market Institutions in Sub-Saharan Africa. MIT Press, Cambridge, MA, USA.

Hunt, S.D. and Morgan, R.M. (1995). The Comparative Advantage Theory of Competition. Journal of Marketing 59: 1-15.

Ingenbleek, P.T.M. and Immink, V.I. (2010). Managing Conflicting Stakeholder Interests: An Exploratory Case Analysis of the Formulation of CSR Standards in the Netherlands. Journal of Public Policy & Marketing (in press).

Ingenbleek, P.T.M. and Van Tilburg, A. (2009). Marketing for Pro-Poor Development: Deriving Opportunities for Development from the Marketing Literature. Review of Business and Economics 54: 327-344.

Jones, G.G. (1996). The Evolution of International Business. McGraw-Hill, London, UK.

Kambewa, E.V. (2007). Balancing the People, Profit and Planet Dimensions in International Marketing Channels. PhD thesis Wageningen University, the Netherlands.

Kirca, A., Jayachandran, S. and Bearden, W.O. (2005). Market Orientation: A Meta-Analytic Review and Assessment of its Antecedents and Impact on Performance. Journal of Marketing 69: 24-41.

Kohli, A.K. and Jaworski, B.J. (1990). Market Orientation: The Construct, Research Propositions and Managerial Implications. Journal of Marketing 54: 1-18.

Sen, S. and Bhattacharya, C.B. (2001). Does Doing Good Always Lead to Doing Better? Consumer Reactions to Corporate Social Responsibility. Journal of Marketing Research 38: 225-243.

Vargo, S.L. and Lusch, R.F. (2004). Evolving to a New Dominant Logic for Marketing. Journal of Marketing 68: 1-17.

Wilkie, W. (2005). Exploring Marketing's Relationship to Society. Journal of Public Policy & Marketing, 24: 1-2.

Witkowski, T.H. (2005). Antiglobal Challenges to Marketing in Developing Countries: Exploring the Ideological Divide. Journal of Public Policy & Marketing 24: 7-23.

Linkages between theory and practice of marketing in developing countries

Aad van Tilburg

The supply or value chain for primary producers in developing countries is as strong as the weakest link whether this is entrepreneurship including marketing, market performance, horizontal or vertical coordination in the supply chain, or combinations of these factors.

Abstract

In this essay, I will look back on my career from both a theoretical and a practical point of view. I discuss the sources in the literature that guided my teaching and research, the theories and key concepts that helped me in finding new ways to approach marketing and market problems and I share the highlights of my field experience in developing countries with the reader to illustrate the development in my thinking in this field. The conclusion is that it is unlikely that a single approach can deal with all problems, but researchers should rather choose a context dependent perspective in their analysis. I end this essay with the recommendation to pay more attention to the roles and functions of entrepreneurs and institutions as key forces that shape markets. I propose to broaden the scope of performance measurement by covering a broader part of the sustainability concept rather than using financial performance only.

Keywords: case studies, market access, marketing in developing countries, market institutions, market performance, primary producers, supply chain, value chain, vertical coordination

1. Introduction

There was little theory and practice on marketing in developing countries when I started with this sub-discipline by the end of the 1970s. I got my first insights into this field from published research in agricultural economics, marketing, anthropology and rural sociology and also from discussions with the few colleagues who were working in the same field of interest. A dominant perspective from early on in my work has been that the inclusion of small scale primary producers in supply chains (be they local, regional, or global) provides a promising avenue towards alleviating poverty in developing countries, provided that it includes a fair distribution of value added to all chain participants. However, I have learned from 30 years of experience that this is not easily achieved. It can be difficult for primary producers in developing countries to become integrated into value chains because of a complex of many bottlenecks. Examples of such bottlenecks are imperfect competition in markets, concentration of power positions in the supply chain and a weak institutional environment. Hence, my proposition is that the supply chain for primary producers in developing countries is as strong as the weakest link whether this is entrepreneurship including marketing, market performance, horizontal or vertical coordination in the supply chain, or combinations of these factors. An experience has been that when one problem has been 'solved', another may arise because of, for example, one or more changes in the institutional environment of the supply chain.

The aim of this essay is to show how, from the late seventies onwards, interaction between theory and practice of marketing in developing countries stimulated my thinking, lecturing and research with respect to the roles that primary producers and traders can play in the supply chain of vulnerable agricultural products. My research has been focussed on the relationship between primary producers and connecting markets for farm inputs, farm services and the products to be sold. The functioning of these markets has been a bottleneck in the economic development of primary producers who faced barriers to access markets or supply chains as is demonstrated by means of several case studies. Consequently, the question arises what are the lessons learnt to improve access to markets or supply chains. The principle question has been how markets or supply chains can service primary producers better with respect to their marketing requirements. In this respect, sub-questions are: What have been main bottlenecks in the supply/value chain? Which theoretical constructs contributed substantially to the problem analysis and the generation of solutions? Which typical case studies regarding marketing or market studies in developing countries illustrate the linkages between theory and practice and which insights did they generate on improved access of primary producers to markets or supply chains.

In this essay I will first list problem areas or bottlenecks in supply chains in developing countries based on my case study research. Next, theoretical constructs relevant for the analysis of these problems are discussed and, finally, problem areas, theories and case studies are linked to generate several lessons learnt.

2. Main bottlenecks in the supply or value chain

The bottlenecks that I encountered in my research, related to marketing and markets in developing countries, are listed in Table1. Each bottleneck is connected to at least one case study in which I was involved. Typical examples of the connection between a particular bottleneck and a particular case study are as follows:
- A supply orientation without taking needs of customers into account with respect to potato marketing in Bhutan (2000s) where farmers offered ungraded potatoes to traders and traders were sorting these potatoes into three lots: the small ones to be used as seed potatoes, the big ones to be used for the potato chip industry and the intermediate-sized potatoes to be used as ware potatoes.
- Reducing transaction and transport costs with respect to the marketing of vegetables and fruits in Costa Rica (1990s) would open up new markets and strengthen a product's competitive advantage both within and outside the country.
- 'Getting institutions right' by strengthening the institutional environment of the supply chain with respect to the marketing of rice in Sierra Leone (1980s) where formal institutions directed to rice farmers were better accessible for farmers living near the service centers than for farmers living in more remote areas.
- Developing improved links between supply and demand with respect to fish marketing from the shores of Lake Victoria in Kenya (2000s) where fishermen were denied proper market information because of the power positions of traders or processors in the supply chain.
- Improving the distribution of value added in the supply chain with respect to rice marketing in Malaysia (1980s) where the government fixed prices in all stages of the supply chain.

- Improving market performance by affecting both market structure and market conduct in the various stages in the supply chain of highland vegetables in West Java (1970s-1980s) where competition and market transparency was relatively high in rural assembly markets and relatively low in urban wholesale markets. Another example concerns the degree of price integration between periodic markets in the maize market of Benin (1980s-1990s) which was relatively high in the long run but relatively low in the short run.
- Improving access to unique resources with respect to fish marketing from the shores of Lake Victoria in Kenya (2000s) where fishermen were confronted with overfishing of the common pool resource.

Linkages between problem areas or bottlenecks, relevant theoretical constructs and illustrating case studies are summarized in Table 1.

Table 1. *Linkages between bottlenecks, theoretical constructs and illustrating case studies with respect to marketing in developing countries.*

Bottlenecks in developing countries	Useful theoretical constructs	Illustrating case studies
Supply orientation without taking needs of customers into account	Marketing theory	All case studies
High transaction costs reducing market opportunities	• Commodity approach	
Underperformance of formal institutions: 'How to get institutions right'	• Functional approach • Institutional approach • Marketing management approach	
'No' supply chain: Optimal links between supply and demand need to be developed	Marketing theory	Rice marketing in Malaysia
Uneven distribution of value added in the supply chain: How to obtain a more balanced distribution?	• Vertical coordination in supply chains or distribution channels through: – Ownership – Contractual – Networks	Rice marketing in Sierra Leone Fish marketing in Kenya
Spot markets are underperforming because of deficiencies in either market structure and/or market conduct of actors	Organizational economics • Perfect or workable competition in markets • Market structure analysis • Market integration analysis • General equilibrium analysis	Potato marketing in Bhutan Vegetables marketing in Java Rice marketing in Malaysia Maize marketing in Benin Agricultural produce marketing in Costa Rica
Lack of access by entrepreneurs to needed and unique resources: How to improve access?	Marketing theory • Market orientation Organizational economics • Resource-based view	Vegetables and fruits marketing in Bhutan Fish in Kenya
Weak institutional environment: How to strengthening the institutional environment of the supply chain?	Organizational economics • Transaction and contract theory	Rice marketing in Sierra Leone Fish marketing in Kenya

3. Theoretical constructs contributing to analysis and solutions

The start-up phase

When I started to lecture and to do research on marketing in developing countries in the late seventies, the sub-discipline was a relatively new field of academic knowledge. Early theoretical work that I used included publications by: Abbott and co-authors (1958, 1966, 1979) – working at the marketing section of the economic division of the United Nations Food and Agricultural Organization – who were publishing on marketing problems and improvement programs in the tropics; Slater (1968) on marketing processes in Latin America; Bain (1959), Clodius and Mueller (1961), Scherer (1970), Cubbin (1988) and Baumol *et al.* (1988) on market competition and market performance; Bucklin (1965, 1970, 1977) on vertical marketing systems and food retailing in Asia; Harriss (1979, 1981, 1982, 1983) on food marketing in the semi-arid tropics; Colman and Young (1989) on markets and prices in developing countries; Van der Laan (1986, 1987, 1989) on marketing boards in Africa and Meulenberg (1986) on the evolution of agricultural marketing theory. With respect to market research and field work in developing countries I benefited from publications of Des Raj (1972) and later Harriss-White (1999) on the design of surveys. Early applications related to marketing theory in developing countries included Geertz (1963) on social development and economic change in two towns in Java who discussed both the firm type and the bazaar type of economy; Bijlmer (1987) on strategies of petty traders in Surabaya, Indonesia; Moser (1977) on upward migration of market sellers in Bogota, Colombia; Siamwalla (1978) on agricultural marketing in Thailand; and Bryceson (1985a, 1985b) on food marketing in Tanzania.

My initial interest and research regarded the kind of marketing problems that farmers in developing countries face as primary producers. Field work in this respect regarded farmers in a rice irrigation scheme in Malaysia in 1982 (Kalshoven *et al.*, 1984) and in a tidal rice growing area along the Great Scarcies river in Sierra Leone in 1985 (Borren, 1986; Van Tilburg and Hamming, 1999; Van Tilburg, 2001a). My interest regarded also the functioning of rural assembly and urban wholesale markets in Indonesia in 1979 (Van Tilburg, 1981), Benin in 1987 (Lutz *et al.*, 1995; Van Tilburg and Lutz, 1992), Senegal in 1988 (Van Bergen *et al.*, 1989) and Costa Rica in the early nineties (Van Tilburg *et al.*, 1992). Meanwhile, I noticed the important role of market institutions involved in vertical coordination in the supply chain such as the marketing board for paddy and rice in Malaysia. Gradually, my interest regarded more and more the role of channels connecting primary producers in developing countries to consumers at local, national, regional or international level. These channels - labeled as marketing channels, supply chains or value chains (e.g. Van Tilburg *et al.*, 2007) – were subject of research in several PhD studies, for example, with respect to cassava in Colombia (Janssen 1986) or China (Zhang, 1999), vegetables in Kenya (Dijkstra, 1997, 2001), marketing systems in relation to sustainability in Colombia (Castano, 2001, 2002, 2005), Nile perch in Lake Victoria, Kenya (Kambewa, 2007, 2008), or weaver products in India (Bhagavatula, 2009, Bhagavatula *et al.*, 2008).

What follows is a summary of theoretical notions that stimulated my thinking with respect to lecturing and research in marketing in developing countries. There are two lines of theory that I will discuss with respect to the supply chain: marketing as an entrepreneurial activity and the governance mode. The theoretical constructs to be discussed are summarized in Table 2.

Table 2. *Marketing in the supply chain and supply chain governance as theoretical constructs (to be) used in marketing studies in developing countries.*

Source in theory	Theme	Specification
Marketing in the supply chain		
Marketing	Schools of thought	Commodity approach
		Functional approach
		Institutional approach
		Marketing management approach
Organizational economics	Resource-based view	Access to unique resources?
Supply chain governance		
Vertical coordination		
Marketing	Coordination in the supply chain or distribution channel	Ownership
		Contractual
		Network
Organizational economics	Coordination through transactions or contracts	Contracts in a weak institutional environment
Spot market coordination		
Organizational economics	Industrial organization: market performance	Market structure analysis
		Market integration

Marketing as an entrepreneurial activity in the supply chain (upper part of Table 2)

Marketing theory originated as a discipline dealing with the process of getting agricultural commodities from farmer to consumer (Bartels, 1970). Before 1950, three schools viewing marketing as a socio-economic process were developed and gradually integrated: the commodity school focusing on the nature of the product, the functional school focusing on the functions needed in marketing and the institutional school focusing on institutions or organizations facilitating the marketing functions (e.g. Hill and Ingersent, 1982; Meulenberg, 1986; Stoelhorst and Van Raaij, 2004).

The commodity school dealt with the terms necessary to bridge the gap in place, time and product form between producer and consumer for general product classes such as cereals, coffee, tea, vegetables, fruit, meat or fish. The functional school focused on three functions to bridge the gap between producers and consumers: the exchange function including buying and selling operations and negotiating a contract, the physical function including contracting for transport, storage or processing; and the facilitating function including trade financing (credit, insurance) and market information. The institutional school took into account how institutions may contribute in facilitating the flow of products from producer to consumer in terms of marketing governance such as put in practice by a cooperative or a marketing board; standardization of products and processes such as weights, measures, quality classes and contract forms; market information services; finance institutions providing trade credit and insurance; and commodity exchanges providing tools to reduce price risk.

After 1950, the management approach became central in marketing analysis (e.g. Kotler and Keller, 2009). It is focusing on strategies and tactics of the entrepreneur to produce products or services that meet customer needs (e.g. Meulenberg, 1986; Stoelhorst and Van Raaij, 2004). The related resource-based view of entrepreneurship (e.g. Kraaijenbrink *et al.*, 2010; Locket *et al.*, 2009) is focusing on a firm's unique resources, competences and opportunities to attain competitive advantage in the market. Can a firm obtain *distinctive resources or competences* so that it can do particularly well in particular market segments relative to its competitors? Examples of unique resources can be raw materials, skills, competences, procedures, networks, market opportunities and brands. Examples of costly-to-copy resources are capabilities leading to pro-active innovation, insights in positional advantages in market segments, skills how to cope with imperfect market information, special organizational learning capabilities or building unique brands.

Governance in the supply chain (lower part of Table 2)

Supply or value chain analysis deals with vertical coordination of activities in marketing channels connecting supply and demand. With increasing globalization, thinking about types of horizontal or vertical coordination in the supply chain became of particular interest (e.g. Bucklin, 1970; Ruben *et al.*, 2007; Stern *et al.*, 1996).

Vertical coordination

A value chain between primary producers and consumers can be characterized by its governance structure. *Spot market* coordination of economic activities is governed by markets in which supply and demand is cleared through price discovery. Market prices embody a crucial signaling device which is directing decisions of market participants. *A hierarchy of economic activities* can be obtained through ownership, e.g. in the Chiquita supply chain, by means of contract, e.g. in case of franchising, or by means of the action of a channel leader who takes the initiative to arrive at a common marketing plan. *A network of economic activities*, e.g. among relatives or business partners, consists of informal relationships between agents lubricating economic activities. Based on this, common types of coordination in marketing channels (Stern *et al.*, 1996: Chapter 6) are labeled as conventional marketing channels where competition in spot markets prevails in each stage of the chain, vertical marketing systems (hierarchies) in which at least two subsequent stages in the chain cooperate through voluntary or contractual coordination, or networks based on people trusting each other. Key features in the coordination of economic activities are given in Table 3.

Traders link subsequent stages in the supply chain. Collecting traders, also called petty traders, itinerant traders, or rural merchants, perform a vital function in linking the farmer with a market at a level of turnover that is generally unattractive to a large merchant. Wholesalers buy in bulk from collecting traders or sell in bulk to retailers. Traders can adjust the discrepancy of assortments needed in the various stages

Table 3. *Key features in coordination mechanisms of economic activities (Adapted from Powell, 1991).*

	Market	Hierarchy	Network
Normative basis	contract	employment	trust
Communication	prices	routines	relational
Flexibility	high	low	medium
Commitment	low	higher	higher
Climate	suspicion	formal	mutual benefits
Choices	independent	dependent	interdependent

in the marketing channel from initial supply to retail by applying the sorting function (Bucklin 1965). The 'sorting function' includes sorting out which implies breaking down of a heterogeneous supply in homogeneous lots, 'accumulation' which implies bringing similar stocks from a number of sources together, 'allocation' meaning the breaking down a homogeneous supply into smaller lots and 'assorting' which means building up of an assortment for resale.

Contracts and trust relationships as coordination mechanisms

A contract, a written or spoken agreement, represents a transaction between seller and buyer given a particular contract environment in terms of formal and informal institutions. Stages in the contract process are contract preparation, contract conclusion and contract enforcement (Table 4).

Transaction costs (e.g. Rindfleish and Heide, 1997) tend to be high in developing countries (e.g. Fafchamps, 2004) because of a lack of standardization of products, procedures and market information, market transparency, horizontal and vertical coordination in value chains, access to collateral to obtain trade credit and economies of scale. These transaction costs can be reduced by improving market transparency to reduce *search costs*, by standardizing weights, measures, procedures, contracts, markets to reduce *negotiation costs,* and by reducing contract *enforcement costs* by taking proper precautions for a successful transaction, or by using arbitrage instead of a judicial procedure in the court system.

In legal contracts transactions are arranged in a written form and contract enforcement tends to be formal in case of default (e.g. arbitrage, court case). Transactions in developing countries tend to be more trust-based than legal-based. Trust is the willingness of at least two persons to enter in a negotiated agreement, to incur *obligations* and to acquire *rights* that have a low level of legal protection. In trust-based exchange transactions are based on trust levels obtained through reputation of the contract partners or mutual personal relationships. They tend to know each other's morality or ethics, preferences, motivation for doing business and endowments. Shortcomings in formal institutions can be partly bypassed through trust-based exchange where trust can be the result of a history of successful exchanges leading to relational contracting. Relational contracting is expected to arise in markets where product-screening costs are high, and *personal trust* is a substitute for *external contract enforcement* (Fafchamps, 2004; Grosh, 1993).

I benefitted much from the work of Fafchamps and co-authors (e.g. Fafchamps, 2004) on theory and evidence with respect to the functioning of market institutions in Sub-Saharan Africa. The message of this work is that the trade and marketing characteristics differ considerably between supply chains operating in a weak or strong institutional environment. Prevalent differences in the institutional environment between less and more developed countries regard, amongst others, the level of purchasing power, the degree of market transparency, the level of transaction costs and the degree of access of actors in the supply

Table 4. *Stages in realizing a contract.*

Stage in the process	Action	Type of transaction costs	Stage in the agreement: written or spoken
'Before'	Information search	Search costs	Contract preparation
'Agreement'	Negotiation	Negotiation costs	Contract conclusion
'After'	Enforcement	Enforcement costs	Contract enforcement

chain to both resources and markets. Transactions in a weak institutional environment – to be beneficial – need to be embedded in trust relationships. These relationships can be based on reputation, participation in (business) networks, family relationships, a common location of origin, common ethnicity, or sharing the same religion, e.g. hadji traders or marabouts in Senegal. Market institutions tend to be relatively weak in less developed countries.

This approach with respect to transactions and contracts in a weak institutional environment fitted very well in the course Microfinance and Marketing in Developing Countries which we lectured (initially with Henk Moll and, after his retirement, with Robert Lensink) at Wageningen University, but also several years in the European Microfinance Program, a Master of Science programme at Solvay Business School, l'Université Libre de Bruxelles supported by three universities including also l'Université Paris Dauphine. The point of departure has been that marketing and finance are narrowly related which can be illustrated with many types of credit relationships in trade. For example, assembly traders in developing countries may be pre-financed by wholesalers to be able to give smallholder farmers credit in the lean season under the condition that they will sell their crop in the harvest season, usually at a relatively low price (e.g. Van Tilburg and Hamming, 1999). This phenomenon is known in the literature as locked in transactions or interlocked product and credit markets.

Spot market coordination

Market structure analysis

Theory about the coordination of economic activities through markets (e.g. Bain, 1959; Cubbin, 1988; Hill and Ingersent, 1982) has been based on the model of perfect competition and has been extensively applied in both agricultural economics and marketing studies. Market performance in the real world has been evaluated by comparing the actual patterns of competition in a spot market with the theoretical characteristics of perfect, workable or contestable competition. The model of perfect competition (e.g. Henderson and Quandt, 1980) is characterized by homogeneous demand, perfect market information, divisible and mobile resources, many buyers and sellers being price takers, costless transactions and, consequently, buyers and sellers maximizing welfare. Conditions of workable competition are close to perfect competition, e.g. products are rather homogeneous, there are sufficient buyers and sellers for a level playing field, market transparency is of a reasonable level and small barriers to entry or exit are small. The main condition of 'contestable' competition is that market entry and exit are free resulting in traders (incumbents) who take in their strategies also potential competition by new market entrants into account. The basic hypotheses of market structure analysis are that *market structure → market conduct → market performance* (→ means is affecting).

Main characteristics of market structure are the degree of competition in a market represented by the number of suppliers and buyers and the degree of market transparency. Market conduct represents the degree of competitive behavior in the market which is, for example, reduced by joint pricing by suppliers or buyers (collusion). Market performance, for example profitability, represents the welfare effects of changes in the market structure or the market conduct by market actors. A weakness of this theory is that it is principally static implying that it is not clear how the market can be a 'change factor' in development (e.g. Jansen and Van Tilburg, 1997).

Market transparency is necessary to facilitate proper decision-making by producers, traders, consumers and public authorities to invest and to reduce market risks. Market transparency can be improved (e.g. Abbott, 1958) by standardizing product quantities and qualities, delivery options, contracts and market information with the aim is to lower transaction costs. To increase market transparency, many governments in developing countries set up a Market Information Service for their main food commodities during the eighties. A Market Information Service is a (public) service, collecting and processing data on prices and supply of agricultural commodities, and disseminating relevant information on a timely and regular basis.

4. Illustrating case studies on marketing in developing countries

In this section summaries of the case studies regarding marketing or market studies in developing countries are presented. These studies illustrate linkages between theory and practice and have been instrumental in generating insights on how access of primary producers to markets or supply chains can be obtained.

The case studies

The theoretical constructs discussed in previous section are linked to case studies in which I was involved, usually both in field work, analysis and reporting, often in close cooperation with colleagues or students. The selected illustrating case studies regard the trade or marketing of:
- Highland vegetables in West Java, Indonesia
- Rice in peninsular Malaysia
- Rice in Northwest Sierra Leone
- Maize in Benin in close cooperation with colleague Clemens Lutz
- Agricultural produce in Costa Rica
- Vegetables and fruits in Bhutan
- Nile perch from Lake Victoria, the PhD study of Emma Kambewa (2007)

These case studies are characterized in Table 5 by commodity, location and time frame of the study, the main problems or bottlenecks encountered, the focus of the study, the units of analysis, the relative strengths of formal and informal market institutions and the main causes of performance differentials. The quantitative analysis for several of these studies, notably with respect to market integration analysis in Benin and Bhutan benefited much from close cooperation with colleague Erno Kuiper.

Trade and marketing of highland vegetables in West Java, Indonesia: an experiment with an alternative marketing channel

The impression of the research team was that the asymmetric power position of primary producers versus collecting and distributing wholesalers in the supply chain was a main bottleneck. Another problem was the lack of standardization in the trade and the lack of proper packaging of vulnerable vegetables to be transported over large distances which resulted in considerable product losses. The following summary of the case study (Van Tilburg, 1981) relates the assumed bottlenecks to reality.

Highland vegetables like cabbage, tomatoes and potatoes are grown in the mountains around Bandung and Bogor in West Java. These vegetables are mainly marketed to the capital Jakarta. The Indonesian government was not satisfied with the performance of the private marketing system because of a lack of market transparency, highly fluctuating prices, considerable post-harvest losses and assumed malpractices of traders notably in the wholesale market of Jakarta. The study evaluates the traditional marketing system of highland vegetables in the light of a market structure analysis. An experiment of an Indonesian-Dutch project team with an alternative marketing channel for properly sorted and packed vegetables took place between March and May 1980. Private traders could offer highland vegetables to retailers in a time span

Table 5. *Illustrating case studies on marketing in developing countries.*

Commodity location, period	Main problems	Focus of research	Units of analysis	Relative strengths of formal versus informal market institutions	Causes performance differentials
Vegetables in Java, 1970s-1980s	Asymmetric power positions in the chain; Lack of standardization and packaging	Functioning of markets	Producers, traders, markets	Weak - Strong	Product quality; Packaging; Transport time
Rice in Malaysia, 1980s	Fixed paddy prices, no relation to the quality offered	Functioning of market institutions	Producers; Market institutions	Strong - Weak	Quality: moisture content
Rice in Sierra Leone, 1980s	Interlocked product and credit markets; Services mainly to near-by farmers	Transactions between farmers and traders	Producers; Markets	Weak - Strong	Distance of farmers to market centers
Maize in Benin, 1980s-1990s	Lack of price integration among markets, lack of market information	Functioning of maize markets	Producers; Traders; Markets	Weak - Strong	Market transparency; Distance of farmers to markets
Agricultural produce in Costa Rica, 1990s	Trade and spatial barriers in the flow of agricultural produce	Markets and trade flows, macro level	Market demand and supply; Trade flows	Strong - Weak	Market access
Vegetables and fruits in Bhutan, 2000s	Lack of access to markets including border auctions	Functioning of auction markets for potatoes	Traders	Strong - Weak	Post-harvest treatment: grading and sorting
Fish in Kenya, 2000s (Kambewa, 2007)	Lack of resources to implement sustainable practices	Focus on upstream part of the value chain	Fishermen; Assembly traders	Weak - Weak	Quality of storage facilities; Market power of fishermen

of 24 hours instead of the 48 hours needed by the project. The experiment did not succeed in selling vegetables at a profit because of limited trade experience; sophisticated and expensive cleaning, grading and packing methods, and high handling costs. The relatively high quality of the vegetables offered was not sufficiently compensated for. The farmers received fixed prices not directly related to the ruling market price. The conclusion of the analysis was that the ruling marketing system of highland vegetables was more efficient than expected but that improvements could be obtained by group action of growers and more standardization of products and procedures to improve market transparency. Evidence of entry barriers in the urban wholesale market was obtained as wholesalers were able to limit market entry for newcomers. The lesson learnt was that it appeared to be difficult for a pilot project that was initiating an alternative marketing channel for primary producers of vegetables to compete with the private sector that was supposed to under-perform.

Trade and marketing of rice in the North-east of peninsular Malaysia

The impression was that uniform prices paid all over the value chain by the public marketing board, irrespective of the quality of paddy delivered by the farmers, was a problem. The following summary of the case study relates the assumed bottleneck to reality.

The marketing system for paddy rice (Kalshoven *et al.*, 1984) was analyzed from the perspective of the paddy farmers because of their dependency on middlemen or public or cooperative rice mills. Data on the marketing behavior of farmers, middlemen and rice mill managers were collected and analyzed with market structure analysis in 1982. Conclusions about the performance of the marketing systems were that there was strong competition among traders to buy paddy from farmers but many farmers were locked-in with their sales to traders because of debt obligations (valid for about 20% of the farmers) or because the quantities of paddy sold were too small to be sent to a rice mill (valid for about 25% of the farmers). The paddy and rice market was quite transparent due to the annual publication of prices set for these commodities in all stages of the supply channel. Many farmers were not able to relate these official prices to the price net of transport costs and subsidies that they received from traders. The uniform prices paid for paddy, irrespective of the quality delivered, did not stimulate farmers to offer paddy of higher quality. The private sector offered higher prices than the officially announced prices during the dry season when the properly dried paddy was of good quality, but it did not have interest in buying paddy during the wet season because of the costs involved to dry the wet paddy of lower quality. The lessons learnt were that the public channel absorbed the bulk of the wet season paddy whereas the private sector channel was absorbing most of the dry season paddy resulting in considerable underutilization of the storage and processing capacities in the region and, related to this, that the marketing system for paddy and rice did not stimulate farmers and traders to deliver better quality paddy in the wet season.

Sources and uses of rice by farming households in Northwest Sierra Leone

The impression was that rice and credit markets, just like the previous case in Malaysia, were interlocked for many farmers. A second point of concern was whether rice farmers had equal access to services such as mechanization and credit provided by formal institutions. The following summary of the case study relates these assumed bottlenecks to reality.

This study (Borren, 1986; Van Tilburg, 2001a; Van Tilburg and Hamming, 1999) dealt with rice transactions of 372 farming households in Northwest Sierra Leone in 1985. Three stretches along the Great Scarcies River, an upland/upstream area, a midstream area and a downstream area, were selected as research area reflecting variation in farming ecology, livelihood system and distance to rice market centers.

The upland farmers cultivated both rain-fed rice and rice naturally irrigated during high tide of the nearby sea. In the midstream and downstream area rice was mainly cultivated on the extended river banks that were flooded two times daily. A rice balance sheet was constructed for each household with the sources of rice at the left side and its uses on the right side. The sources of paddy – in the sequence upland-midstream-downstream area – originated for 64-46-69% out of production, for 28-42-21% from purchases and for 2-6-7% from receipts in kind as a compensation for renting out land or giving rice on credit terms. The uses of paddy were for 55-29-28% for household consumption, 5-31-25% for sales, 10-18-19% for payments in kind to obtain additional land, labor or capital, 11-8-8% for gift-giving to the village chief, relatives, friends or the mosque, 7-6-9% to be used as seed rice for next crop and 7-5-5-% for particular events such as funerals and marriages of members of the household. Upland farming households appeared to be the most subsistence-oriented class of farmers whereas both the midstream and downstream farming households represented the more trade-oriented class. The study concluded that rice had many functions in the economic, social security and cultural system of the region and that services provided to farmers by rural institutions with regard to improved seed, sales outlets, extension, mechanization and credit reached only a small part of the farming population, especially those living close to the service centers.

The analysis showed that product and credit markets were interlocked for 36% of the transactions (n= 424 transactions). The prices that farmers received for the locked-in rice transactions were substantially lower than for their free sales, partly in compensation for the credit obtained. The lessons learnt were that interlocked product and credit markets had a positive effect: access to working capital, but also a negative effect: relatively low prices for the part of the harvest sold, and that access to formal market institutions was far from optimal for the farmers living remote from centers providing agricultural services.

Trade and marketing of maize in Benin, in close cooperation with Clemens Lutz (Lutz, 1994)

The assumption was that the regional periodic market system was quite competitive in buying agricultural produce but that the degree of price integration between markets might be less than optimal because of a lack of proper market information. The following summary of the case study relates the assumed bottlenecks to reality.

The research in Benin, a joint project between the Faculty of Agriculture of the University of Benin (Abomey-Calavi) and three universities in the Netherlands, was concentrated in the southern part of Benin with two rainy seasons in a year and, consequently, two crops and harvests. The physical infrastructure has been improved during the research period which resulted in reduced transport costs. Master of Science students and faculty cooperated in collecting primary data on market prices, marketing costs, and the level of competition, collusion practices and entry barriers in the maize marketing system (Van Bruggen and Van Tilburg, 1999; Fanou et al., 1997; Van Tilburg, 1990). Data on transactions at periodic spot markets were collected by trained enumerators.

Spot markets

The rural assembly and wholesale markets for maize were characterized as 'contestable'. Traders who were normally dealing in other products than maize were spotting maize prices to enter the maize market during times that trade margins were increasing and they left this market in periods that trade margins were decreasing. These traders knew how to deal with potential entry barriers such as trade customs or practices (e.g. non-standardized volume measures and product grades), lack of market information and working capital (Lutz and Van Tilburg 1992ab, 1997; Van Tilburg and Lutz 1992).

Spatial networks

The initial assumption was that large wholesale markets in Bohicon and Cotonou were price-leading markets in the sense that wholesalers in these markets were able to set prices based on their estimates about the ruling supply and demand conditions. However, this appeared not to be the case when the results of a co-integration analysis became available. Traders in the wholesale markets in the south of Benin appeared to interact in such a way that the ruling price level resulted from their joint activities (Kuiper *et al.*, 1999; Lutz *et al.*, 1995). Long-term price integration, meaning that prices at different markets were moving gradually in the same direction, was the rule but short-term price integration was slow. However, an IFPRI study on reforming agricultural markets in Africa (Kherallah *et al.*, 2002: 90-91) concluded – based on Lutz *et al.* (1995) and other studies – that arbitrage between markets took place in a relatively short time frame in the Benin market, particularly in comparison with the Malawian case. This study on market performance of the maize market in Benin by measuring the degree of price integration fitted into a series of co-integration studies reported in the literature (e.g. Palaskas and Harriss, 1993).

Marketing channels

The hypothesis was that maize wholesalers were influencing the price level more than maize retailers. This was only partly true. Wholesalers appeared to affect the price level more than retailers in rural markets, whereas retailers influenced the price level more than wholesalers in urban markets (Kuiper *et al.*, 2000, 2003).

Recommendations for stakeholders

Relevant price information is difficult to obtain without proper standardization of measures and product grades (Shepherd *et al.*, 1997). Price information about each quality class of the underlying lot is necessary to be able to assess its value. The FAO published already in the 1950s and 1960s documents about proper marketing standards in developing countries (e.g. Abbott, 1958). Abbott recommended private-public partnerships, backed by proper marketing institutions, to initiate required changes in agricultural markets in developing countries.

The analysis showed that competition with respect to maize was contestable in rural periodic markets and that price integration between markets was sluggish mainly due to lack of standardization and market information resulting in insufficient capacities of traders to be involved in market arbitrage. The lesson learnt was that there was a need to improve market transparency by strengthening the formal market institutional infrastructure, notably through standardization and market price information.

Market analysis and market performance in Costa Rica

The impression was that trade flows within Costa Rica and with import and export markets might contribute more to national welfare when particular trade barriers such as import tariffs or bottlenecks in the national road system would be lifted. The following summary of the case study relates the assumed bottleneck to reality.

The study in Costa Rica (Jansen *et al.*, 1996) was a joint research of CATIE, the Universidad Nacional (UNA), the Universidad de Costa Rica (UCR) and Wageningen University. It was an integrated approach in which soil scientists, agronomists and social scientist cooperated in developing and testing tools to analyze market performance and regional development. The research activities were concentrated in the Atlantic Zone where farmers complained about missing markets because it happened that they could not sell their produce. For example, traders in roots and tubers did not pass by the farms, or the transport costs to assembly markets were prohibitive. Apart from cattle auctions, operating at rural and national level, there was not much direct arbitrage between spatially separated wholesale markets, mainly because of thin markets, large distances and a high mountain ridge (the sierra) in between major markets. The supply chain for non-export crops was a conventional marketing channel whereas the marketing of export crops tended to be well organized in a corporate or contractual vertical marketing system, e.g. coffee by a marketing board, fruits by multinationals and tubers by export companies.

An agricultural sector analysis for Costa Rica demonstrated that the sector has been highly dependent on world market prices for export commodities and on domestic transport costs for the non-export commodities. Such an agricultural sector analysis (Roebeling *et al.,* 2000) can be used by decision-makers to assess the effects of alternative scenarios on land use patterns, trade flows and shifts in welfare of producers and/or consumers. Alternative scenarios regarded trade liberalization, an improved transport infrastructure, shifts in demand or shifts in technological developments in agriculture. Typical questions were: What will be the expected effect of an improved road network, improved market transparency, or lower export or import tariffs on trade patterns? The spatial equilibrium analysis included 17 main agricultural commodities, 6 regions covering Costa Rica and 'the rest of the world'. A first scenario assumed trade liberalization where producers face FOB (free on board) export prices and consumers are confronted with CIF (cost, insurance and freight) import prices. A partial liberalization scenario implying free trade in basic grains (notably rice, maize and beans) resulted in gains in producer welfare at the expense of consumer welfare. Another scenario assumed reduced transport costs leading to a decline in pasture area for beef production and favoring milk and crop production. A third scenario assumed demand shifts based on income growth in case of pessimistic (0.0%), normal (2.5%) and optimistic (5.0%) income growth scenarios, given an expected 2% annual population growth rate. The outcomes depended largely on the income elasticities for the commodities under review and included that the area allocated to more income elastic products would increase; domestic production of commodities with high import prices, e.g. basic grains, would increase; the expected area of crop cultivation would increase at the expense of beef production; and a deterioration of the balance of trade although the area allocated to banana was hardly affected. This analysis showed the effects of trade measures on producer and consumer welfare in Costa Rica. Trade liberalization would benefit producers at the cost of consumers because of the ruling policy to keep consumer prices relatively low. The lesson learnt was that government's policy to affect food prices distorted markets with benefits for consumers at the cost of producers.

Trade and marketing of vegetables and fruits in Bhutan

The impression was that a main problem of farmers was the lack of access to market outlets such as the auctions at the Bhutanese/Indian border. Market access was hindered by the rough mountainous landscape and the remoteness of many farmers from accessible roads. The following summary of the case study relates the assumed bottleneck to reality.

This study consisted of two components. The first one regarded the development of a marketing plan for the horticultural sector in Bhutan on request of the ministry of Agriculture and covered mainly vegetables, e.g. potato, chilies, beans and mushrooms, and orchard products such as apples, mandarins and walnut (Van Tilburg, 2001b). The aim of this study was to identify strengths, weaknesses and risks of the vegetable and fruit marketing system and to suggest interventions to make the marketing system more effective and efficient. The second study concerned a market integration study with respect to potato prices at three border auctions (Van Tilburg *et al.,* 2008).

Bhutan's agriculture has been facing challenges dealing with the vulnerability of fresh agricultural products in relation to the rough environmental conditions. Challenges in the domain of product quality have been shortages in human resources because of out-migration in the rural areas, lack of good farm management practices, inadequate harvest and post-harvest operations and a lack of knowledge of farmers about prevalent market conditions. Challenges related to the required speed of delivery of agricultural products to (distant) markets have been large distances between farms and rural markets, a vulnerable national road system and increased competition in Bhutan's traditional export markets India and Bangladesh because of compliance with WTO regulations. Major opportunities were the increasing demand for high-quality and organic products both in Bhutan and its major export markets because of consumers becoming more critical on food safety and health aspects, the process of rural-urban migration and the rise of new communication technologies facilitating the promotion of Bhutanese agricultural products abroad. Potential threats were stricter food safety regulations in the countries to which Bhutan has been exporting agricultural products and liberalized export markets facilitating the entry of competitors. Major strengths of the agricultural sector of Bhutan have been that off-season production supplemented the diet of consumers in north India and Bangladesh and the good taste related to the organic characteristics of Bhutanese agricultural products. Major weaknesses of the agricultural sector in Bhutan have been little vertical coordination in supply chains, insufficient systematic knowledge about export markets, lack of entrepreneurial capacities throughout the supply chain, absence of group marketing, insufficient investments in both harvest and post-harvest operations and relatively high transport and labor costs. Recommendations were summarized in six items: exploit off-season markets, exploit premium product markets, exploit opportunities for vertical coordination in the supply chains and generate quality products for specific market niches (e.g. organic medicine).

The degree of market price integration was tested on potatoes. It was assumed that imperfections in market infrastructure, market structure and market conduct would prevent an optimal price for deliveries at the three border auctions. Market performance was assessed by testing the law of one price for three series of auction price data. The conclusion was that, based on monthly data covering the period 1996-2000, the auction prices between three border auctions were interrelated both in the long- and short run with one of the three auctions as the price-leading market but that the price integration came under pressure in the period 2001-2005 indicating the rise of market imperfections. Notice that short-run integration in the context of this study means price integration within one month. This is because only monthly data could be used which is not in line with the decision horizon of traders who base their trade decisions on daily or weekly rather than monthly prices.

From this analysis, we learned that market access and the lack of adding value in post-harvest operations were main bottlenecks for farmers to obtain a higher share of the value added in the potato supply chain.

Nile perch in Kenya

The impression was that the main bottleneck was the fishermen's lack of resources to implement sustainable practices. The following summary of the case study relates the assumed bottleneck to reality.

The case (Kambewa, 2007; Kambewa *et al.,* 2007, 2008) deals with inclusion of small-scale primary producers in international supply chains. Few insights existed about how to build sustainable and inclusive food chains when natural resources are scarce. The case investigates whether small-scale primary producers would engage in contracts that oblige them to implement sustainable and quality-improving practices and if so under what conditions. In the analysis, several homogeneous segments of fishermen willing to engage in similar contracts were found.

Segment 1, the smallest, is the only cluster that has a high utility for contracts with middlemen. This cluster was called a *clan* because middlemen belonged to the same local communities as the fishermen. This may compel some fishermen to continue trading with the middlemen. *Segment 2* had the highest preference for contracts in which ice for quality improvement is provided. This cluster is called *quality* sensitive. *Segment 3,* the largest cluster, comprised fishermen that would primarily engage in contracts in which good fishing gear is provided. Given their strongest willingness to engage in contracts in which good fishing gear is provided, this cluster was called *green* fishermen that seek sustainability above anything else. *Segment 4* comprised fishermen that cannot be uniquely identified by the contracts they would engage in. Due to lack of decisive types of contracts, this cluster was called *opportunists* who may want to grab anything that comes their way. *Segment 5* comprised fishermen who would primarily engage in contracts in which fish prices are fixed to minimize price risks. This cluster was called *price risk-averse*.

To identify fishermen that prefer particular contracts, the segments were profiled according to their demographic characteristics. Segment 1: the clan had the highest proportion, i.e. 4 out 12 (33%) fishermen that have kinship relations (e.g. brother, sister, parents or direct cousin) with middlemen they trade with. This suggests that the clan fishermen are willing to engage in contracts with middlemen due to their kinship relations. Segment 2: the quality sensitive fishermen were on average the youngest (27 years) compared to the rest of the fishermen. They had the least average monthly income probably explaining their need for quality improvement to boost their income. Segment 3: the green fishermen had the highest proportion of fishermen (about 63%) that had no other income generating activities than fishing. This may explain why they wanted to have good fishing gear to promote sustainable fishing to protect their only major source of livelihood. The Green fishermen also had the lowest proportion (about 11%) of fishermen with kinship relations with middlemen. Segment 4: the opportunists could not be uniquely profiled by their demographic characteristics. Although segment 5: the price risk averse fishermen, had the highest number of fishermen that own fishing gear and also have other income generating activities, they still wanted to minimize price risks by willing to engage in contracts that provided price information.

The lesson learnt was that the main bottleneck consisted of the fishermen's lack of resources to implement sustainable practices. Fishermen appeared to be open to sustainability-quality enhancing contracts provided that such contracts also enhance their welfare and economic benefits.

5. Discussion

In this essay, I was looking back on my career from both a theoretical and a practical point of view and I discussed the sources in the literature that guided my teaching and research. Theories and key concepts that helped me in finding new ways to approach marketing and market problems in developing countries were discussed and I shared the highlights of my field experience with the reader to illustrate the development of my thinking in this field.

With respect to entrepreneurship and marketing, evidence for my proposition at the beginning of the essay was presented in case studies on the marketing for agricultural produce in Java, Costa Rica and Bhutan as well as for fish in Kenya. Regarding market performance, evidence for the proposition was generated in case studies on marketing of agricultural produce in Java, Sierra Leone, Benin and Bhutan by means of market structure analysis and/or market price integration analysis. The best example of horizontal and vertical integration in the supply chain – in a period that public marketing of agricultural produce by a marketing board was prevalent all over the world – is presented in the case study of rice marketing in Malaysia. Effects of market institutions on the marketing of agricultural produce were discussed in all case studies but typical examples are the cases regarding Sierra Leone and Costa Rica.

The following linkages between theoretical constructs, case studies and lessons learnt were sketched. *Market structure analysis* was applied to assess to what extent there was a level playing field in the markets under study. Competition in rural agricultural markets appeared to function to a certain extent but market imperfections were prevalent due to lack of market transparency and asymmetric market power between producers and traders (e.g. the Benin case). *Market integration analysis* was applied to assess the association in price developments among markets. Evidence that there must be something wrong in spatial separated markets is when the price of a commodity is increasing in one market and decreasing in another market. Markets tended to be reasonably well-integrated in the long-run but to be sluggish in integration in the short run (e.g. the Benin case). *Exchange or transaction theory* was applied to assess factors influencing the outcome of a transaction between trade partners. The lesson learnt was that many transactions between primary producers and assembly traders have been locked in because of credit ties or small quantities to be offered, reducing product prices for primary producers (the cases of Malaysia and Sierra Leone). *General equilibrium analysis* was applied to assess the effect of policy measures in agriculture. It appeared that consumers benefitted from public subsidies at the cost of primary producers (the Costa Rica case). *Analysis of vertical coordination in the supply chain* was applied to assess opportunities for primary producers to improve their market access and to streamline the flow and quality of products between primary production and final consumption. Lessons learnt are that it is not easy to substitute an existing supply chain by an alternative one without cooperation of the stakeholders involved (the case of Java, Indonesia), and, primary producers lacking resources to implement profitable and sustainable production and marketing practices have difficulties in adhering to the requirements of international supply chains (the Kenya fish case). *Marketing planning* to prioritize investment plans in agriculture were fruitfully applied in Bhutan. The theory on the roles of – and balance between – *formal and informal institutions* as important facilitators of the marketing process of agricultural produce was applied in all presented case studies. The conclusion of this review can be that it is unlikely that a single theoretical approach can deal with all problems, but that researchers should rather choose a context dependent perspective in their analysis.

For the near future, my impression is that more attention needs to be paid to the roles and the functions of entrepreneurs – being primary producers, traders or processors – in the development process of notably disadvantaged sectors in the rural economies of developing countries. In this respect, the analysis will increasingly use management and marketing constructs such as *market orientation* and *the resource based view* (e.g. Ingenbleek and Van Tilburg, 2009) to explain performance differentials between entrepreneurs or among value chains. Performance criteria will increasingly be related to sustainability criteria: profitability (Profit), sustainability (Planet) and contribution to pro-poor development (People). The studies of Kambewa (2007) and Bhagavatula (2009) are examples of how this road can be taken. Also, more attention need to be paid to strategies and tactics of entrepreneurs in weak institutional environments. Forthcoming PhD studies in the Marketing and Consumer Behaviour group of Wageningen University on the impact of the institutional environment on the governance and performance of supply chains in West Africa take these views into account. New in these studies is that seeking and testing weak links in supply chains, supported by scenario analysis, can sketch the way forward of how to build sustainable and inclusive supply or value chains.

References

Abbott, J.C. (1958). Marketing problems and improvement programs. Food and Agriculture Organization of the United Nations, Rome, Italy.

Abbott, J.C. and Creupelandt, H.C. (1966). Agricultural Marketing Boards, their establishment and operation, FAO Marketing Guide no. 5, Rome, Italy.

Abbott, J.C. and Makeham, J.P. (1979). Agricultural Economics and Marketing in the Tropics. Intermediate Tropical Agriculture Series, Longman Group Limited, London, UK.

Bain, J.S. (1959). Industrial organization. Wiley, New York, NY, USA.

Bartels, R. (1970). Marketing theory and metatheory. R.D. Irwin, Homewood, IL, USA.

Baumol, W.J., Panzar J.C. and Willig, R.D. (1988). Contestable markets and the theory of industry structure, revised edition. Harcourt, Brace, and Jonanovich, New York, NY, USA.

Bhagavatula, S. (2009). Weaving social networks: Performance of small rural firms in India as an outcome of entrepreneur's social and human capital. PhD thesis Vrije Universiteit (Free University), Amsterdam, the Netherlands.

Bhagavatula, S., Elfring, T., Van Tilburg, A. and Van de Bunt, G.C., (2008). How Social and Human Capital Influence Opportunity Recognition and Resource Mobilization in India's Handloom Industry. Journal of Business Venturing: 1-16.

Bijlmer, J. (1987). Ambulante straatberoepen in Surabaya. Een studie naar kleinschalige economische aktiviteiten. VU Uitgeverij, Amsterdam, the Netherlands.

Borren, C.E. (1986). Collecting Rice Trade in the Great Scarcies Area of Sierra Leone. MSc.-Thesis, LU-Wageningen, vakgroep Marktkunde en Marktonderzoek.

Bryceson, D.F. (1985a). The Organization of Tanzania Grain Marketing: Switching Role of the Cooperative and the Parastatal. In: K. Arhin, P. Hesp and L. Van der Laan (eds.), Marketing Boards in Tropical Africa. KPI Limited, London, UK.

Bryceson, D.F. (1985b). Food and urban purchasing power: the case of Dar Es Salaam, Tanzania. African Affairs 84: 499-522.

Bucklin, L.P. (1965). Postponement, speculation and the structure of distribution channels. Journal of Marketing Research 2: 26-31.

Bucklin, L.P., ed. (1970). Vertical Marketing Systems. Scott Foresman, Glenview, IL, USA.

Bucklin, L.P. (1977). Improving Food Retailing in Developing Asian Countries. Food Policy (May): 114-122.

Castano, J. (2001). Agricultural Marketing systems and sustainability. Study of small-scale Andean hillside farms. PhD Thesis Wageningen University, also published as Mansholt Studies, Nr. 22.

Castano, J., Meulenberg, M. and Van Tilburg, A. (2002). A new method of measuring the adoption of soil conservation practices: theory and applications. Netherlands Journal of Agricultural Science 50: 95-114.

Castano, J., Meulenberg, M. and Van Tilburg, A. (2005). The Impact of Marketing Systems on Soil Sustainability of Agriculture in Developing Countries: A Method and an Application. Agricultural Economics 33: 51-66.

Clodius, R.L. and Mueller, W.F. (1961). Market structure analysis as an orientation of research in agricultural economics. Journal of Farm Economics 43: 515-553.

Colman, D. and Young, T. (1989). Principles of agricultural economics; Markets and prices in less developed countries. Cambridge University Press, Cambridge, UK.

Cubbin, J.S. (1988). Market structure and performance, the empirical research. Taylor&Francis, Abingdon, Oxford, UK.

Dijkstra, T. (1997). Horticultural marketing channels in Kenya: Structure and Development. Ph.D. thesis Wageningen Agricultural University/ African Studies Centre, Leiden, the Netherlands.

Dijkstra, T., Meulenberg M. and Van Tilburg, A. (2001). Applying marketing channel theory to food marketing in developing countries: A vertical disintegration model for horticultural marketing channels in Kenya. Agribusiness 17: 227-241.

Fafchamps, M. (2004). Market Institutions in Sub-Saharan Africa. The MIT Press, Cambridge, UK.

Fanou, L., Clemens, K., Lutz, H.M. and Van Tilburg, A. (1997). Les marchés régionaux de produits vivriers. In: J. Daane, M. Breusers and E. Frederiks (eds.), Dynamique paysanne sur le plateau Adja du Bénin. Karthala, Paris, France, pp. 153-188.

Geertz, C. (1963). Peddlers and princes: Social development and economic change in two Indonesian towns. The University of Chicago Press, Chicago, IL, USA.

Grosh, B. (1993). Contract Farming in Africa: an Application of the New Institutional Economics. Journal of African Economies 3: 231-261.

Harriss, B. (1979). There is a Method in my Madness or is it Vice Versa? Development Studies Discussion Paper 54, University of East Anglia, Norwich, UK.

Harriss, B. (1981). Transitional Trade and Rural Development: the Nature and Role of Agricultural trade in a South Indian District. New Delhi, Vikas, India.

Harriss, B. (1982). Agricultural marketing in the semi-arid tropics of West Africa, East Anglia, Development Studies Discussion Paper.

Harriss, B. (1983). Implementation of food distribution policies. Food Policy (May 1983): 122-130.

Harriss-White, B., (ed.) (1999). Agricultural markets from theory to practice. Field experience in developing countries. MacMillan Press Limited, New York, NY, USA.

Henderson, J.M. and Quandt, R.E. (1980). Micro-economic theory; a mathematical approach. 3rd ed. McGraw-Hill, London, UK.

Hill, B.E. and Ingersent, K.A. (1982). An economic analysis of agriculture. 2nd ed. Heinemann Educational Books, London, UK.

Ingenbleek, P.T.M. and Van Tilburg, A. (2009). Marketing for pro-poor development: Deriving opportunities for development from the marketing literature. Review of Business and Economics 54: 327-344.

Jansen, H.G.P. and Van Tilburg A., with Belt, J. and Hoekstra S. (1996). Agricultural marketing in the Atlantic Zone of Costa Rica. Centro Agronómico Tropical de Investigación y Ensenanza (CATIE), Serie Técnica, Informe Técnico, No. 271, Costa Rica.

Janssen, W.G. (1986). Market Impact on Cassava's Development Potential in the Atlantic Coast Region of Columbia. CIAT, Cali, Colombia.

Janssen, W.G. and Van Tilburg, A. (1997). Marketing analysis for agricultural development: suggestions for a new research agenda. In: B. Wierenga, A. van Tilburg, K. Grunert, J-B.E.M. Steenkamp and M. Wedel (eds.), Agricultural marketing and consumer behaviour in a changing world, Kluwer Academic Publishers, Boston, MA, USA, pp: 57-74.

Kalshoven, G., Daane, J.R.V., Fredericks, L.J., Van den Steen van Ommeren, F.A.J. and Van Tilburg, A. (1984). Paddy farmers, irrigation and agricultural services in Malaysia. A case study in the Kemubu Scheme. Papers of the Departments of Sociology 11, Wageningen University, the Netherlands.

Kambewa, E.V. (2007). Balancing the people, profit and planet dimensions in international marketing channels. A study om coordinating mechanisms in the Nile perch channel from Lake Victoria. PhD thesis Wageningen University. Commercially published as: Kambewa, E.V. (2007), Contracting for sustainability: An analysis of the Lake Victoria – EU Nile perch chain. Wageningen Academic Publishers, Wageningen, the Netherlands.

Kambewa, E.V., Van der Lans, I.A.C.M., Van Trijp, J.C.M., Ingenbleek, P.T.M., Van Tilburg, A. and Van Boekel, M.A.J.S. (2007). Restructuring international food chains: Building sustainable and all-inclusive food chains at the primary stages. Paper prepared for presentation at the 106th EAAE Seminar on Pro-poor development in low income countries: Food, agriculture, trade, and environment, 25-27 October 2007, Montpellier, France.

Kambewa, E., Ingenbleek, P. and Van Tilburg, A. (2008). Improving Income Positions of Primary Producers in International Marketing Channels: The Lake Victoria EU Nile perch Case. Journal of Macromarketing 28: 53-67.

Kherallah, M., Delgado, D., Gabre-Madhin, E., Minot, N. and Johnson, M. (2002). Reforming agricultural markets in Africa. The John Hopkins University Press, Baltimore, MD, USA.

Kotler, P. and Keller, K.L., (2009). A Framework for Marketing Management. Pearson, Upper Saddle River, NJ, USA.

Kraaijenbrink, J., Spender, J.-C. and Groen, A.J. (2010). The resource-based view: A review and assessment of its critiques. Journal of Management 36: 349-372.

Kuiper, W.E., Lutz, C. and Van Tilburg, A. (1999). Testing for the law of one price and identifying price-leading markets: An application to corn markets in Benin. Journal of Regional Science 39: 713-738.

Kuiper, W.E., Lutz, C. and Van Tilburg, A. (2000). Price setting power among wholesalers and retailers: Maize in Benin and sorghum in Burkina Faso. In: A. van Tilburg, H.A.J. Moll and A. Kuyvenhoven (eds.), Agricultural markets beyond liberalization. Kluwer Academic Publishers, Boston, MA, USA, pp. 159-172.

Kuiper, W.E., Lutz, C. and Van Tilburg, A. (2003). Vertical price leadership on local maize markets in Benin. Journal of Development Economics 71: 417-433.

Lockett, A., Thompson, S., Morgenstern, U. (2009). The development of the resource-based view of the firm: A critical appraisal. International Journal of Management Reviews 11: 9-28.

Lutz, C.H.M. and Van Tilburg, A. (1992a). Spatial arbitrage between rural and urban maize markets in Benin. In: L. Cammann (ed.), Traditional marketing systems. German Foundation for International Development (DSE), Feldafing, pp. 90-100.

Lutz, C.H.M. and Van Tilburg, A. (1992b). Concurrentievormen op rurale en urbane maïsmarkten in Zuid-Bénin. Tijdschrift voor Sociaal Wetenschappelijk Onderzoek van de Landbouw 7: 195-221.

Lutz, C. (1994). The functioning of the maize market in Benin: spatial and temporal arbitrage on the market of a staple food crop. University of Amsterdam, Regional Economics, Amsterdam, the Netherlands.

Lutz, C., Van Tilburg, A. and Van der Kamp, B. (1995). The process of short-and long-term price integration in the Benin maize market. European Review of Agricultural Economics 22: 191-212.

Lutz, C. and Van Tilburg, A. (1997). Framework to assess the performance of food commodity marketing systems in developing countries with an application to the maize market in Benin. In: W.K. Asenso-Okyere, G. Benneh and W. Tims (eds.), Sustainable Food Security in West Africa. Kluwer Academic Publishers, Boston, MA, USA, pp. 264-292.

Meulenberg, M.T.G. (1986). The evolution of agricultural marketing theory: towards better coordination with general marketing theory. Netherlands Journal of Agricultural Science 34: 301-315.

Moser, C. (1977). The dual economy and marginability debate, and the contribution of micro analysis: Market sellers in Bogota. Development and Change 8: 465-489.

Palaskas, T.B. and Harriss, B. (1993). Testing market integration: New approaches with case material from the West bengal food economy. Journal of Development Studies 30: 1-57.

Powell, W.W. (1991). Neither market nor hierarchy: Network forms of organization. In: Thomson, G., J. Frances, R. Levacic and J. Mitchell (eds.), Markets, hierarchies and networks, SAGE Publications, p. 265-276.

Raj, D. (1972). The design of sample surveys. McGraw-Hill, New York, NY, USA.

Rindfleisch, A. and Heide, J.B., (1997). Transaction Cost Analysis: Past, Present, and Future Applications, Journal of Marketing 61: 30-54.

Roebeling, P.C., Jansen, H.G.P., Van Tilburg, A. and Schipper, R.A. (2000). Spatial equilibrium modeling for evaluating inter-regional trade flows, land use and agricultural policy. In: B.A.M. Bouman, H.G.P. Jansen, R.A. Schipper, A. Nieuwenhuyse and H. Hengsdijk (eds.), Tools for land use analysis on different scales; with cases studies for Costa Rica. Kluwer Academic Publishers, Boston MA, pp.65-96.

Ruben, R., Van Boekel, M., Van Tilburg, A. and Trienekens, J. (2007). Tropical Food Chains; Governance Regimes for Quality Management. Wageningen Academic Publishers, Wageningen, the Netherlands.

Scherer, F.M. (1970). Industrial market structure and economic performance. 1st ed., Houghton Mifflin Company, Boston, MA, USA.

Shepherd, A., Lutz, C. and Van Tilburg, A. (1997). Market information services, the theory. In: A.W. Shepherd (ed.), Market information services. Theory and practice. FAO Agricultural Services Bulletin 125, FAO, Rome, pp. 5-15.

Siamwalla, A. (1978). Farmers and Middlemen: Aspects of Agricultural Marketing in Thailand. Econ. Bulletin for Asia and the Pacific, Vol. 29, No. 1, 38-50. Republished in: Agricultural and Food Marketing in Developing Countries; Selected Readings, J. Abbott, ed., CAB International, Wallingford, UK.

Slater, C.C. (1968). Marketing Processes in Developing Latin American Societies. Journal of Marketing (July): 50-55.

Stern, L.W., A.I. El-Ansary and A.T. Coughlan (1996). Marketing Channels, 5th ed. Prentice Hall College Div, NJ, USA.

Stoelhorst, J.W. and Van Raaij, E.M. (2004). On explaining performance differentials: marketing and the managerial theory of the firm. Journal of Business Research 57: 462-477.

Van Bergen, A.P.L., M.G. Roelands, Van Tilburg, A. and Warner, R.B. (1989). Voedselhulp in relatie tot de graanvoorziening in ruraal Senegal. Vakgroep Marktkunde en Marktonderzoek, Landbouwuniversiteit in opdracht van het Ministerie van Buitenlandse Zaken, DGIS/IOV.

Van Bruggen, L. and Van Tilburg, A. (1999). Maize and bean marketing in Benin (West Africa): The choice of marketing outlet of larger peasant farmers. In: H.L. van der Laan, A. van Tilburg and T. Dijkstra (eds.), Agricultural marketing in tropical Africa, Ashgate Publishing, Surrey, UK, pp.153-168.

Van der Laan, H.L. (1986). The Selling Policies of African Export Marketing Boards. African Affairs 85: 365-383.

Van der Laan, H.L. (1987). Marketing West Africa's Export Crops: Modern Marketing Boards and Colonial Trading Companies Compared. Journal of Modern African Studies 25: 1-24.

Van der Laan, H.L. (1989). Export Crop Marketing in Tropical Africa: What Role for Private Enterprise? Journal of International Food & Agribusiness Marketing 1: 41-62.

Van Tilburg, A. (1981). Evaluation of the performance of the marketing system for highland vegetables in West Java, Indonesia. Proceedings the Annual Conference of the European Marketing Academy, Copenhagen, Demark.

Van Tilburg, A. (1990). Les commerçants du maïs et du gari des grands marchés dans le nord de la province du Mono, Bénin. Vakgroep Marktkunde en Marktonderzoek, Landbouwuniversiteit.

Van Tilburg, A. Mulder, M. and Van Dijken, G. (1992). Fresh snap beans for urban markets: The performance of some vegetable marketing systems in developing countries. In: G. Henry and W. Janssen (eds.), Snap beans in the developing world. CIAT publucation 195, Colombia, South-America, pp. 103-126.

Van Tilburg, A. and Lutz, C. (1992). Competition at rural markets in South Benin. In: L. Cammann (ed.), Traditional marketing systems. German Foundation for International Development (DSE), Feldafing, pp. 101-112.

Van Tilburg, A. and Hamming, I. (1999). Primary rice marketing in Northwest Sierra Leone: market and non-market transactions. In: H.L. van der Laan, T. Dijkstra and A. van Tilburg (eds.), Agricultural marketing in tropical Africa, Ashgate Publishing, Surrey, UK, pp.131-152.

Van Tilburg, A. (2001a). Livelihood diversification of farming households in Northwest Sierra Leone. Wageningen-UPWARD Series on Rural Livelihoods 3.

Van Tilburg, A. (2001b). The Bhutan National Agricultural Marketing Plan, Report for the Ministry of Agriculture of Bhutan in co-operation with the Agricultural Marketing Section, Policy and Planning Division of the Ministry of Agriculture, Bhutan and the Netherlands Development Organisation SNV.

Van Tilburg, A. Trienekens, J., Ruben, R., and Van Boekel, M. (2007). Governance for quality management in tropical food chains. Journal on Chain and Network Science 7: 1-9.

Van Tilburg, A. Kuiper, W.E. and Swinkels, R. (2008). Market performance of potato auctions in Bhutan. Journal of International Food and Agribusiness Marketing 20: 61-87.

Zhang, X. (1999). Agricultural marketing in a country in transition. Case of sweet potato products in Sichuan, P.R. China. Mansholt Studies 13, Wageningen Agricultural University. Wageningen, the Netherlands.

About the authors

Tina Beuchelt is Research Associate at the University of Hohenheim and Chair of Rural Development Theory and Policy in Stuttgart, Germany. Her current interest lies in business models of farmers and cooperatives, upgrading and governance in agrifood chains, costs and benefits of standards and certifications regarding poverty and rural development, impact evaluation. Aad van Tilburg's research on tropical food chains and marketing in developing countries has very much inspired her research.

Erwin Bulte is professor of development economics at the universities of Wageningen and Tilburg. He is a fellow of OxCarre (Oxford Center for the Analysis of Resource-Rich Economies) and the Department of Land Economy at Cambridge University. His research interests include natural resource economics, the economics of conflict and post-conflict recovery, and institutional economics. In addition he contributes to the domain of paleoeconomics: economic decision-making in the stone age. Together with Aad he has been a member of the European Microfinance Programme.

Marijke D'Haese is post-doctoral assistant at the Department of Agricultural Economics, Ghent University and visiting researcher of the Development Economics Group of Wageningen University. Her research interests are in market access of agricultural producers in developing countries and the influence of market failure on food security and farm productivity. She works on similar research topics as Aad and she has taught together with Aad (and Henk Moll) in the courses on microfinance and marketing at Wageningen and in the European microfinance program in the ULB Brussels.

Grahame Dixie is a Senior Agri-Business Specialist in the South Asian Agriculture and Rural Unit of the World Bank based in Washington D.C. He is currently working on several investment projects in South Asia with a focus on raising farm incomes through improved market access including in Afghanistan, India and Sri Lanka. In particular, he is in charge of a research project to quantify the impact of an agricultural information service in India which is feeding information directly to farmers and field extension officers.

Divine Foundjem-Tita is a PhD student at the Departments of Plant Production and of Agricultural Economics of Ghent University. The topic of his PhD research (and Msc dissertation finished August 2009) is the potential of group sales for improved market access of smallholder producers of non timber products in Cameroon. His PhD research is on policy, institutional arrangements and performance of non timber forest products value chain in Cameroon and falls within the research topics on which Aad has worked during his career.

Andy Hall is a Senior Researcher, United Nations University-MERIT. He has written extensively on agricultural innovation and he operates a global agricultural innovation network.

Franz Heidhues is Prof.(em.) of development economics at the Hohenheim University, Department of Agricultural Economics and Social Sciences in the Tropics and Subtropics and member of the University's Center for Tropical and Subtropical Agriculture, in Stuttgart, Germany. He taught and conducts research on poverty, rural development and natural resource management; food and nutrition security; and rural finance, primarily in Sub-Sahara Africa and Southeast Asia. Before joining the University Hohenheim Franz Heidhues worked from 1969 to 1982 at the World Bank in Washington, D.C., in the fields of macro-economic country studies and agricultural sector reviews, project preparation and appraisal of rural development projects. His research interests widely coincided with those of Aad van Tilburg with whom he is closely associated within the European Association of Agricultural Economists.

Wim Heijman is affiliated with Wageningen University since 1981. In 2001 he has been appointed to the chair of Regional Economics at Wageningen University. He is conducting research in the areas of general and regional economics. He is especially interested in the area of rural development in Central and East Europe. He has been the chairman of one of the study programme committees at Wageningen University. In this position he has been cooperating with Aad van Tilburg intensively when he was Director of the Educational Institute.

Sascha Huijsman is an M.Sc student (Finance) at the University of Groningen, and she holds a B.Sc degree in International Economics and Business. For her B.Sc thesis she focused on the impact of the macro economy on microfinance. The current financial and economic crisis offered an opportunity to test this relation during a period of distress as a key component of her M.Sc thesis. She met Aad van Tilburg in Benin, Africa, when she was three years old. They both lived there at the time.

Paul Ingenbleek is assistant professor in marketing at Wageningen University and researcher at the Agricultural Economics Research Institute (LEI-WUR). He studied history of society at the Erasmus University Rotterdam with majors in business history and history of nonwestern societies. He obtained a PhD in marketing from Tilburg University (2002). His research interests focus on the domain of marketing strategy and include among others agricultural marketing systems in developing countries, marketing institutions for sustainable development, and corporate social responsibility. In recent years he was introduced at many occasions by Aad van Tilburg as 'my successor'.

Hans Jansen is a Senior Agriculture Economist in the South Asian Agriculture and Rural Unit of the World Bank. He is currently based in the Bank's Country Office for Afghanistan in Kabul where his work focuses on agricultural investment projects and food security issues. Together with Prof. van Tilburg he has published a monograph on agricultural marketing issues in the Atlantic Zone of Costa Rica and worked with him on the development of a spatial equilibrium model for Costa Rica.

Willem Janssen is a Lead Agricultural Specialist at the World Bank. He focuses on Latin America where he oversees investment activities and analytical studies. Most of his work concerns the strengthening of national agricultural innovations systems and the integration of climate change considerations in economic development. Willem was Aad's first 'promovendus' (in 1986) in the field of agricultural marketing for developing countries at Wageningen University. They worked together extensively in Colombia, where Willem was working at CIAT (International Center for Tropical Agriculture) and later in 1992 at Wageningen University when Willem spent a sabbatical year in the department of Marketing and Market Research.

Emma Kambewa is Social Scientist at the WorldFish Center, Malawi office. Emma worked with Aad for 4 years (2004-2007) when he was a supervisor for her PhD thesis at Wageningen University, Marketing and Consumer Behavior Group. Emma and Aad have jointly published journal articles and refereed book chapters. They are still working together on more publications. Emma's research interests include smallholder market access: mechanisms for linking smallholders to markets, corporate social responsibility and sustainable natural resource management.

Anna Kiemen is Research Assistant at the University of Bonn, Institute for Food and Resource Economics in Bonn, Germany. Aad van Tilburg's work on governance and quality issues in food supply chains has been insightful for her own research.

Robert Lensink is Professor of Finance and Financial Markets at the University of Groningen. He is also part-time Professor within the Development Economics Group, Wageningen University. His research mainly deals with Development Finance, with a special focus on microfinance. In Wageningen he teaches the course Microfinance and Marketing. He did this for several years together with Aad van Tilburg.

Clemens Lutz is associate professor at the Faculty of Economics and Business of Groningen University. His current research focuses on small business in developing countries, in particular SMEs (including farmers) in food markets and global value chains. His first cooperation with Aad van Tilburg dates back to the beginning of the 1980s. Aad launched him in the world of food marketing in developing countries while Clemens was working on his master thesis. The cooperation developed through a large number of co-supervised master thesis projects, research projects, a.o. Clemens' PhD, and several co-authored publications on market integration. More recently they shared their interest in research on global value chains and the inclusion of smallholders.

Joseph Nagoli is a Senior Research Analyst at WorldFish center, Malawi Office. Joseph briefly interacted via e-mail with Aad in 2007, when the Marketing and Consumer Behavior group and WorldFish Center wrote a joint proposal on Integrated Aquaculture – Agriculture in Southern Africa that was submitted to Wotro for funding. Joseph would have done a PhD research if the proposal had been funded. Joseph is interested in farming systems research and vulnerability assessment among small-scale farmers in Southern Africa.

Ajuruchukwu Obi is a Senior Lecturer in the Department of Agricultural Economics and Extension of the University of Fort Hare in Alice, Eastern Cape Province of South Africa. Obi's current research interests include institutions and smallholder farming, particularly in relation to factors influencing market access and technology adoption. Obi and Aad met in 2004 as research collaborators on a project funded by the South African Netherlands Research Programme on Alternatives in Development (SANPAD) to which Aad serves as Dutch Collaborator.

Eija Pehu is an Adviser at the World Bank. Her interests are in the fields of agricultural innovation, biotechnology and gender in agriculture.

Joost Pennings is the AST professor in commodity markets in the Department of Marketing and Consumer Behavior at Wageningen University, a professor in Marketing and the Alex Investment Bank professor in Finance at Maastricht University and a Research Fellow in the Office for Futures & Options Research at the University of Illinois at Urbana-Champaign. Current research deals with understanding *revealed* economic behavior by studying the decision-making behavior of *real* decision-makers (market participants, consumers, managers etc). Both descriptive and normative models are developed in order to explain and predict behavior. Special attention is given to decision-making under risk and uncertainty. Dr. van Tilburg's work is characterized by having a in-depth understanding of the decision context; having spend a long time in least developed countries he is able to enrich theoretical en empirical research. His work and approaches have guided many students and professors, including myself.

Stephan Piotrowski obtained a Master degree in agriculture from the University of Göttingen and was awarded a Ph.D. in Agricultural Economics from the University of Hohenheim. The topic of his doctoral dissertation was the analysis of land property rights and natural resource use in China. He currently works as an agricultural economist in the private sector. His research focus is natural resource management and the analysis of agricultural markets.

Nigel Poole is currently Associate Dean for Learning and Teaching in the Faculty of Law and Social Sciences, School of Oriental and African Studies, University of London. Among other things, he continues to conduct research on marketing systems from a value chain perspective, focusing on how agricultural smallholders can access markets and create sustainable business enterprises. He has shared research interests with Aad for a number of years.

Riikka Rajalahti is a Senior Agricultural Specialist at the World Bank who coordinates the World Bank's activities in the field of agricultural innovation.

Donald Ricks is Professor Emeritus in the Department of Agricultural, Food and Resource Economics at Michigan State University. He has devoted much of his career to improving the performance of vertical coordination in horticultural value chains in the United States. Working collaboratively with value chain participants in the fruit industries, through his dual role with the Michigan State University Cooperative Extension Service and with problem-oriented research, he has helped to create and coordinate value chain participant councils. He has spent his career addressing similar issues of market coordination as those Aad van Tilburg worked on.

Ruerd Ruben holds the Chair in Development Studies and is Director of the Centre for International Development Issues (CIDIN) at Radboud University Nijmegen, the Netherlands. He previously worked at Wageningen University and Free University Amsterdam, and was visiting fellow at the International Food Policy Research Institute (Washington D.C.). He spent a considerable part of his career working abroad in Latin America and sub-Saharan Africa. His research interest include studies on poverty and food security, sustainable value chains, rural cooperation and micro-finance. Recent studies address the development impact of Fair Trade and the contribution of smallholding to sustainable poverty alleviation in less-favoured areas. He worked extensively with Dr. Aad van Tilburg in studies on supply chain governance and quality management in (inter)national agro-food networks.

John Staatz is Professor Emeritus in the Department of Agricultural, Food and Resource Economics at Michigan State University. He has spent much of his career carrying out research, teaching, and outreach on improving the performance of agricultural markets in developing countries, particularly in Sub-Saharan Africa. In that process, he has greatly profited from the work of Aad van Tilburg on this topic area.

Eric Tollens is professor emeritus (since October 1, 2009) of agricultural and food economics at the Faculty of Bioscience Engineering of the Catholic University of Leuven (K.U. Leuven), Leuven, Belgium. He obtained his M.A. in economics (1970) and Ph.D. in agricultural economics (1975) at Michigan State University, East Lansing, USA. He started his academic career as professor of agricultural economics at the National University of Zaïre (Kinshasa and Yangambi), followed by four years at EUROSTAT, European Commission, Luxemburg and since 1983 full time at K.U. Leuven. His main research interests are in agricultural technology evaluation and food marketing, particularly focused on sub Sahara Africa.

His research interests overlap with those of Aad van Tilburg, which he met on several occasions and with whom he shares research interests in food marketing.

Máximo Torero is Director of the Markets, Trade and Institutions Division in the International Food Policy Research Institute (IFPRI) based in Washington DC. His research interests rest mainly in the areas of poverty and inequality, analysis of public investments, social and institutional aspects on the delivery of public services, impact analysis of infrastructure investments, and project evaluation.

Martinus van Boekel holds the chair Product Design & Quality Management in the cluster Food Sciences of the Department Agrotechnology & Food Sciences of Wageningen University. The central theme in research and education in the chair group concerns quality of food. The approach taken is a techno-managerial one, implying many links with social sciences, such as marketing and consumer behaviour, development economics, management studies. The approach means that it is investigated how food quality can be defined on the product level in terms of consumers' desires and how it can be controlled and influenced by technological and managerial measures. The author worked closely together with dr. Aad van Tilburg in projects on quality management in international agro-food chains.

Guido Van Huylenbroeck is professor at the Department of Agricultural Economics, Ghent University. His research focuses on institutional development and transaction cost economics in supply chains, farming and environmental economics in Belgium, Europe and developing countries. He knows Aad from different international meetings and lectures, invited him for lecturing on micro-finances in Ghent and shares his research interests.

Johan van Ophem works in the field of Economics of consumers and households at Wageningen University. His research is mainly conducted in this very broad field. He has met and discussed with Aad van Tilburg on various aspects of curricula design and study program development when Aad was director of the Educational Institute for the Social Sciences.

Aad van Tilburg has been associate professor in the Marketing and Consumer Behaviour group at Wageningen University (1974-2010). His research interests included the functioning and performance of market actors, markets and value chains. He published in *Agribusiness, Agricultural Economics, European Review of Agricultural Economics, Journal of Business Venturing, Journal of Development Economics, Journal of Regional Science, Journal of African Economies , Journal on Chain and Network Science, Netherlands Journal of Agricultural Science and Review of Business and Economics* and he was co-editor of *Agricultural Marketing and Consumer Behavior in a Changing World* (1997, Kluwer Academic Publishers), *Agricultural Marketing in Tropical Africa* (1999, Ashgate Publishing), *Agricultural Markets beyond Liberalization* (2000, Kluwer Academic Publishers) and *Tropical Food Chains* (2007, Wageningen Academic Publishers). He has been visiting professor in the European Microfinance Master of Science programme in Brussels, a joint activity of the Université Libre de Bruxelles (Solvay Business School), Université Paris Dauphine and Wageningen University where he focused on relationships between trade transactions and microfinance in rural areas in developing countries.

Hans van Trijp holds the Chair in Marketing and Consumer Behavior (MCB) within the Social Sciences Group of Wageningen University and a part-time affiliation at Unilever in Vlaardingen. His key research interest lies in the complex interconnections between marketing strategy, consumer behavior and societal values, with a specific emphasis on consumer behavior with regards to health and sustainable development.

He has been a colleague of Aad since 1986, when he first joined the MCB group. When Hans returned to Wageningen in 2001 to take up the position of Full Professor he worked closely with Aad, both in the supervision of several PhD students with Aad and in the management of the MCB group. He is very grateful for all of Aad's scientific contributions as well as the senior management role that he has played for so many years within the MCB group.

Jacques Viaene is professor emeritus at the Department of Agricultural Economics, Ghent University. He specializes in marketing, competitiveness, structural development and innovation in the agro-food sector in Belgium and abroad. He cooperated with Thieu Meulenberg and Aad on different EU-projects and on marketing related to developing countries.

Berend Wierenga is Professor of Marketing at the Rotterdam School of Management, Erasmus University. He graduated from Wageningen University, and he is the Founding Editor of the *International Journal of Research in Marketing*. Over time, his research has covered various domains of marketing, including brand choice processes, consumer decision models, and marketing models. The main focus of his recent work is marketing decision making and marketing management support systems. He is the editor of the *Handbook of Marketing Decision Models* (Springer 2008) and he is also (co)author of *Marketing Management Support Systems: Principles, Tools and Implementation* (Kluwer 2000). His journal publications include articles in *Communications of the ACM, Decision Support Systems, European Journal of Operational Research, Journal of Management Studies, Journal of Product Innovation Management, Interfaces, International Journal of Research in Marketing, Journal of Marketing, Journal of Marketing Research, Management Information Systems Quarterly, Management Science*, and *Marketing Science*.
Berend Wierenga keeps excellent memories of the period 1975-1983, when he was a colleague of Aad van Tilburg at the marketing department of Wageningen University. This was the time that Aad decided to specialize in marketing of developing countries. He is very impressed by what Aad has accomplished in this field, which, unfortunately, is not always visible to mainstream marketing.

Manfred Zeller is Professor at the University of Hohenheim and Chair of Rural Development Theory and Policy in Stuttgart, Germany. His current research interest is in costs and benefits of social or environmental standards in agrifood chains, and the performance of cooperatives and microfinance institutions. Aad van Tilburg and Manfred were members of the international program committee for EAAE seminars that were held in Montpellier in 2007 and Florence in 2004.

Index of the keywords

Printed in the United States
by Baker & Taylor Publisher Services